MW01174613

Verdi, Milan And Othello: Being A Short Life Of Verdi, With Letters Written About Milan And The New Opera Of Othello

Blanche Roosevelt

In the interest of creating a more extensive selection of rare historical book reprints, we have chosen to reproduce this title even though it may possibly have occasional imperfections such as missing and blurred pages, missing text, poor pictures, markings, dark backgrounds and other reproduction issues beyond our control. Because this work is culturally important, we have made it available as a part of our commitment to protecting, preserving and promoting the world's literature. Thank you for your understanding.

VERDI:

MILAN AND "OTHELLO."

BEING A SHORT LIFE OF VERDI, WITH LETTERS WRITTEN
ABOUT MILAN AND THE NEW OPERA OF OTHELLO:
REPRESENTED FOR THE FIRST TIME ON THE
STAGE OF LA SCALA THEATRE, FEB. 5, 1887.

BY

(BLANCHE ROOSEVELT,

AUTHOR OF "COPPER QUEEN," "STAGE STRUCK," "LIFE OF LONGFELLOW,"
"LIFE OF GUSTAVE DORÉ," ETC. ETC.

"The man that hath no music in himself,
Nor is not moved with concord of sweet sounds,
Is fit for treasons, stratagems, and spoils.
The motions of his spirit are dull as night,
And his affections dark as Erebus :
Let no such man be trusted.—Mark the music."
Merchant of Venice, Act v. Sc. 1.

WARD AND DOWNEY,

12 YORK STREET, COVENT GARDEN, LONDON.

1887.

[*All rights reserved.*]

LIFE OF VERDI.

THE NEW YORK
PUBLIC LIBRARY
749952
ASTOR, LENOX AND
TILDEN FOUNDATIONS
R   1916   L

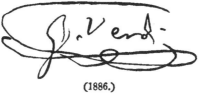

(1886.)

TO

WILKIE COLLINS.

My dear Friend,

When I left England for Italy, you said, " Do write me
all about Verdi, Milan, and the new opera *Othello*." I have
taken you at your word ; only the letters, like most feminine
epistles, have stretched away into limitless pages, and from a
few vagabond sheets have grown into a volume. I am sure
you will never again ask a woman to write to you, even from
Paradise ; but in the mean time, here is the result of your
amiability, and, knowing that the work never would have
been written without you, I dedicate it to you. I hope also
that it may recall to your mind not alone a composer, a country,
and a people whom you have long so professedly admired, but
likewise the humble colleague who, with the world, owes you
more delightful hours than any pen—not your own—could ever
hope to repay.

With expression of sincerest regard,

Affectionately yours,

BLANCHE ROOSEVELT.

Paris, June 1887.

LIFE OF VERDI.

CHAPTER I.

THE Duchy of Parma has given birth to some of Italy's greatest men. Not alone Mazzuoli and Correggio, but Joseph Fortunio François Verdi, known to all the world as Giuseppe Verdi, the greatest living Italian composer. Verdi was not born in Parma, or in any of those charming cities which have made the old duchy so renowned ; but he first saw the light of day in a poor little hamlet called Roncole—a wretched place near to another almost as wretched called Busseto, this latter counting about four thousand inhabitants, and situated at the foot of the Apennine range.

Roncole, to-day famous, was at the time of Verdi's birth a village which claimed, perhaps, three hundred souls. Amongst that number was a young couple, Carlo Verdi and his wife, who kept an unpretending hotel and shop, selling the usual supplies to be found in village stores—heterogeneous collection of heterogeneous wares, amazing to the eye of childhood, and which formed equally the delight of the hardy peasants in and about Roncole.

It is a proud thought that the greatest gifts bestowed by Nature—genius, intellect, and intellectual power—have their birthright in the humblest soil : the seeds are sown irrespective of caste, person, or social standing. The humblest peasant's child, like the son of a Cæsar, may ascend a throne, or bind his brows with the laurel of immortality. The 10th of October 1813, just as the sun was sinking behind the golden Apennines, Signora Verdi gave birth to the babe whose name rings, as it has done for the best half of a century, from one end of the land of song to the other. Nature may be regardless of the clay whereon she scatters her germs of genius, but it is always well to know the moral status of a great man's parents.

Giuseppe's father barely knew his letters, was a contadino, but renowned for his uprightness and honest dealing. Signora Verdi, daughter of the same humble race, had no book-learning, but a warm heart, generous impulses, and noble courage. M. Pougin says that in 1814, when Prince Eugène of Savoy and his armies were retreating before the Austrian and Russian troops, the village of Roncole shared in the general devastation ; the women and children hid in churches, caves, and corners. Signora Verdi fled from her home with little Giuseppe in her arms ; the way was perilous, the sound of cannonading filled the air, and shots rained into the streets like hail ; once they barely escaped death ; but, fainting with fatigue and terror she finally reached the old church, hoping to find therein a safe asylum. She hid herself in a farther corner of a little chapel, but the mob soon invaded this sacred spot ; the altars were defamed, blood ran in rivers in the sacred aisles, a horrible yelling mob seized upon and massacred every creature, right and left, who had taken refuge in the church, and yet in this general carnage two souls were saved—that of Giuseppe Verdi and his brave mother, who, while the scene of butchery was at its height, managed to escape into the streets, thence to a safer refuge, and, finally, to a haven of safety. Truly there is a destiny which shapes our ends, rough hew them

THE HOUSE WHERE VERDI WAS BORN,

Roncole, Duchy of Parma, Oct. 10th, 1813,

THE NEW YORK
PUBLIC LIBRARY

ASTOR LENOX
TILDEN FOUNDATIONS

as we will. Signora Verdi and the future author of *Rigoletto* and *Othello* were probably the sole persons who out-
lived this memorable revolt. Giuseppe Verdi's mother was
a low-born peasant, yet she had in her the stuff which has
given Jeanne d'Arc a place in history. Twice she saved her
son's life ; twice was the instrument in the hands of that Fate
which had destined one more name to its galaxy of glory.

At an early age little Giuseppe showed an extreme fond-
ness for music, and a, wandering minstrel called Bagasset was
the first to awaken divine inspiration in the child's soul.
Bagasset, travelling here and there about Busseto, sleeping in
barns and begging on the highway, played a wretched violin, but
one which was Giuseppe's delight, and every time Bagasset
came to Roncole he used to stop before the Verdi osteria, and
send little Carlo into absolute paroxysms of joy. It was
impossible not to notice the child's love for music, and although
his parents hoped to make a good cobbler or farrier out of him,
Giuseppe persisted in showing a preference for this beloved
calling. At seven he was altar-boy in the church, and on one
occasion was so distraught that the priest vainly called for
water a third time : Verdi still remained so deaf the irate
prelate then handed him a blow which sent the inattentive melomaniac spinning to the foot of the sacred shrine. M. Pougin
says: "Verdi's fall was so violent that he fainted, and was
carried home unconscious." After this circumstance Giuseppe begged very hard to be allowed to study music, and his
father not only accorded him the desired privilege, but bought
an ancient spinet from an old priest, and presented his son
with it, in order that this latter should have every possible
chance to devote himself to the profession of music. At the age
of fifteen we find him playing an organ in the great church at
Busseto, a dim cathedral whose nave, presbytery, and aisles
were veiled in eternal shadow, and where on a high seat in the

great organ-loft sat a diminutive young organist, invisible to, and certainly almost ignored by, the smart citizens of Busseto.

At that time Verdi was going to the village school, where he learned to write, and pursued the usual form of a peasant boy's studies, viz. casting up accounts, geography, &c.

Although the boy was very intelligent in music, he never displayed remarkable intelligence in anything else. He had the shrewdness common to his class, called by the pretty name of astuzia, and we are told there were few sharper lads in Busseto than this same Giuseppe Verdi.

He conceived an early friendship for Barezzi, a shopkeeper of Busseto, who sold various wares to Verdi's father, and who never ceased on every occasion that brought him to the hotel at Roncole to speak of the little Giuseppe's talent, and his belief in a great musical career for the lad. Verdi spent a great deal of his time with Barezzi and his family, and was almost brought up with this latter's children. He grew very fond of Barezzi's pretty daughter Margherita, a clever, quick, and sympathetic child somewhat younger than himself, but certainly older in comprehension and ripened intelligence.

The old spinet which Verdi's father had bought him at seven was soon replaced, and we find the maestro the happy possessor of a fine piano made by the celebrated house of Fritz in Vienna. At this time Verdi was still organist in the little village of Roncole, and was diligently studying harmony under the organist Baistrocchi, a man of very fair talent, like most Italians an inborn musician, and naturally quoted as the greatest musical authority in his native village.

Verdi had attained his twelfth year when his professor disappeared from the scene, and we find the little student replacing his teacher in the dusty old organ-loft, where Baistrocchi had spent the greater portion of his life: Carlo Verdi's son taking his master's place, and for the first time conducting

VILLAGE CHURCH AT RONCOLE,

Scene of the famous massacre, when Verdi's life was twice saved by his mother.

THE NEW YORK
PUBLIC LIBRARY

ASTOR LENOX
TILDEN FOUNDATIONS

the Mass in that same village church where his life was once
saved by a miracle.

His salary then was fixed at the annual sum of thirty-six
lire, or three francs sixty centimes, or less than half-a-crown a
month. The second year his diligence, fidelity, and increased
ability gained him the additional sum of four lire, raising his
salary from thirty-six to forty lire per annum.

Verdi gives to Antonio Barezzi absolutely the honour of
having started him in his career : he also declares that he
was indebted to him for permission to study his art ; and,
more still, that supreme impetus towards developing talent
which sometimes the humblest, least considered, and most un-
important friend may unconsciously be instrumental in giving.

Barezzi, although a shopkeeper, was a real dilettante in
music ; he filled his house with such artists as came in his
way, and sometimes these were very good ones. Art in those
times occupied a more humble position than it does to-day.
Composers were not considered very safe people to know ;
pianists, and the usual wandering tribe of piano performers
found in Italy, were looked upon as a sort of musical banditti,
rather to be kept out of the house than encouraged to come into
one's home. The musician who to-day would aspire to sit at a
duke's table, to drink Extra Dry, and devour cheese-patties,
with the same talent, might have been very glad, fifty years
ago, to have drunk the native Italian wine, and imbibed the
succulent macaroni of even a Signor Barezzi's hospitable
board.

Through this good man's intervention Verdi was soon made
choirmaster at the church, and Ferdinando Provesi, who
lived in Busseto, an artist of admirable musical talents, con-
ceiving a sudden caprice for little Verdi's musical disposition,
began giving him lessons without payment. Verdi seemed destined
not alone to succeed his early masters, but almost to oust

them from the humble position where it had been in their power to aid the little student. At the age of sixteen we find Verdi taking Provesi's place, and shortly after becoming director of the Philharmonic Society of Busseto. At this time the master told his pupil that he had no longer anything to teach him. He advised Verdi to try and do his best to go to Milan, and not only aided him with counsel and money, but through his kindness obtained for him the "Home" prize given to the musician of the highest talent in the town of Busseto. This was a premium offered by the head of the Monte di Pietà Society, a charity which had been enriched by several important legacies, and which gave the sum of six hundred lire a year as a reward to the chosen pupil of the society's musical competitors.

At the age of nineteen Verdi found himself suddenly transplanted to Milan, the charming Lombard capital, home of arts and sciences; above all, that cradle of music which has rocked on its bosom the greatest names in Italy's world of art. He was surprised and delighted at the sight of the beautiful city, but he left gallery, palace, and promenade, to wander into the great cathedral, and naturally his first wish was to play the organ in that divine temple. Roaming about the streets, looking in the shop-windows, or pausing before the bric-à-brac in the De Cristoforis Gallery, Verdi still seemed to have eyes and ears for nothing but music: it was not strange that he had little time either to contemplate or reflect on any of Milan's beauties. This city was then the great musical centre of Europe. It is so to-day, but very much less than it was at the time when little Verdi was sent there to complete his musical education. The Conservatorio di Musica bore a very just renown, was, and still is, one of the most splendid art-schools in the world.

This was in 1832, and Verdi had just attained his nineteenth year. By the peculiar providence which seems to place in the footsteps of genius unheard-of obstacles in early life, Verdi, an authority in Busseto, a celebrity at Roncole, finished pupil in all that Master Provesi could teach him, came to Milan the prize pupil of the Monte di Pietà Society of Busseto, to be told that he had no talent, and to be refused admission at the Milan Conservatorio ; in short, his powers were deemed unworthy of cultivation in this celebrated but critical school. The knowledge of this has since raised a whirlwind of discussion throughout Italy, but the fact remains, and Verdi, for one, has never forgotten it. The musical directors pretended that after the age of fourteen no scholar could be admitted to this academy, and that as the date of leaving was fixed at the age of twenty, Verdi, having attained the age of nineteen before he applied for admission, was considered too old to be accepted as a pupil.

Francesco Basily was the censor, or head, of the Milan Conservatorio, reputed witty, well-read, supposed to be always just, and a fair protector of gifted youth ; but it is certain that he found Verdi possessed of little or no talent : naturally in virtue of the extraordinary development of this lad's genius Basily and his friends have since tried to excuse their haste and lack of judgment, by making the accepted rules of the school the real reason of young Verdi's non-reception in the class. The explanation is sufficient in one sense, but it is also certain that Basily might very well have overstepped traditional boundaries had he found in the talent of young Verdi the wherewithal to authorise him to such a step. This happened many years ago : there always has been, and probably always will be, the same mystery about the affair. In a letter which Verdi wrote from Sant' Agata, 13th October 1880, addressed to M. Caponi, the justly celebrated Folchetto of the Milan Perseveranza, and the Fanfulla of Rome, the composer said :

" It was in the month of June 1832—I had not yet attained my nineteenth year—when I made a demand in writing to be admitted as a paying scholar at the Milan Conservatorio di Musica; more than that, I underwent a sort of examination at the school itself, in presenting some of my own writing, and playing a composition for piano before Basily, Piantanida Angeleri, and others, amongst them the old master Rolla, to whom I had been specially recommended by my master at Busseto, Ferdinand Provesi. About a week after I went to Rolla's house, when he said to me quite suddenly, ' *Give up thinking of the Conservatorio.* Choose a master in the city. I advise you to take Lavigna or Negri.'

" I heard nothing more of the affair, my demand was not even responded to, and no one either before or after my examination ever mentioned or spoke to me of rules. I know nothing of the Basily judgment spoken of by Fétis.*

" That is all. I write you in haste and briefly, because you are in a hurry to know; however, I have told you all that I know myself. My wife thanks you, and I shake you affectionately by the hand. VERDI."

* *Universal Biography of Musicians :* Fétis speaking of Verdi.

CHAPTER II.

FOLLOWING Rolla's advice, Verdi chose as a professor Lavigna, a splendid and practical musician, a fine harmonist, and composer of several works which had obtained real success in Italy ; but as they no longer find a place in to day's operatic repertory, and having nothing whatever to do with this history, it would be quite unnecessary to mention them. Lavigna was enchanted with Verdi's talent. He found his pupil unpretentious, very studious, and very prudent. He also said that Verdi possessed great intelligence, and added, " Some day he will not only do himself great honour, but likewise his country."

Pougin in his little anecdotal life of Verdi tells a story which at the time the circumstance took place must have greatly confused Basily, and, in spite of this latter's position, have cast a rather serious reflection on his perspicacity. Every evening Verdi did not pass at the Opera, La Scala, or some other theatre, he spent with his master Lavigna, and on one occasion he found Basily present. The professor was complaining of the deplorable result which had been obtained by the music and chapel master of the Church San Giovanni de Monza ; for out of twenty-eight young students who had taken part in this competition not one competitor had properly, or even correctly, .developed the subject, a study from the fugue proposed and written by the master Basily himself.

Lavigna, not without certain malice, said to his friend,

" Really this is very extraordinary. Now look at Verdi ; he has only been studying fugue two years, but I would be

ready to lay a wager that he would have done better than any
of the twenty-eight competitors."

"Indeed?" queried Basily, in ironical tones.

"Certainly, without doubt," responded Lavigna. "Do you
remember your subject?"

"Yes."

"Well, write it, and let us see."

Basily wrote a few bars, and Lavigna, handing the theme
to Verdi, said,

"Sit down at that table, and work a little on this."

In the mean time the two friends took up and spun out the
thread of their conversation, when Verdi approached and interrupted, saying simply,

"Here you are; I have finished it."

Basily took the paper, examined it, and as he read showed
evident signs of amazement. When he reached the end he
could not do otherwise than compliment Verdi on his work.
Although chary of praise, he even could not help adding—only
by way of observation,

"But how does it happen that you have written a double
canon on this theme?"

Verdi looked him straight in the eye. The young man, who
without doubt had a faint remembrance of the welcome which
once upon a time had been extended to him by the renowned
school so ably presided over by Basily, responded slowly,

"The reason? The reason is, I found it rather bare, and I
wished to adorn it a little."

Basily bit his lip and made no response, but perhaps he
remembered having heard somewhere that vengeance was a
pleasure of the gods.

Lavigna and his pupil accompanied the old master back to
the Conservatory door. Their good-nights were cordial, but
they looked deep into each other's eyes and smiled. That

smile was all, for never in his lifetime, either before or since, with the exception of the letter sent M. Caponi, has Verdi ever made allusion to the maestro Basily or his first musical checkmate.

Verdi had been studying in Milan during the whole of two years when Provesi's death at Busseto forced the citizens to choose his successor as director of the Philharmonic Society and organist of the great cathedral. Verdi was a favourite with the chief authorities of the town, still he had a competitor, Giovanni Ferrari, whose talent was vastly inferior to Verdi's, but who was warmly advocated by two bishops and the church in general. In spite of his talent, Verdi found himself vanquished by the priests' protégé ; however, the Philharmonic Society as a body protested against this injustice, and rushing to the church carried away all the music and all that had been composed by Verdi. The war fairly raged amongst the townspeople, between Verdi's and Ferrari's partisans, until peace was declared, and Verdi was finally named by the municipal council master of the Philharmonic Society with a salary of 300 francs a year, obliged to compose marches for the city, the municipal and military bands.

CHAPTER III.

A GREAT man's youth must always be more or less interesting. It is interesting especially to know the first steps which led him to success, and to follow little by little the lanes of obscurity and darkness whence he ultimately emerged into the broader paths of honour and glory. Verdi may tell of his youth in his own words, about the success of his first opera, his life in Milan, and the real first step which led to his recognition as a man of talent.

Monsieur Pougin in his life of Verdi has made use of stenographic notes taken by the Ricordis, father and son, many years ago, after a conversation held with Verdi, and I cannot do better than draw my inspiration from the same source. The young master relates the following :

" About 1833 or '34 there existed in Milan a Philharmonic Society composed of very good musical elements. It was directed by a master called Masini, who, while he did not shine through his eminent musical knowledge, at least had patience and tenacity ; that is to say, the necessary qualities requisite for the conductor of an amateur musical body. At that time they were organising at the Theatre Philodramatic a performance of Haydn's oratorio *The Creation*, and my master Lavigna asked me, for my own benefit, if I would not like to go to the rehearsals. I need not say I accepted with pleasure. I went, but no one paid the slightest attention to the little youngster who seated himself modestly in an obscure corner. Three masters, Perelli, Bonoldi, and Almasio, conducted

these rehearsals, but one fine morning, by a singular coincidence, none of the three was present. The public was
getting impatient, when the leader, Masini, not feeling
himself capable to sit down to the piano and accompany the
full score, turned towards me and begged me to be accom-
panist. He was so little confident in the ability of the young
musician that he said to me, ' It will be sufficient to accompany
with the bass only.'

"At that time I was fresh from my studies, and certainly I
would not have felt very much embarrassed before any orchestral score living. I accepted Masini's offer, and sat down to the
piano to commence the first measures. I well recall several
ironical smiles on the faces of certain amateurs, for it seems
that my juvenile physiognomy, my lank body, and shabby
dress were not of a nature to inspire great confidence. However that may be, we began the opening number; little by
little, warming up to it and beginning to feel the excitement
myself, I was not alone satisfied with accompanying the bass,
but I commenced to direct the orchestra with my right hand,
at the same time playing the score with the left. When the
rehearsal was finished, from every side I received felicitations
and compliments, but particularly from the Conte Pompeo
Belgiojoso and Conte Renato Borromeo. To close this incident,
whether the three masters of whom I have already spoken
were too occupied to continue the task of conducting for the
Philharmonic Society, or whether from other reasons, I know
not, but the Society finished by confiding the direction of the
concert entirely to me. The public performance was such a
success that we gave a second performance in the great room
of the Casino dei Nobili, in the presence of the Archduke and
Archduchess Ranieri, and the grand society then residing in
Milan. The success was so great that the Viceroy himself

expressed a wish to hear *The Creation*, and a third concert took place in the palace, again under my direction.

"Immediately after, Conte Renato Borromeo gave me a commission to compose the music of a cantata for voice and orchestra—if I remember rightly, on occasion of the marriage of a member of his family. While on this subject, I may also remark that I had no pecuniary profit therefrom, and my help was absolutely gratuitous."

It is rather curious to remark that the Borromeos, one of the richest and most powerful families in Milan, should have taken this occasion to profit by the talent of a young compatriot who lived on a franc a day in the most convenient pot-house, and yet not realise that if his work was worth almost a royal marriage, it certainly was worth some pecuniary benefit to the nearly starving composer. On the celebration of this wedding, as is the custom throughout Italy, if I remember rightly, the usual gifts were given to the poor, but Verdi never had so much as a wedding *ricordo*, or a halfpenny, or even a wedding-favour to recall his presence on this memorable festivity. I suppose it was considered honour enough to allow him to appear in person at so aristocratic a gathering.

Verdi *loquitur* continues:

"Masini [who, it seems, had great confidence in the young artist] proposed to me to write an opera for the Philodrammatica Theatre, of which he was the director; and soon after gave me a libretto, which, particularly changed and modified by the poet Solera, became *Oberto di San Bonifazio.*

"I accepted this offer with pleasure, but I was obliged to return to Busseto, where I was engaged as an organist. I stopped there perhaps three years. My opera completed, I again undertook a voyage to Milan, carrying with me my complete score perfectly in order, from which I had taken the care to make a copy myself of all the vocal numbers."

CHAPTER IV.

I HERE stop Verdi's recital to give one reason why he was obliged to return to Busseto.

In all this time we have followed only the fortunes of Verdi, the student, the faithful, conscientious boy, who, having embraced an art, had given himself up wholly and entirely to his career ; but what is it Tennyson says about springtime and a young man's ideas turning lightly to thoughts of love? We now see Verdi playing a new rôle we find him leaving his desk and spinet to stroll down fair valleys in the moonlight, or walk idly about the village roads of Busseto ; his companion one whom he had known in youthful days, one who had joyed or sorrowed with him, who had shared all his hopes and fears, whose smile of friendship and never-failing word of praise, from earliest childhood, had been the guardian angel of his dearest dreams and fondest illusions ; one with whom he had ever exchanged his dearest thoughts and sympathies : none other than little Margherita Barezzi, old Antonio Barezzi's daughter ; little Margherita, grown from a charming child to be a charming young woman, the pride of her father Barezzi, beloved by all the village, and especially by her father's humble protégé Giuseppe Verdi. One fine morning the cathedral bells rang out a merry harmony. It was Verdi's wedding-day ; friends came from far and near, within and without Busseto ; above all, those of his youth and poverty gathered round to wish the young organist God - speed, and to kiss the soft cheeks of Margherita Barezzi his bride. Father and mother Verdi

left the little hotel at Roncole. Even Bagasset, the wandering
minstrel, dragged his weary feet, not only to the city walls, but
to the very church-door, where he finally got near enough to
see kind old Antonio Barezzi giving away his daughter, and
Verdi, the boy whom he had loved and protected, stretching
forth his hand to receive the brightest jewel in his bene-
factor's home-crown. Bagasset looked proudly on; his eye
dimmed and his lip fell only when he saw father Barezzi put
the musician's hand in that of his daughter, and heard him say
with his deep voice,

"To no one in the world would I give her with so much
joy as to you."

The young couple set up housekeeping, but Verdi, now being
a married man, wished for a more lucrative career than that
of a simple country bandmaster or organist. He decided to
attempt writing for the theatre, and with that idea in view
returned alone to Milan. He very soon made acquaintance
with Themistocles Solera, a young poet, and together they
wrote an opéra comique called *Oberto, Conte de San Bonifazio.* Verdi was living at Busseto in a house called Palazzo
Rusca — do not be surprised; if you have ever been to
Italy you will know that the name of palace is often given
to barns of places, and during the winter of '37 and '38, Verdi
in his Palace Rusca, orchestrated the score of his first opera.
When all was finished he came to Milan, confident—at least
hopeful, as has been every Italian composer since Pergolesi—
of bringing out this work at the grand opera-house of La Scala.

Everything was arranged for its production in the spring
of 1837, with Signora Strepponi, the magnificent soprano ;
Moriani, a fine tenor ; and the world-renowned basso-buffo,
Giorgio Ronconi. But Milan, in the outset of Verdi's career,
seemed to be the one city where he was destined to know the
most disappointment and chagrin. Moriani fell ill during the

rehearsals, and there was no more talk of the opera. Verdi was thoroughly disheartened, for he was no longer a poor artist struggling alone, but a married man and father of two children presented him by his beloved wife Margherita. In the autumn, however, Merelli, the well-known manager, proposed to give Verdi's opera, and on the 17th November 1839, *Oberto, Conte di San Bonifazio* made its first appearance on the stage of La Scala, with the well-known artists, Ranier-Marini, Shaw, Marini, and Salvi.

I will now leave Verdi to go on with his reminiscences, taken up at the point where he spoke of returning to Busseto.

" My difficulties now began," he says. " Masini was not long the director of the Philodrammatica, and he no longer there, it was not possible for me to bring out my opera. However be it, whether he really had confidence in me, or whether to show his gratitude after the performance of *The Creation*— I had aided him on several occasions to prepare and direct various performances, among others *Cinderella*, always, be it understood, without any recompense whatever, and whether he wished to show me his gratitude in some way or not I never knew ; but certainly he was not discouraged by any ordinary difficulties, and promised to use his efforts to have my opera performed at La Scala on the occasion of the annual benefit usually given to the Milanese Pio Istituto. Count Borromeo and the well-known barrister Pasetti promised to help Masini on this occasion, but to tell the exact truth, I must say that this help produced nothing for me beyond a few scanty words of recommendation. On the contrary, Masini gave himself a great deal of trouble, and he was aided by the violinist Minghi, whom I had known whilst he was a member of the Philharmonic Society's orchestra, and who had every belief and confidence in me.

" Finally we managed to arrange things for the spring of

'39, and they were done in such a way that I had the double
fortune to bring out my work at the Scala theatre and to have
for interpreters four really extraordinary artists—La Strepponi,
soprano; Moriani, the tenor; the baritone, Giorgio Ronconi;
and the great basso, Marini.

"The rôles had barely been distributed, and the rehearsals
barely commenced, when Moriani fell seriously ill; then, of
course, everything was interrupted. It was not possible to even
dream of giving my opera. I was absolutely disheartened, and
was preparing to go back to Busseto, when one morning, as I
was entering my door, one of the employés of the La Scala
came towards me and said in a brutal tone : ' Are you that
maestro from Parma who was to have given an opera for the
Pio Instituto ? If so, come to the theatre; the manager is waiting for you.'

"' Is it possible ? ' I cried.

"' Yes, signor; they ordered me to go and hunt up the master from Parma who was going to give an opera; if you are
the man, come ;' and—I went.

"The manager of La Scala at that time was Bartolomeo
Merelli. One evening in the flies he had overheard a conversation between Signora Strepponi and Giorgio Ronconi, conversation in the course of which La Strepponi had spoken
favourably of the music of *Oberto di San Bonafazio,* and Ronconi had likewise found it very much to his taste.

"I presented myself at once to Merelli, who, without other
preparation, told me that, owing to the favourable opinion
which he had heard expressed about my work, he was willingly disposed to bring it out the forthcoming season; but if I
accepted his terms I should be obliged to make some changes
in my score, as the artists who were to perform it could not be
the same as those which I had at first counted upon. The
offer was a brilliant one for me. Young and unknown, I had

found a manager who dared put upon the stage a new work without requiring of me any sort of indemnity, which, by the way, I need not add, it would have been impossible for me to pay.

" Merelli took upon himself to pay all expenses, and proposed to me to divide half the sum which, in case of success, I might obtain, if he sold the score. Don't imagine for a moment that the proposition was a poor one. Merelli was speaking of the work of a beginner, but in fact the result was so gratifying that the editor, Giovanni Ricordi, consented to make himself sole proprietor of my opera, which he bought for the price of 2000 Austrian lire."*

* 2000 lire come to between 75*l.* and 80*l.* sterling.

CHAPTER V.

" *Oberto di San Bonifazio* obtained a success, if at least not very considerable, certainly good enough to merit a fair number of representations, which Merelli happily augmented by giving several extra performances not included in the subscription nights. The work was sung by Marini, a mezzo-soprano; Salvi, the tenor; and by the basso Marini. As I have before mentioned, it had been necessary to make several modifications in my music, in order to adapt it to the special voices of my new singers. I also wrote an extra number, a quartette, the dramatical situation of which was given me, or indicated, by Merelli himself, and for which Solera had written extra verses. This quartette turned out one of the best pages of the opera.

" Merelli then made me a superb proposition for that time; that is to say, he offered to sign a contract in which I engaged myself to write every eight months three operas, which should be represented at La Scala or at the Imperial Theatre of Vienna, of which he was also director. He engaged to give me 4000 Austrian lire for each of these operas, and the result of the sale of the complete scores was to be equally divided between us. I immediately accepted this proposition, and some time after Merelli, going away to Vienna, commissioned the poet Rossi to furnish me a libretto, which happened to be that of *Il Proscritto*. This book did not completely satisfy me, and I hadn't even began to put it to music, when, in the early months of 1840, Merelli returned to Milan, and told me that in accordance with the special obligations of his repertory, he had absolutely need of an opera-buffa for the autumn season. I consented: he added that he was immediately going to hunt me up a book; while, if I liked, I might occupy myself later with composing music to *Il Proscritto.*

" I could not refuse, and he then gave me several complete librettos by Romani, which, whether they had been forgotten, or whether they had never been successful, or whether they for some other reason had been laid aside, I never could discover. I did my best to read and re-read them, but not one pleased me. However, circumstances pressing, I selected the one which seemed to me the least bad. Its title was *Il Finto Stanislao,* a title which was afterwards replaced by that of *Un Giorno di Regno.*

" At that time I occupied a modest, even tiny, apartment in the environs of Porta Ticinese, and I had with me my little family; that is to say, my young wife, Margherita Barezzi,* and our two little children. I had barely commenced my work when I fell gravely ill with malignant sore-throat, which obliged me to keep my bed for a very long time. I was just entering on convalescence when I remembered that the quarter's rent, for which I was obliged to pay fifty scudi (10*l*.), would fall due within three days' time. At that period, if the sum was not a slight one for me, it was, nevertheless, a very grave affair; my long and painful illness had prevented my thinking of it in time, and the state of postal communication with Busseto was one of equally painful uncertainty. There was at that epoch a courier but twice a week, and knowledge of this prevented me writing to my excellent father-in-law, Barezzi, to beg him to send me the necessary money in time. Cost what it might, I wished to pay my rent on the day due, and although very

---

* V. rdi was so fond of, and grateful to, his father-in-law, that he rarely ever referred to his wife by any other appellation than that of Margherita Barezzi.

much annoyed to be obliged to have recourse to a third person, in spite of myself I decided to beg the kind barrister Pasetti to ask Merelli for the fifty scudi of which I stood in need. Whether in advance, on the condition of my contract, or whether as a loan for eight or ten days, any way he liked, only to give me time to write to Busseto and receive the above-named sum. It is useless to recapitulate by what fatal circumstance Merelli, perhaps through no fault of his own,* did not advance me the money in question. However, I was deeply chagrined to let my rent-day go by, even but for a few hours, without being able to settle everything in full. My wife, seeing my unhappiness, then took the few poor jewels she possessed, went out, and I never knew how she managed, but she got together the necessary money, and brought it back to me. I was profoundly touched by this proof of affection, and promised myself to lose no time in giving her back her trinkets, which happily before long, thanks to my contract, I was able to do.

" At this time, however, my greatest misfortunes began : my baby fell ill in the beginning of April; the doctors could not discover what ailed him, the child daily grew weaker, and finally died in the arms of his mother. She was simply crazy with anguish and despair. That was not enough ; a few days later my little girl likewise fell ill, and her malady also ended fatally ; and yet—and yet that is not all : on the first day of June my young companion was seized by acute encephalitis, and on the 19th June 1840 a third corpse was carried out of my house. I was alone, alone : in the space of two months three loved beings had disappeared, had gone out of my life, for ever. I had no more family, and in the midst of this terrible anguish, in order not to neglect the engagement

---

* Verdi is really too generous. I should say, through every fault of his own : was he not named Merelli ?

which I had solemnly contracted, I was obliged to sit down
to work to complete a comic opera.

" *Un Giorno di Regno* did not succeed ; a part of this failure
certainly was on account of the music, but the other part belongs to the executants. My soul torn by the unhappiness
which had overwhelmed me, my mind embittered by the
failure of my work, I began to persuade myself that I should
find no consolation in art ; I resolved never to become a composer, and I even wrote to my friend, Pasetti, who, by the way,
since the failure of *Un Giorno di Regno*, had given no signs of
life, and begged him to obtain for me the annulment of my
contract.

" Merelli sent for me and treated me as if I were a capricious child : he would not admit that by one failure I could be
disgusted with art, &c. &c. ; but I insisted so strongly that he
finished by giving me back my agreement: then he added, ' Listen, Verdi. I cannot oblige you to work by force ; still, my confidence in you is undiminished. Who knows but some day you
will decide to take up your pen ? In that case, it will only
be necessary to give me notice two months before the beginning
of any operatic season, and I promise you that whatever opera
you bring me shall be represented.'

" I thanked him, but his words did not make me retract my
determination, and I withdrew. I then fixed myself in quarters
near the De Cristoforis Galleria* (one of my favourite walks
in Milan). I was utterly discouraged, and thought no more of
music. One evening, however, coming out of the gallery, I
met Merelli face to face ; he was on his way to the theatre.

" It was snowing in big flakes, and Merelli, slipping his arm
into mine, induced me to accompany him as far as La Scala,
and to the director's cabinet. We talked freely on our way
there, and he told me he was very much embarrassed for a

* One of the oldest arcades, or covered public galleries, in Milan.

new opera which he wanted to give. He had commissioned
Nicolai to write this opera, but Nicolai had not been satisfied
with the libretto furnished him.

"'Imagine,' said Merelli, 'one of Solera's librettos, superb,
magnificent, extraordinary; the most grandiose dramatic situa-
tions, full of interest, with such beautiful verses, and that
beast Nicolai will listen to nothing of it. He declares that
the story is impossible, and so on. I don't know where to put
my head to discover or get hold of another libretto.'

"'O, I can relieve you of some embarrassment there,' I
said; 'did you not have the poem of *Il Proscritto* written
for me? I haven't set a note of music to it. It is absolutely
at your disposal.'

"'Ah! bravo! that is really great luck!' he cried; and,
chatting amiably, we finally arrived at the theatre-door.

"Merelli instantly called Bassi, general factotum, poet,
stage-director, librarian, and I don't know what beside, and
told him to hunt in the archives to see if he could not find the
manuscript of the *Proscritto*. It was found in an obscure
corner; but at the same time Merelli took up another manuscript and showed it to me.

"'Here!' he cried, 'here! look at this; it is Solera's libretto
—such a grand subject, and to refuse it! Here you are; take
it, and read it.'

"'What on earth do you expect me to do with it? No, no;
I have no wish whatever to read this libretto.'

"'Ah! come now. I suppose it won't hurt your feelings
just to look at it? Read it, I say; then you can bring it back
to me.'

"He placed the book in my hands; it was a big pamphlet
written in big characters, as was the style in those days. I
rolled it up, and saying 'good-bye' to Merelli, wended my way
homewards.

CHAPTER VI.

"WHILST walking thither I was seized with an indefinable feeling; a profound sadness, a veritable anguish seemed to wall up my heart. I reëntered my house, and with an almost violent gesture threw the manuscript on the table, but some way I also straightened myself and stood upright before it. In falling on the table it had opened itself, and without knowing why or wherefore my eyes fell upon the open page before me, precisely upon this verse,

'Va pensiero, sull' ali dorate.'
(Fly away, thought, on golden wings.)

" I quickly ran over the following verses, and somehow felt deeply impressed, all the more so as they were really a paraphrase from the Bible, the reading of which had ever been one of my dear employments.

" I read a fragment, I read two fragments, but strong in my resolution to compose no more, I gained command over my feelings, shut up my book, and went to bed. But how account for it ? *Nabucco* kept running in my head, and sleep did not visit my eyelids. I arose, read the libretto, not once or twice, but *three* times, and so carefully that the next morning I knew Solera's poem by heart, and could repeat it from one end to the other. In spite of this I did not feel disposed to change my mind about composing, and during the day I went back to the theatre to give Merelli his manuscript.

" ' Ah !' he said, ' is it beautiful?'

" ' Very beautiful.'

" ' Well, set it to music.'

" ' Not at all. I wish to do nothing more in the way of composition.'

" ' Set it to music, I say; set it to *music*,' he repeated, particularly emphasising this last word. He took the book and thrusting it into my overcoat pocket, seized me by the shoulder, and not only briskly put me outside his study, but he actually shut the door and locked it in my face.

" What was to be done? Nothing but to go home, which I did. I went back with *Nabucco* in my pocket.

" One day one verse, one day another verse, here a note and there a phrase, and little by little the opera was written. We were then in the autumn of '41, and remembering my promise to Merelli, I went to him to announce that *Nabucco* was finished, and that in consequence he could have it performed the forthcoming carnival and Lenten season at La Scala. Merelli declared that he was as good as his word, but at the same time reminded me that it would be impossible to give this work the very next season, because his programme was quite made up, and he had already selected three new operas from three celebrated composers to be the chief attractions. To give a fourth new work by an author who was almost a beginner would not only be dangerous for everybody, but particularly so for me. According to Merelli it would be much better to wait for the spring season, when he would not only be free from obligation to give other new operas, but when, he assured me, he would be able to engage some excellent artists to perform in mine. I refused, saying that it should be during this carnival or not at all, and I had very good reasons for my refusal; because it would have been impossible to have found two artists better suited to my opera than Signora Strepponi and Ronconi, both of whom I knew were engaged at La Scala.

that moment, and upon whom I had founded the greatest hopes and aspirations.

"Although well enough disposed to be agreeable to me, I cannot say that Merelli was altogether in the wrong. Four new operas one after the other was a great risk to run; while I on my side had some strong artistic arguments to put forward in my own favour. To make a long story short, between yes's and noes, protestations, embarrassments, half-promises, &c., a huge poster was published, and *Nabucco* was not announced amongst La Scala's attractions for that season.

" I was young and I was hot-blooded. I wrote Merelli an idiotic letter, a letter in which I exhausted all my rage ; and I must confess that the document was but barely posted when I felt a sort of remorse, and trembled for fear that by my manner of acting I had brought irretrievable ruin upon myself.

"Merelli sent for me, and when he saw me, cried out briskly :

" ' Now, I ask you, is that the way to write to a friend ? But, nonsense ! perhaps you are right ; and we will produce this famous *Nabucco*. However, I am obliged to tell you that as I shall have terrible expenses to run into for the other operas, in consequence, I cannot furnish any new scenes or costumes for yours, and you must content yourself with the best properties we can find in the Scala storehouse.'

" So deeply was my heart set on giving my opera that I consented to everything, and shortly I saw appear a new *cartellone* (poster), upon which at last I had the joy to read *Nabucco*.

" I remember with regard to this a comical scene which took place between Solera and myself. In the third act he had written a little love-duet between Fenella and Ismaele, but this duet did not please me, because it seemed to throw cold water on the action, and diminish the biblical grandeur which

characterises the subject. One morning Solera was at my
house, and I mentioned the above idea to him. He would not
give in. I was right, however, because then he would have
been obliged to recommence work, for him already done. We
warmly discussed our reasons, first one and then the other;
but I stuck to mine and he stuck to his. He finally asked me
what I would like in place of this duet, and I suggested
the idea of the prophecy of Zacharias, which idea did not seem
to him wholly a bad one. However, he was full of buts, ifs, and
perhaps's; he would not yield, but finally said that he would
think it over, and that he would write the scene at once.
That did not suit me : knowing Solera, I also knew that he
would allow any number of days to pass before he could decide
himself to write a single verse, so I quietly turned the key in
the lock, and half seriously, half laughingly said to him, " You
don't go out of this room until you have written the prophecy ;
here is a Bible, here are the words ; all you have to do is to
versify. Come !"

" Solera had a hasty nature, and he did not take kindly to
the affair. A flash of anger brightened his eyes, and, I admit,
I passed a bad quarter of a minute. To begin with, he was a
sort of colossus, and might well have revenged himself on me
by taking it out of my frail person ; but suddenly he laughed,
bit his lip, and then sat down. He began to write tranquilly,
and a quarter of an hour after the prophecy was finished.

" At last, near the end of February '42, the *Nabucco* rehearsals
began, and twelve days after the piano rehearsal, on the 9th of
March, the first representation took place. I had for interpreters Signora Strepponi and Bellinzaghi, Ronconi and
Miragli.

" It is with this work my artistic career commenced, and
even if I had to struggle against innumerable difficulties, it is
likewise certain that *Nabucco* was born under a happy star ;

even the very things which might have been hurtful to its success by some chance were the very things which happened to be favourable. To begin with, I had written a villainous letter to the manager, from which it was highly probable that the said manager would have sent the young composer to the devil; but just the contrary happened. The old and patched-up costumes, rearranged with taste, became simply splendid. The old worn-out scenery, touched up and readjusted by the painter, Perrani, produced extraordinary effect; especially on the first representation, the scene of the temple caused such an overwhelming enthusiasm, that the public applauded certainly not less than ten minutes. At the last rehearsal we did not even know whether the military band was to come on, or where, and the leader, Tutsch, had been very much embarrassed. I indicated a measure to him at rehearsal, and on the first night the music came on the stage with such precision in the crescendo that the public burst out into the wildest storm of applause I had yet heard." Verdi concludes : " You see, it is not always well to confide in benevolent stars, and experience has proven to me the justice of our proverb : " Fidarsi è bene, ma non fidarsi è meglio " (To trust oneself is well, but to distrust oneself is better).

CHAPTER VII.

THE opera of *Nebuchadnezzar*, or *Nabucco* as it was called in Italian, has a great many inferior numbers, but likewise a great many sublime inspirations. It was given all over Italy, and still has a place in the Italian repertory of to-day. The *Illustrated Italian Journal* of February 6th, 1867, gives us a very succinct idea of what Verdi's habits of life were at that time of his economy—his studiousness, and marvellous patience. He lived in Via Andegari, a short street which those who know Milan will remember as running into Via Alessandro Manzoni. After working all day, Verdi and some friend would go to a little restaurant called Osteria di San Romano, in a little court just at the left of Via Durini. The master and his companion never spent more than twenty or twenty five Austrian soldi—a soldo is not quite one cent in American money—for their dinner. Verdi was coming from this very hotel when he met the old Merelli on that night when they walked to the opera-house and afterwards began talking about *Nabucco*. The opera was a triumph, and from that day forth we see Verdi on the high-road to success. *Nabucco* was given at the Carcano Opera House in Milan several years ago, and I was struck by its many beauties. I must leave this work, however, to speak of *I Lombardi, or the First Crusades*, an opera containing exquisite Verdinian measures, which followed the *Nabucco*, and one which settled beyond a doubt the master's fertile genius and art. Nothing he had ever previously written could at all compare with the success of *I Lombardi*, which was brought out in Venice in 1844.

Verdi was at that time considered one of the most gifted of living Italian composers. Without possessing either so spiritual an inspiration as Donizetti or Bellini, or so masterly a talent as Rossini, there was something in his composition which had power to move, which touched the popular heart, and the abundance of melody, sometimes vulgar but always graceful, seemed to furnish, at that time, music specially adapted to such singers' voices as those of Mesdames Pasta, Grisi, Persiani, and Frezzolini. Verdi was looked upon as the legitimate successor of the above-named masters, and the one on whose shoulders this triply-bordered ermine was to fall. His works and name were received everywhere with strange enthusiasm; Donizetti was betrayed into praising him, and Rossini said, "I can't get that fellow Verdi's music out of my head."

So much has been written and said about Verdi as a patriot that it would be wrong not to refer to the subject here, and again, it would be impossible not to find some qualities in his writing synonymous with the stirring times in which Italy then found herself. Victor Emmanuel was not yet sovereign of the united kingdom. The Austrians were masters of Venice, and the country was overrun with factions: every time a tune was heard that had anything warlike or patriotic in its measures, the Italians were moved to the very depths of their souls, and most willing to laud the writer thereof to the skies. They looked upon him as a second evangelist, and Verdi by some strange fatality was this human instrument in the House of Savoy's destiny. In 1842, the police sent word to Merelli and Verdi to tell them they must modify something in the *Lombardi's* libretto. An archbishop had heard that there were certain things in the opera which touched the faith, and were the words and situation not changed, he threatened to write to the Austrian Apostolic

Emperor and make a full statement of his grievances. Verdi refused to obey the call of the chief of police, and he said that he would give his opera as it was written or would not give it at all. A war of words and discussion ensued. Sentiment ran so high with Church on one side, civil and military authorities on the other, that they were really in danger of a battle. A compromise was, however, effected. Several insignificant variations were admitted, the Archbishop was appeased, and Verdi's artistic soul satisfied.

It is certain that Verdi succeeded in raising patriotic enthusiasm, and it is very probable that he did this intentionally. In the *Lombardi* a chorus, "O signori del tetto natio," when sung in the streets of Milan and Venice, caused one of the famous political uprisings which finished in the separation of Italy from Austrian rule. In 1846 Verdi wrote *Attila*, an opera which was received with the wildest enthusiasm. Again, Verdi's measures are used for political purposes; sets of patriotic words are readjusted to his tunes, and in Venice when the grand solo, "Cara patria, già madre e regina," was sung, it raised such wild enthusiasm that another political demonstration took place on the very steps of the theatre. Verdi then wrote *Macbeth*, an opera which contains some of his most magnificent and soul-stirring music. It seems almost ridiculous to add that when the great tenor Palma sang

> "La patria tradita
> Piangendo c'invita,"

the people arose with one voice and interrupted the tenor, joining with him in singing the stirring and peculiarly appropriate words. As I am on the subject of Verdi, patriotism, and the influence his music had on the Italians, I must add one more curious anecdote. At the time when the Austrians entered Milan, and Victor Emmanuel, then King of Sardinia, had placed the hopes of Savoy deep in the heart of the Lombardian province, the desire to shout, "Long live King Victor Emmanuel!" was the wish of many at soul ; but the city in the hands of Austrians, Austrian spies, and Imperial sentinels at every outpost, patriotic cries were born stifled in many an Italian throat. In spite of enemies, however, the watchword was given to many ; in spite of Austrian emperors and Austrian domination, the composer's name, VERDI, formed the initials for Victor Emmanuel, Rè d'Italia; and the cry, " Long live Verdi, viva Verdi !" rang from one end of Lombardy to the other. When they cried " Viva Verdi, Verdi viva !" it was equivalent to saying "Long live Victor Emmanuel, King of Italy !" The streets were filled with placards in white, red, and green, the Italian colours ; Verdi in such big letters that nothing else was visible on the posters. Perhaps this was his baptism at the font of Italian liberty and independence. Verdi is adored and even worshipped in a country which although had he never existed would still have been united ; yet Italy always remembers the excitement caused by his magical music, and the enthusiasm aroused in every heart whenever an Italian voice shouted forth his magical name. Whoever liked could have screamed in the very face of the Archduke Francis himself " Viva Verdi !" and feel that while he was honouring the musician, at the same time he was giving vent to his private feeling as an Italian and a soldier. Whilst the country was still in a state of constant alarm and uproar Verdi was again requested to put his pen to a patriotic subject. He had been to Paris to see about the opera called *Jerusalem*, new name for *I Lombardi*, and on his return was given the libretto called *The Battle of Legnano*: but when it was finished it was not possible to represent it in Milan, at that time still under Austrian dominion. Verdi decided to bring

D

it out at Rome, and the first performance took place in the Argentina Theatre, 27th January 1849.

The opera was not a success, but two scenes particularly pleased—naturally those bearing special reference to the tumultuous times and Italian patriotism in Lombardy. These numbers were the war counsel of the Lombardy delegates and the great patriotic finale. This opera, although written under extraordinary circumstances and in a very short time, was scarcely worthy of Verdi, and very little attention was paid to it. It was even baptised with another name and called *Astiglio*, but since very many years has disappeared from the Verdinian repertory.

Verdi's fame and fortune had grown considerably. He still had to struggle against the music of Bellini, Donizetti, and Rossini, which held the first place in the Italian heart; but with all his faults, his incorrectness, and sometimes frivolous melodies, there was something so stirring, so theatrical in everything he wrote, that it touched the popular heart, and every opera that came from his hand was received with the greatest favour and enthusiasm. At this time he was asked to write a work for the Paris Grand Opera House, and he selected the libretto of the *Sicilian Vespers*, of which opera we shall speak later.

We next come to Verdi's greatest success, *Ernani*, one of the most truly inspired and glorious creations in the Italian musical repertory.

It would be useless to speak of *Ernani*, an opera which is so widely known. Verdi quickly followed this with another effort. While *Ernani* was a triumph, the new opera, *I Due Foscari*, was almost a failure. It has entirely disappeared from the stage of to-day.

The next work which brought Verdi success and money was his *Giovanna d'Arco*, whose chief interpreter was the beautiful, brilliant, and never-to-be forgotten Erminia Frezzolini. I met Madame Frezzolini many years later, shortly before her death, and in spite of time and its terrible ravages, was amazed both at her personal appearance, voice, and still exquisite singing. Such expression, such delicacy, such sweetness, such perfection of execution I rarely remember ever to have heard. This incomparable soprano was then close upon, perhaps, sixty, and yet she sang snatches of *Giovanni d'Arco*, the long and elaborate arias of the *Sonnambula* and *Puritani* in a way that no singer of to-day has ever been able to approach. I cannot do justice to her musical expression, which was something unique, original, and evidently a part of herself. Singing was in her one of those divine natural gifts which neither age, disease, sickness, nor sorrow could modify, but also just one of those musical organisations which, alas! no amount of study or culture can give.

If she sang thus at sixty, what must she have been as the intrepid and beautiful Joan of Arc, the passionate Elvira in *Ernani*, or the unhappy Leonora of the world-sung *Trovatore?* Verdi was certainly very happy in having had such an artist to interpret his even mediocre operas. *Giovanna d'Arco* has no longer a place in the Italian repertory, yet people remember many magnificent numbers; and later, Verdi used the overture for an opera which was brought out in Paris, and has since made the tour of the world—namely, the *Sicilian Vespers*.

Erminia Frezzolini was born in Tuscany about the year 1818. Her parents were not specially given to music or the fine arts, but she came into the world a veritable daughter of the gods; a perfect Pandora in beauty, grace, and talents. From her earliest childhood she showed her love for music, and at the age of fifteen made a triumphant début in a Rossinian opera at La Scala, Milan. Thence she was speedily called to Paris, where her success was still more complete. And her personal appearance—how she looked, you ask ? I can see her now--slender, well made, and graceful as a fawn ; great black eyes lighting up a face of purest oval, a small mouth laughing over the whitest of teeth, a nose that would have shamed the most perfect of aquiline models, and an expression of countenance in itself another's sole beauty : and this at the age of fifty. I really could not believe her older. She was a rare picture set in a rare frame. An old house in the Faubourg St. Germain of Paris ; rooms with oak-panelled walls were hung with the Old Masters ; French windows opened on to a terrace and most seductive garden ; birds sang in leafy trees, and the hottest of June suns poured golden rays athwart the dense shubberies ; water kept trickling in a hidden fountain ; domestic, even wild, animals went skipping to and fro on the grass ; a huge black cat lay blinking on a post of the terrace ; and—shall I ever forget it ?—an enormous green parrot, who, hearing Erminia Frezzolini's voice, seemed to burst through the sunshine and green, straight into the drawing-room, thence straight on to his mistress's shoulder. The next instant this thing of evil, prophet still, or bird, or devil, interrupted her singing. She was breathing forth the " Ah, non credea " of *La Sonnambula :* the bird interrupted her, and on the word *amore* broke into as blood-curdling a trill as it has ever been my lot in this life to listen to. She half stopped, but he, she, or it continued. " You see one of my favourite pupils," she added : " now hear him in ' Ah, non giunge.' " I listened, and seem still to be listening. Of all unearthly sounds, a parrot singing Italian opera is the climax. After an inimitable series of measures, this " bird or devil " looked at his mistress.

" What on earth does your pupil want now ?" I asked.

" 'Ernani involami' is his favourite," she said ; then began the tum-*tum*-TUM waltz accompaniment to this brilliant cabaletta. The green parrot's eyes positively glowed with joy. He slightly

lifted his feathers, half closed his orbs, waved his head in imitation of a prima donna beginning her air, and making a movement with one claw, as if to pose it on a troubled breast, began
a series of dainty staccati which nearly killed me.   Never—no,
never—have I heard such an extraordinary artist, and—and—

Poor parrot ! who knows what has become of him ?   Erminia Frezzolini is dead ; her favourite pupil will never sing
Sonnambula again : he had an unnatural organ, yet alone
imitated to perfection a cantatrice who in life, as in art, by
human beings was inimitable.

CHAPTER VIII.

VERDI'S next great opera was the *Sicilian Vespers*, written for the Paris Grand Opera—the old house in the Rue le Pelletier, destroyed by fire in November of '73, the excitement of which caused many to cry "Henry V. is coming in from Versailles with a white flag to proclaim himself King of France." But about the opera. Paris possessed a delightful prima donna, called Sophie Cruvelli, at present the Viscountess de Vigier, one of the two sisters, Germans, the Misses Cruell with Italianised names. The girl Sophie certainly possessed the most remarkable musical abilities of any artist of the nineteenth century.

Old Mr. Ullman, the late well-known manager, told me a great many things about Sophie—of her beauty, her voice, her accomplishments, but above all of her overwhelming capriciousness. I have often seen her portrait at his house : a fair young woman with a face like an old Flemish portrait, laughing eyes, laughing mouth, and a figure and form of exceptional beauty. Verdi's opera *Attila*, which had been brought out in Venice with very fair success, was sung in London with very great success, and there are plenty of opera-goers to-day who remember its remarkable cast, with Cruvelli, Gardoni, Beletti, and Coulon: and yet the opera was never a favourite. *Attila's* latest interpreters were Lagrange, one of the greatest living singers ; Grisi, then in the splendour of her voice and talent; Frezzolini and Lablache, the great Lablache; and the delicious Persiani, whose voice and singing more nearly represented the perfection of a musical box than any human instrument. Verdi had heard of the name and fame of Cruvelli; he also heard her sing his *Ernani* at the old Italiens, and was very desirous of—in fact, did write the opera of the *Sicilian Vespers* for her. After a great deal of trouble, the poem of the *Sicilian Vespers*, which was written by Scribe and Duveyrier, was pronounced complete in June of 1854, and the music, specially written for the Cruvelli's pheno-menal voice, was orchestrated and ready for band rehearsals.

This artist had been singing at the Italian Opera, in *Luisa Miller*, but in *Ernani* had scored one of the most remarkable successes ever known to have taken place under the roof of the old theatre, Les Italiens. Mdlle. Cruvelli was speedily en-gaged at the Grand Opera House, and was paid the enor-mous sum of 100,000 francs a year, at that time remarkable in French lyric annals. Verdi coming to Paris found in this great theatre the artist who had done so much towards the success of his works at the Italian Opera.

Everything was ready for rehearsal on the 9th of October. The *Huguenots* was to be given, with Mdlle. Cruvelli in the part of Valentine. The theatre was packed, the excitement such as only could have been possible in France on the first night of a Meyerbeer's opera, the enthusiasm was universal, when it was discovered that Mdlle. Cruvelli had disappeared ; had gone none knew whither, and that without even giving her-self the trouble to inform the theatrical director of her depar-ture. As this is not a life of Mdlle. Cruvelli (dead), or the Viscountess de Vigier (alive), I will refrain from any special remarks either on her position, her talent, emoluments, or conduct. The fact was, that as she could not be found after a fortnight's strict research, it was impossible to bring out the opera of the *Sicilian Vespers*. Verdi then declared officially that he could not give this work without Cruvelli, and begged to retract his engagement with the Paris manager. As Cruvelli was not there he refused to confide the rôle, written exceptionally for her powers, to any other dramatic singer at the Grand Opera. The fact is, Mdlle. Cruvelli had run away to Brussels and entered into another engagement, not theatrical, but matrimonial, with M. George Vigier (the second son of Baron Vigier), whom she married that same week; and some time after, the *Courier* of Strasburg contained the following paragraph :

. " Mdlle. Cruvelli, the fair fugitive of the Paris Grand Opera, was last night seen at the theatre (at Strasburg), and assisted at a brilliant representation at the Grand Opera. Mdlle. Cruvelli is only a bird of passage in our city, and returns to Paris at once."

Finally, after many pros and cons, we find capricious Cruvelli making her peace with the Parisian managers, and at last studying the *Sicilian Vespers* with Verdi in person; he not only teaching the refractory prima donna her rôle, but accompanying her at the piano. Nearly a year slipped by before the *Sicilian Vespers* was ready for the public, and it is certain, when the opera finally did appear, its success was triumphant. The scene was one of indescribable enthusiasm, amongst the stars. Cruvelli, of course, carrying away the most brilliant honours.

; The *Sicilian Vespers* as a musical work may be placed amongst Verdi's second-best compositions; there are very brilliant airs and finales, and some very celebiated concerted music, which enjoyed great success in Paris, in London, and from one end of Italy to the other. It is so well known in England and America that I shall not attempt to give a description of it. For those in London, the old familiars of Covent Garden and Drury Lane, well remember Madame Angiolina Bosio and the brilliant Grisi singing in the opera; whilst those in America recall Mesdames Parepa, de Wilhorst, Lagrange, and of to-day's renown, Agatha States, all remarkable heroines in this celebrated opera. . . .

CHAPTER IX.

Verdi composed a number of operas, the following amongst the best known : *Un Giorno di Regno,* failure at La Scala ; *I Due Foscari,* moderate success at Rome ; *Algira,* failure at Naples ; *Attila,* a success at Venice; *Il Corsaro* and *La Battaglia di Legnano* were failures at Trieste ; *Luisa Miller* was a *succès d'estime* at Naples ; *Simon Boccanegra,* a success at Venice ; and *Stiffeglio,* transformed into *Araldo,* was again a failure at Florence ; *Un Ballo in Maschera, Don Carlos,* and *La Forza del Destino,* all great works, were triumphant and lasting successes. Few of these earlier operas hold a position in the repertory of to-day, and have had so little to do with earning Verdi his great fame I shall pass them by, to get on to the master's most important productions.

After *Ernani* and the *Sicilian Vespers,* Verdi's most triumphant work was *Rigoletto,* which was given for the first time in Venice the 18th March 1851.

Solera was no longer librettist ; but young Piave, an excellent Italian poet, who has since furnished most of the librettos of Verdi's recent works, had made a study from Victor Hugo's *Le Roi s'Amuse,* and the opera's first title was *The Malediction;* but Victor Hugo had no intention of seeing his poem put into operatic form, and opposed himself to this defamation so strenuously that it was a very long time before the opera of *Rigoletto* in its present form could be perfected. There was enough of the new work to belong to the Italian poet, and yet the scenes were the original *Le Roi s'Amuse,* but so disguised that even Victor Hugo could not legally take exception to the opera. Again Verdi had the old political troubles to encounter, viz. the Austrian censorship and interference of certain Austrian nobles. It seemed impossible to hit upon any subject which had no allusion, direct or indirect, to the Austrian or Italian Government, and to the sad political state of affairs. To make matters worse, Italy learned that Piave had taken his inspiration at the fount of Victor Hugo's poetry. The censor informed author and poet that their opera could not be represented, as, to begin with, the title was an offence in itself: however as there is a certain amount of worry and fretting and incredible things which crop out when a work seems absolutely completed, so there is always a good fortune which protects genius and helps to pull it through the most turbulent waters. A second commissary of police was found named Maletto, who came to hunt up poor Piave, and indicated to him certain modifications, secondary in themselves which would not hurt the poem, and which would give the poet an outlet to escape the Austrian censorship; for instance, the rôle of the King of Sicily was to be changed to that of the Duke of Mantua, and instead of calling the opera *La Maledizione* it could be called *Rigoletto, the Court Jester.* Piave was satisfied, but Verdi remained to be appeased. At last, however, things were satisfactorily arranged, the changes were made, Verdi ran off to Busseto, where he usually worked, and in an incredibly short space of time came back to Venice with a complete score in his pocket. M. Pougin tells a curious incident relative to the production of the opera. When they began to study the fourth act, the tenor, Mirate, charged with the rôle of the Duke of Mantua, discovered that the solo which he ought to have sung was missing.

"One number is not here," he said to the composer.

"There's time enough," said Verdi; "I will give it to you soon."

But the rehearsals went on, and each day Mirate was obliged to repeat his demand; each day the response was the same " *telo daro.*" Mirate began to be very nervous, and said to Verdi,

" What shall I do to learn this solo ?"

It was but two days before the first performance when Verdi brought him a paper on which was written the famous song " La Donna e Mobile."

" Here," said the composer, " read it."

Mirate opened the paper, saw that the solo was easy, and appeared enchanted.

" Mirate," said Verdi, " give me your word of honour that you will only sing this in your own house, that you won't hum it, that you won't breathe a word or whistle a measure of it, nor let it be heard by any human being whatever before to-morrow night."

" I promise you," said Mirate; but he could not understand why, and seemed much mystified.

Verdi became quiet and said no more.

The reason of the mystery on this occasion was a very simple one. Verdi counted a great deal on the effect of this number for a portion of the success of that act of the opera. He knew that it was a taking facile melody, very easy to catch up, and realising the peculiar talent of the Italians, he feared that if it were heard once before the night of the first performance, the whole populace would immediately be singing it in the streets : in consequence, on the very first night when the opera would be given, he might be accused of plagiarism instead of being applauded for a genuine and happy inspiration.

Verdi's instructions to Mirate had not been useless, and the day for the very last general rehearsal he addressed himself not only to orchestra, but to all the persons of the theatre, to keep it the most absolute secret. It was difficult to do, for

Italians sing without knowing why; still the secret was kept, and that particular solo was a veritable triumph on the first night: when the performance was concluded, as is usual with a new opera, Verdi was not surprised to hear them already humming, in aisle and lobby, on staircase and under portico, " La Donna e Mobile."

Rigoletto is also so well known that I shall not attempt any general description of it here. The success of the opera was great, but nothing to be compared to what the success of *Ernani* had been. In fact, in Paris, where it was brought out some time after by the Escudier Brothers at Les Italiens, many journals, and even celebrated musical critics, went so far as to say that it was one of Verdi's most feeble works. This is not strange when we remember that *Norma* was hissed on its first representation, and that many other world-renowned masterpieces enjoyed a similar fate.

Verdi has never done anything so incomparably fine as *Rigoletto.* The whole score is not only replete with gems of the loftiest inspiration, but musically considered, it is the grandest work Verdi has ever composed. Verdi is always Verdi, and everything from his pen bears the original stamp of his own unique and original talent. In *Rigoletto* there are some few strains of a frivolous, perhaps vulgar, nature, still the whole opera, from the first number to the last, is composed with an elegance as uniform as conspicuous : a sublimity of art and inspiration to which Verdi has in no other score attained ; yet, strange to say, *Ernani* was talked about and sung from one part of the Continent to the other, while *Rigoletto* was successful only at Venice; and even then certain Italian critics of that time show more a spirit of favouritism in speaking of the work, than a real knowledge of its many superlative beauties.

CHAPTER X.

GIUSEPPE VERDI was now in a perfect vein—so to speak, a perfect fever—of composition. He was also very intelligent in his choice of a subject, and usually was the one to suggest to the librettist what was thought would be well suited to an operatic composition. After the *Rigoletto* came following upon its heels the perennial *Trovatore*, which was represented at the theatre in Venice immediately after the performance of *Rigoletto*.

Verdi worked in an incredibly short space of time, and at the moment of finishing *Rigoletto* had already well under way the opera which has been the fortune of barrel-organs and Italian pianinos for more than three decades. The *Trovatore* is the one of all Verdi's works which has, perhaps, the greatest renown. A few notes regarding it may not be amiss. Piave was not the librettist for this score, but a certain poet named Cameranno : he had come across a Spanish play called *El Trovador*, written by a young Spanish patriot named Garcia Guttiriez, a gifted man who had offered several pieces in verse to the Royal Theatre of Madrid. A curious story is told by M. Pougin anent the young Guttiriez. He had barely written his drama of *Trovador* when he presented it to the theatre Del Principi, and the rehearsals were barely begun when he was drafted ; too poor to buy a substitute, he found himself obliged to join the army as a conscript. He was getting ready to wear his uniform in the service of Spain when his play obtained such a success that he was able to procure

the long-desired exchange, and devote himself entirely to a
literary career. This is as much as is known of *El Trovador,*
which, while it furnished the subject for a thrilling melodrama,
is not exactly the subject of the opera libretto.

Il Trovatore was produced at the Apollo Theatre, Rome,
19th January 1853, two years from the representation of
Rigoletto at the Venetian Opera House, La Fenice. The success
of this work was something absolutely unprecedented in Italian
operatic annals. Those who have seen Rome will remember
the Apollo Theatre, which overlooks the Tiber, and is just a
stone's throw from the bridge and castle of St. Angelo. *Trovatore's* success had been so great, that the morning after the
first performance the streets were filled with an immense
affluence of people: not only surging to and from the theatre
doors, but the crowd was so great that it covered the bridge
from one end to the other, whilst the shoutings and echoes
were heard across the water even to the very door of the
castle. The whole day long the Roman streets, which had once
resounded to the cries of tribunes and triumvirs, reëchoed to
the name of this Cæsar in art, Verdi. "Long live Verdi, the
greatest composer Italy has ever known!" The excitement
was kept up until nightfall. People even went to the theatre
to look at the bare walls—and Heaven knows they are bare
enough to look at from the outside—they stared and stared at
the dull columns and plaster, as if they could coax new enthusiasm from out the gray stone pillars and porticoes of L'Apollo.

Madame Penco, a fine dramatic soprano, was the Leonora;
Grossi, the tenor, was Manrico, and several celebrities were
intrusted to the creation of the chief rôles. If I pay so much
attention to *Trovatore*, it is because the airs of this favourite
score are as well known throughout the length and breadth of
the land as the legendary cradle or nursery song with which
we were rocked to sleep in our babyhood. I have met and

spoken not only with eye-witnesses of its extraordinary success, but two of America's most remarkable artists, Mr. and Mrs. Henry Squires, having given me an interesting account of the first production of *Trovatore* in Naples, I cannot do better than repeat their words.

Mrs. Squires, then known as Lucy Escott, was the delightful Prima donna at the Teatro Nuovo in Naples. She was the favourite pupil of the great Florentine master, Romani, and was the first American to sing in Italy : she it was for whom Mercadante wrote his opera of *Violetta*, more than that, her charms, voice, and talent had been the attractions which had actually built up the fortune of the Teatro Nuovo. Her most remarkable personations up to that time had been Gilda in *Rigoletto*, and Violetta in Mercadante's opera of that name.

Mrs. Squires not only remembers about *Trovatore*, but she created the rôle of Leonora at this charming Neapolitan theatre, and was the cantatrice to create the part in English when it was given for the first time at old Drury Lane.

The following conversation may be irrelevant in one sense, but cannot be in another. The condition of Neapolitan society, the exaggerated enthusiasms and wildfire successes, the attitude of certain composers and certain theatre-goers, all represent an epoch which shows us the gulf stretching between the stage of to-day and the social position of artists thirty years ago. The political state of the country then bore directly upon Verdi's life and his electric renown. Could the second half of the nineteenth century ever see a parallel case?

Mrs. Squires began :

" My dear, you have asked me about *Trovatore*, but I can't tell of that without bringing up a host of recollections. In the first place, everything was different then from what it is now : artists were slaves, and the public their masters. Milan, and Venice, and Florence were difficult enough, but in Naples they were simply terrible. The poet said ' see Naples, and die,' but sing in Naples and you may sing anywhere—*Passa Napoli, passa tutto.*

"But speaking of the singers. The license accorded certain artists and professionals to-day brings very forcibly to mind Naples in 1850 — the State and the Theatre : the liberty enjoyed by the former, and an artist's abject slavery under old King Bomba's reign.

"It was in one of Verdi's operas that the tenor, as the Duke, having been hardly treated by the public, conceived the idea of singing and playing at one of his Majesty's households, for which offence he was arrested, and spent a week in prison. One prima donna, after being hissed, had the ill-grace to shrug her shoulders and turn her back on the public. She was not allowed to finish her song, but was hustled off the stage. She was taken from the theatre straight to gaol, where she spent three days in solitary confinement, being brought back every night, however, and forced to sing her part. This only thirty years ago."

What would the Italians have done to a certain West End actress, who, if my memory serves me right, not only evinced displeasure at the inattention of a first-night public, but so forgot herself as to have the audacity to address the delinquents from behind the footlights—that bar dividing the social from the theatrical world which so far no talent has absolutely levelled? Mrs. Squires continued: "Naples of 1850 was the boiling, artistic city to which Naples of to-day bears little resemblance. Not alone have the Bourbons descended from the throne, but art itself is less firmly seated on her imperious platform. At the time Verdi was first sung in Naples there were three opera-houses in constant play; to-day the great San Carlo barely drags out a short Carnival and Quaresima season. But I have to do with years ago, and remember as

distinctly as if yesterday all that happened. Verdi had conquered northern Italy, but in Naples Mercadante reigned
supreme. He would not listen to the sound of the former's
name. He declared even *Rigoletto* was bosh—you know I
was then singing Gilda at the Teatro Nuovo; he had the court
and highest society for his patrons, and managed to set everybody against poor Verdi. Things went so far that he organ-
ised a cabal against him at Court, and when *Trovatore*—which,
by the way, after Rome, the people would have — was
brought out at San Carlo, Mercadante had so ingratiated
himself with the censor Lord Chamberlain, and I don't know
who else, that they only allowed two acts of *Trovatore* to be
sung, and there was a perfect revolution in the town until the
third and fourth acts were accorded the management.

"I was the first one to sing the full score at little Teatro
Nuovo; the subscribers who were three nights at San Carlo
were the other three nights at my theatre; and to my dying
day I shall never forget the success it had. Happily, Teatro
Nuovo was the earliest in the field with the complete opera.
You may imagine the rage, the force of Verdi's music, after
Rigoletto had been so long kept out of the city, when I tell
you that three theatres in Naples insisted on giving *Trovatore*
at about the same time: the San Carlo, Teatro Nuovo, and
Teatro di San Ferdinando, formerly a royal playhouse, where
Mr. Squires created the part of Manrico, the first American
tenor, by the way, to sing this rôle. This latter hall had
been taken by an amateur troupe for the express purpose
of giving *Trovatore*, and the *Trovatore* rage was so great,
directors brought out the new work with such success, that
the theatre became a regular opera-house, like the others in
the city.

"It is impossible to conceive the tricks and cabals against
Verdi put up by old Mercadante. One would have thought

E

that as he was old and nearing his grave, and his last opera at San Carlo had been a failure, he would have had some consideration for the young and struggling artist ; but, on the contrary, *he kept Verdi out of Naples as long as he could :* the people finally wouldn't stand it any longer ; they weren't going to put up even with Mercadante at his best when there was a fresh new composer taking Italy by storm, when every Italian capital was singing his operas, and Naples, according to all, the very *seat* of fine arts, the only city deprived of hearing Verdi and acclaiming his works."

Mrs. Squires went on :

" When not singing we never went to our own theatre on the first night of a new opera: first, it was not considered etiquette; and secondly, it was not desired by the management. I have already told you about that, but to come to *Il Trovatore.* After the opera had been such a success at Rome, nothing would do but we must bring it out at Naples ; it was during the time of old King Bomba's reign.* He was an ardent patron of music and the drama, and nothing would do but *Trovatore* must be given at once in the city. The town was simply wild, talking *Trovatore, Trovatore* here, there, and everywhere. Rome is so near to Naples that the enthusiasm seems to have come in one straight breeze blown from the Tiber to Vesuvius. Of course, we had to learn our parts from manuscripts, and I never shall forget the curiosity to get hold of those sheets of music-paper. I guess no artists ever learned their rôles so quickly before. At the end of the second rehearsal everybody knew his or her part, and our heads were so filled with the music that it was a simple impossibility in going from one room to another not to break into some snatch of song; from the ' Tacea la Notte ' to the ' Addio, Leonora ' in the last act, it ran like wildfire in our heads. But the worst of all was

* King of the Sicilies : Ferdinand IV., House of Bourbon.

to see that poor Mercadante. In spite of the eulogies which
rang out on every hand fcr Verdi, it was impossible for me to
say a word in his favour. I had been singing a year every
night in Mercadante's *Violetta*, but even that success was
feeble compared with the enthusiasm over the new work ; as we
say in America, Mercadante went about growling like a bear
with a sore head. It was impossible to reconcile himself to
the success of *Trovatore*, to Verdi, the sound of his name,
or the overwhelming interest excited by Verdi's works.

" But the most unhappy people were the artists. You know
Italy was not in those days what it is now ; the performers
were treated like slaves, and when they were about to sing
were not allowed even to absent themselves from the city
without a special permit given by the directors. They were
even carried back and forward to the theatre in sedan-chairs.
San Carlo had one carriage which the prima assoluta always
took, while the others walked or waited. As I say, the singers
were exactly like, in fact *were*, prisoners, and their wills were
simply the wills of whatever manager had them in charge.
I repeat, no artist, however great, was ever expected to appear in
the theatre the first night of a new opera. Imagine what a
howl such a proceeding would set up to-day ; but then it was
not a question of howling ; one merely had to submit, as it was
feared that the others, the non-performers present in the house,
might intimidate or annoy the performers on the stage, and
hinder the success of the performance. Hence they were
usually obliged to stay away. Before the first night of
Trovatore it was something too ludicrous to see the troupes of
the different theatres, and those of Teatro Nuovo not engaged
in the cast, hanging about the stage-doors, begging to be
admitted at rehearsals, trying to catch up a note here, a bar
there, and fairly sick with jealousy, to think that not only
were they not going to perform in this great opera, but that

they couldn't even assist at its failure or triumph. I have assisted at many brilliant successes, but the first night of *Trovatore* at Teatro Nuovo will ever remain one of the memories of my lifetime. We began to speak of Verdi in secret; Austrian spies were everywhere. Why, if we went to Café Donni, we did not dare to say our souls were our own. The Carbonari and secret societies fairly overran Naples. Where I lived Don Antonio was one of old Bomba's spies. Knowing I was a stranger, they used to listen at my door, and after an evening spent at home, the next morning I could go the police-office and read everything which had taken place in my rooms the night before.

" Once I got mad, and said to Musella, my manager, ' Verdi's name means down with the tyrant, his music is a cry for liberty.' When Verdi's brasses went crashing into our ears we out-screamed the instruments, he ruined all the voices extant, but some way we were inspired, *and felt while singing* his music that he was a creature in the hands *of Italy's destiny*. Another curious thing, *no one dared* to change his music. If any artist attempted it the audience would not have it, and howled just as if one were to desecrate Mozart.

" And so it is to this day; one of the greatest tests of Verdi's music was this very fact; even now, to change a Verdi's cabaletta or re-arrange one of his cadenzas makes a shiver run down your back. No, Verdi is a great man ; we shall never see the like of his electric renown repeated in our day."

Trovatore then made the tour of the old and new world. Verdi told me a curious and interesting anecdote of when it was first produced in Paris at the old theatre Les Italiens. It was not alone about the opera, but brought out in striking relief the genius and talent of one of the greatest living women of to-day, Pauline Viardot, the sister of the lamented Malibran. It is of this great woman that the master spoke in such glowing terms.

"The morning arriving for the first performance," said Verdi, " Madame Alboni announced that she was ill, and the opera could not be given that night. What was to be done? Every one was waiting; every seat was sold; I was in despair. Happily, I thought of Madame Viardot. I said to myself, ' She is the only woman in the world who, at a moment's notice, can take the part : if she will only consent to do it.'

"I tore off to her house. It was very early in the morning.

" ' Mon cher,' she said, ' what on earth has brought you at this hour?' I hastily told her the cause.

" ' Alboni is ill.'

" ' But what can I do ?' she said.

" 'You must sing it,' I cried. She interrupted,

" ' I have been so busy I haven't even seen the music ; I haven't looked at it.'

" 'Here it is,' I said, producing a roll, 'it is very easy ; it will be nothing to you.' So laughing and chatting, and protesting that she couldn't, I sat down to the piano. We ran the music of Azucena over from beginning to end two or three times.

"In the afternoon we had another rehearsal, and that evening she sang the part with overwhelming success.

"That is what one may call a quick study," said Verdi, laughing, " to learn such a rôle in the space of eight hours, dress it, and go on the stage and sing it ; but then, you must remember, there is only one Pauline Viardot in all this world."

CHAPTER XI.

AFTER *Trovatore* Verdi's next success was *La Traviata*. I say his next success, as I am speaking of recent judgment only. The *Traviata* on its first performance in Venice was a total failure, and thus described by Verdi himself in a telegram sent to the celebrated musician and composer E. Muzio:

"Dear Emmanuel, *Traviata* last night a fiasco. Is the fault mine or that of the artists? Time will judge.—Yours, VERDI."

It is unnecessary to state that the success of the young Dumas's play, *La Dame aux Camélias*, had made such an impression on the Italian master's mind that he had counted on an equal success for his opera, and was unhappy, naturally, at its utter failure. He had set this charming book to music, and from its completeness it is supposed he took longer than his usual time, four months, to write this score; as in *Rigoletto*, *Traviata* contains some of Verdi's most careful composition, and had he never written but this latter work his name and talent would have been immortalised.

There are plenty of memoirs which tell of this first *Traviata* performance, but I prefer a personal reminiscence, and recall to mind a conversation once held with Randegger, the eminent London singing-master and composer. Maestro Randegger was present at that first performance in Venice, and remembers it as if but yesterday. I readily recall the occasion of his mentioning it. We were at Covent Garden listening to the divine Patti, and saying how lucky even she was in having such an opera to sing.

" O, you think so?" said Prof. Randegger; " but what would you say to hear that once *La Traviata* was a dead failure? I was present in Venice at La Fenice on its first representation, and must say it was a curious experience. The first act was received almost in silence, the finale alone provoking a storm of alternate applause and hisses. This was because of Madame Donatelli's bravura singing, which was simply superb. The second act was almost a greater failure than the first, and the last part of it, which is now the third act of the opera in its present state, was such a total collapse that Verdi was perfectly disheartened.

" It is true that Madame Donatelli, who sang the music of Violetta, was the exact antithesis in personal appearance of the beautifully fascinating but painfully consumptive Marguerite Gautier. Graziani the tenor was very hoarse, and it was almost impossible for him to sing his part ; whilst Varesi, a very eminent baritone of that time, was so displeased with the part of the Father Germont, that he wouldn't give himself the trouble either to act or to sing. Probably for the first time on record Italian opera was seen on the stage with men and women dressed in ordinary habiliments, especially the men, who, instead of wearing Louis XIII. costume, were attired in the more modern swallow-tail and white choker. The father's scene and aria in the second act was simply a lamentable failure. The ball-scene was so replete with ridiculous incongruities, that the public was overcome with a sudden fit of good-humour, and began to find ridicule in everything: we all simply shrieked with laughter.

" Verdi seemed deeply troubled; he hardly knew what to make of it. The wait between the second and third acts was very long, while Verdi kept walking up and down the wings in a state of extraordinary excitement. He must have known that he had put some of his best self into the work, and he was naturally dazed before so curious a judgment. Whilst he was going distractedly back and forwards from the flies to the artists' rooms, he put his hands on my shoulder and said,

"'Now for the last act, and if the prelude doesn't please them, I don't know what will; I'll give up; nothing can satisfy them.'

"The curtain rose for the death-scene, and the public, which was for the moment quiet, listened with ever-growing attention: as Verdi had predicted, the prelude brought forth the most genuine, in fact the only spontaneous applause of the evening. It was then thought that all would go well, but when the poor prima donna appeared in all her strength—great Heavens! she weighed near twelve stone—and when she arose and announced that she was seized with galloping consumption, and had only a few hours to live, the house burst into one roar: with one accord went off into a mad, uncontrollable fit of laughter; that was the ending of the first night of the *Traviata*."

It may be imagined how the poor composer felt, but as we have seen, in speaking of it, Verdi himself said, "time will judge." Time has judged, and decides that *La Traviata* is one of his most exquisitely inspired works, and that the modern Italian repertory will never be complete without this great opera amongst its first attractions.

A very short while after that disastrous season in Venice, the opera was reproduced in the same city, this time with unbounded success. Verdi had altered some things in the score, and changed the entire costuming of the piece. The well-known soprano, Madame Aldigheiri, was one of the most charming Violettas imaginable, and the work, which but a few short months before had been hissed, hooted, and laughed at, now obtained not only a legitimate success, but a veritable triumph. In speaking of *Traviata* it is difficult to confine cur selves to the range of modest enthusiasm. In this work Verdi most admirably displays a musical talent, never in its finest moments one of perfect etherealism, but which, usually replete with a more human passion, here finely expresses the spiritual sense of human love. It is true that Marguerite Gautier was a woman in whom the slightest virtue gained a double reflection. Although she was a lost creature gifted with many good qualities, alone her love for Alfredo was a rare and ennobling sentiment, and reached the point of purest exaltation when it became a living self-sacrifice. All that Verdi has ever felt of passion, of tenderness, of pathos, or of simplicity, all the sensibility he ever may have known, he has put into *La Traviata*. It is true he was writing of a lost woman and man who lived for each other, first drawn together by the senses of purely carnal feeling; but the soul is there, the heart is there, and the contrast between Violetta's life and Violetta's love is depicted by the spiritual tone of this truly inspired music.

Verdi, whose love-duets are always descriptive of the senses and not of the soul, strange to say, in this opera, where he deals of a courtesan's passion, by some inexplicable chord of sympathy, has sounded a note of purer sentiment than he has touched in operas where a purer passion exists. It would be difficult in all the range of Italian opera to find any music so philosophically suited to its libretto, to its character, as this music of *La Traviata*, which at the same time in itself so readily reflects the character, nature, and ability of its composer. To nine-tenths of the music-loving world *La Traviata* and *Rigoletto* will ever come first on the list of Verdi's productions. His isolated works here and there contain gems, and, like the jewels in a broken crown, will gradually be detached from their setting; but it is very probable that as long as we live, and as long as Italian opera lives, these two scores, from their purity, tenderness, and spiritual expression, will have a place amongst the great operatic works of the nineteenth century.

La Traviata made the tour of the world, and opera-goers in London as well as in America will have no difficulty in remembering the finest interpreters which the rôle of Violetta has had: amongst others the gifted Piccolomini, whose success was so great when she sang in this opera at Her Majesty's Theatre that the people ran after her carriage for miles in the street: even when the performance was concluded they stood for hours staring at the door through which she had passed, and the threshold which but just concealed her graceful form.

The late Lord D——y once said to me,

"Madame Piccolomini's success was phenomenal. She was not a perfect singer, but she was the living embodiment of the words ' a perfect opera singer.' I have seen her walking or riding down Regent Street followed by a greater crowd than that which royalty has ever attracted. There was something about her so arch, sprightly, and so thoroughly fascinating that she became the rage, and nothing was talked of but her singing in the *Traviata*. She couldn't trill, she couldn't sing a scale properly, her cadenzas were oftener slovenly than well done, but she was charming, charming—no one ever sang *La Traviata* like Piccolomini."

To speak of Adelina Patti, the most perfect Violetta I have ever heard, seems almost unnecessary, and yet I cannot imagine it possible that any artist could surpass the beauty of her golden voice, charming expression, or her consummate operatic art. For nearly three decades, London, New York, and the world's greatest capitals have done persistent homage to her beauty, gifts, and glorious powers. As long as Adelina Patti sings, *La Traviata* will hold a place in her repertory, and be, as it always has been, her masterpiece.

Verdi composed a great many operas of which it is unnecessary to make even a nominal mention. One, however, deserves a place, as it was the only Italian rôle created by Jenny Lind, the great Swedish Nightingale, in Italy. I refer to *Masnadieri,* which she sang afterwards in London under Lumley's management. The plot was taken from the plot of Schiller's *Brigands :* still, in spite of Jenny Lind and her glorious talent, and the great cast of Drury Lane Theatre, the opera was a flat failure, and completely disappeared from the Verdinian list.

Luisa Miller, brought out about the same time, contains some exquisite bits of writing, and has long been one of Patti's favourite rôles. She has sung it several times at Covent Garden, and tried to revive it recently in America, but the opera has never been a great success, and will not live amongst Verdi's other classics.

CHAPTER XIII.

I PASS over Verdi's intermediate works to come to *Aïda*, his signal triumph, which was written for the Khedive, and brought out at the year of the Franco-Prussian War; also the great *Messa di Requiem*, written in memory of Alessandro Manzoni, and which I heard for the first time in Paris in the year 1875. I take the following account of *Aïda* from the *Chicago Times* of February 11, 1871, as it seems to me a fair, and certainly graphic, description of the opera *Aïda* :

The scene on entering the theatre baffles description. I should like to give you some idea of La Scala, the largest opera-house in the world, although the task is a difficult one. It is entered by an elegant vestibule, flanked on either side by handsome waiting-saloons, where carriages are announced. In the *atrium* the noble statue of Rossini, lately executed by the celebrated Magni, occupies a prominent place. Vast pyramids of orange-shrubs lade the air with a deadly sweetness; camellia-trees, sprinkled with odourless, perfect flowers, clumps of the humble but lovely primroses, that here begin already to predict the spring, clustering at their feet, flank the broad inner entrance. The sense of odour, softly caressed by these perfumes, the eye pleased with their grace, give you faint inner prophecies of the higher emotions you are about to experience, and put you in harmony with the artistic air of the place.

The great house is already packed. The view is magnificent. From the floor to the dome are six tiers of boxes, forty in each tier. All are crowded. Clouds of illusion, silks, satins, lace; blooming faces, and faded ones as well; shining plump shoulders, and withered ones that ought to have discarded the *décollettée* at least ten years ago; youth, age, health, infirmity, roses of nature and roses of the French perfumer; " knots of flowers and ribbons, too;" everywhere animation,

PIAZZA DELLA SCALA.

To the right, Café Martini; centre of the Square, Magni's "Leonardo da Vinci;" and Chief Façade, Opera House of La Scala, Milan.

NEW YORK
PUBLIC LIBRARY

ASTOR. LENOX
TILDEN FOUNDATIONS

light, motion;—all these your eye takes in as it sweeps the vast semi-circle.

The floor is called the *platea*, and corresponds to our parquette, with nearly the same division. There is no dress-circle. The boxes are closed after the European fashion, communicating by a door with the corridor that encircles them, and opens only towards the stage. Nearly all are private property, and many, besides the uniform upholstery of the theatre, are gorgeously and luxuriously fitted up with satin-cushioned walls, elegant mirrors, *fauteuils*, &c. In the rear of each one is a small room where suppers or refreshments are served, if the box is occupied by ladies, or cigars and wines if by gentlemen. The corridors communicate with the *ridotto*, a suite of elegant parlours where ladies and gentlemen from the boxes or stalls are at liberty to promenade and chat between the acts.

The stage is twice as long as the entire auditorium, and of such vast proportions that three hundred persons do not encumber, but only " trim it," as the Italians say. The orchestra numbers two hundred professors, many of them concertists of reputation, and all such finished performers that, at the first reading of the new opera, they played entirely through its extremely complicated instrumentation without once being corrected by the master!—which cannot be said of the singers, with whom the master was so severe that he made every one cry, from the prima donna (the celebrated Stoltz) to the tenor, only his way of crying was good round swearing.

You enter your stall, mercilessly treading on other people's toes— a compliment which will be shortly returned by some later comer than yourself, you may be sure. The immense hum of thousands of merry talkers fills the heated air; some discuss the probabilities of success or failure, for Verdi has made more than one *fiasco* at La Scala. Some opera-glass the ladies in the boxes, among whom very near me I see the Duchess Litta, accompanied by her husband, and surrounded by a brilliant coterie of young men. Among other celebrities, the Archduke Albert of Austria, accompanied by Baron de Kubeck, was pointed out, and, in a box near him, the ex-Chancellor of the Austrian Empire, Count de Beust. The commercial importance of the new work is manifested by the presence of the leading publishers of Paris, Vienna, St. Petersburg, &c.; the artists, by the critics of Rome, Florence, Turin, Bologna, &c.

During the pleasure of looking around on part of the public, the half-hour passes, and the director of the orchestra enters. The first tap of l is bâton is followed by a universal murmur that sounds like the roar of Niagara, heard miles away; and at the second, the stillness of breathless expectation settles over the crowded house. The upraised arm of the director has an unusual fascination; every eye is watching its descent, and unconsciously every ear prepares itself for a grand opening chord. Instead, the violins begin to quiver and melodiously whisper to each other; strange reminiscences of other climes creep over the strings, and beckon to the viols and flutes. Melody becomes perfume; the soft breath of the lotus exhales from these dreamy notes; the heated air of the theatre is a whiff from desert sands; and when, as if drawn by horrible spirits, the curtain rises, the illusion is complete. We are in Egypt.

The epoch, during the might of the Pharaohs, and this, the palace of the king in Memphis. Through the open colonnades of portico you catch glimpses of the fertile plains of the Nile, the mighty pyramid of Cheops in the distance, and the Sphynx, already ancient and mutilated, guarding the entrance to the "desert immense." The walls are covered with hieroglyphic inscriptions, copied with exactitude from archæological remains in the museum of Boulay in Egypt. The designs as well as the argument of the libretto were furnished by Mariette Bey, the celebrated Egyptian archæologist and discoverer of the Cerapeum.

Ramfis, the high priest, announces to Rhadamis, young and valiant warrior, the news of an irruption of the Ethiopians, headed by their formidable king, Amonasro. The sacred oracle of Isis has already designated the leader of the Egyptian hosts, and the high priest bears the sealed decree to the king. Rhadamis, left alone, awaits with suspense the announcement of the choice, desiring that it may be himself, and that he may return victorious to claim from the king the hand of Aïda, the Ethiopian slave of Amneris, daughter of the king. He does not know that Aïda is none other than a princess captured in war, and daughter of the terrible Amonasro, whom he must subdue. Nor does he know that Amneris is also desperately enamoured of him, and as desperately jealous. At the conclusion of the romance for tenor, the king and *cortége* enter the hall, and the sacred oracle is read, while, amid the plaudits of all, Amneris offers to Rhadamis, the chosen leader, the ancient standard of Egypt. This chorus is truly sublime, simple, broad, and powerful in its conception, and written very much after the style of Handel. A regular ovation follows. Deafening cries of " Maestro! maestro!" echo from all parts of the house, and here, for the first time, Verdi appears. He is simply dressed in every-day costume, and holding his hat in his hand, bows bashfully, and smiles as pleasedly as if *Aïda* were the first (instead of the twenty-seventh) effort of his genius, and this applause its chrism. He is fifty-six years of age; middle stature, hair brown, slightly silvered, and face energetic, but not at all what we would call ideal or artistic; quite matter of fact, on the contrary. Milan, the scene of his first great fiasco, and also of his first great triumph with *Nabucodonosor*, is the only city in which he now consents to be present at the first representation of a new opera. In Paris, when *Don Carlos* was given, he superintended all the rehearsals, but left the city before the first representation.

As the court files away, Aïda lingers behind, torn by contending emotions, praying in one moment for the triumph of her father, in the next for that of her lover, and at the closing strains of the exquisitely-mournful plaint, the maestro is again called out enthusiastically.

The next scene opens in the temple of Vulcan, the ancient Ramesseum of Thebes, restored with marvellous perfection. In the midst, the altar of Vulcan, surmounted by the golden idol; through the vast portico the view of the Nile and Libyan range. On the façade of the altar the emblems of Upper and Lower Egypt, the winged Ureus and Vautour (a facsimile of the original in the Louvre). The gods, according to the tradition, turn their back to the altar, the adoring kings face it. Antique Assyrian vases, supported by golden tripods, smoke with incense. Ramfis and Rhadamis stand at the foot of the altar. Within, in the holy of holies of an Egyptian temple, the priestesses of Thermuthis invoke *l'immenso Ftha*—Creator-spirit, the uncreate fire that gives the sun his light; Ftha, who from nothing has drawn the sky and sea—life of the universe—source of eternal Jove! And this conception of God is drawn by Mariette Bey from the palimpsest and hieroglyphics of those ancient times! Who shall bound the heathen and Christian world? The weird chant of the priestesses within is accompanied by the harp, and in the intervals the orchestra and virgins of the temple execute the sacred dance. It is said that these two melodies were sent to Verdi from Constantinople by the brother of Donizetti, director of music to the Sultan. Originally they were only a few strongly-characteristic measures; but they have gained a position of primary importance in the new opera by the infinite art with which they are modulated and interwoven. Nothing could be more sublime than these solemn voices, invoking the immense Unknown; nothing more mystic than the dreamy sacred dances; nothing more graceful than the slowly-moving, chain-laden arms of the priestesses. " Other times, other men—other men, other customs!" an unknown world, a worship of which we were ignorant, a civilisation dimly guessed at even by the scientific, here rises before us with the vividness of reality.

The orchestra, dreamily maintaining the delicious "medium-tint" of the music, seems to change into an opium *rêve*, and the mystic dance becomes a vaporous wreath of smoke, winding and curling in and out among the massive pillars. But as Rhadamis invests the consecrated arms, the former bounds with the superb energy of an unchained lion into the bold crescendo of the finale. The violins in ascending scales scintillate sparks of fire; the viols, reinforced by the brass instruments, execute a design in contrary movement; Rhadamis, supported an octave lower by Ramfis, throws out an upper C of magnificent effect; then the curtain falls on the audience, all spring to their feet as if by an electric shock, and an indescribable roar that soon articulates itself is the cry "Viva Verdi! Verdi! Verdi!" The maestro comes out seven or eight times. At the second call the curtain rises, and a deputation of citizens offer him a magnificent symbolic sceptre.

This gift, which I had the pleasure afterwards of seeing, is of ivory, surmounted by a gold capital of the Roman epoch, supporting a diamond star. Around the ivory runs a ribbon of blue enamel bearing the name of Verdi. The ribbon is entwined with a branch of laurel in enamel, studded with emeralds and rubies. On the other end the arms of Milan and Busseto, his native city, and "Aïda" in precious stones. An address, closely written on parchment, and a crimson velvet cushion, accompanied the gift.

The second act opens in the apartments of Amneris. This apartment is built of wood, according to the archæological inductions of Mariette Bey, who discovered that the ancient Egyptians built only temples and tombs to last for ages. Their every-day houses were lightly built of wood, and covered with rich stuffs. Amneris is surrounded by slaves, who deck her for the festival. Rhadamis has conquered the Ethiopian hordes, and slain their king, so he believes.

In reality the king is a prisoner disguised. A curious and original dance of Ethiopian slaves was received with enthusiasm. Aïda approaches, and Amneris, dismissing the slaves, determines to satisfy her jealous suspicion that Aïda loves the conqueror. She announces that Rhadamis was slain in battle, and, trembling with wrath at the wild outburst of grief of the young slave, accuses her. Aïda confusedly attempts to deny, and Amneris in fury cries, "Look me in the face! I deceived thee! Rhadamis lives!"

Aïda throws herself on her knees, thanking the gods, and Amneris haughtily announces herself her rival, the "daughter of the Pharaohs."

The scene changes to the gate of the city of Thebes. The triumphal procession of the young conqueror enters and files before the king. It would be quite impossible to give you any idea of the extraordinary splendour of this spectacle. There is, I believe, no theatre in the world where operas are so magnificently mounted as at La Scala. The vastness of the stage, the superior arrangements for lighting, &c., and, perhaps, also the cheapness of supernumeraries, account, in some degree, for the fact. In a scene like the above, over three hundred persons are on the stage, and not unfrequently from ten to twenty horses ridden in, not led.

The entrance of the troops in Verdi's opera is heralded by Egyptian trumpeters. These curious instruments are at least five feet long, very thin, and furnished with pistons. They were manufactured expressly for the *Aïda*, and the performers taught to play them. The troops are composed of archers, spearmen, pikemen, and many others, whose uncouth arms I cannot name. Among them, however, my attention was directed to the celebrated "Ichardana," whom the historians say once inhabited the Mediterranean isles, invaded Egypt in the reign of Rhamsis, were conquered, entered the Egyptian army, and in time became the guard of honour of the king. Their superb costumes were exactly copied from bas-reliefs on the tomb of Rhamsis III. After them came four groups of ballet-girls, representing Asia, Ethiopia, Libya, and Egypt, then the priests with the symbols, the sacred cow, the mystic bee, &c. Last of all, announced by the blare of trumpets, his chair borne on the shoulders of twelve officers, Rhadamis, the conqueror, enters, followed by the Ethiopian prisoners, among whom Aïda recognises her father Amonasro. The king recompenses Rhadamis with the hand of Amneris, and, at his request, frees the prisoners, retaining, however, Aïda and her father, who is supposed to be only an officer, as hostages

Act third opens on the shore of the island Philoe, the Nile by moonlight. Here the tender exquisite embroidery of the orchestra expresses, far better than the stage, the quiet splash of the waters, whispers of the wind, rustling of palm-trees—even the clear fine moonlight. Amneris, guided by the high priest, comes to the island temple to invoke the goddess, "immortal mother and spouse of Osiris," before her nuptials. As she enters the temple the plaintive note of the prelude returns to announce Aïda, who comes to this lonely spot to meet

F

Rhadamis.   Instead, her father issues from among the rocks.   He has
marked her love for Rhadamis and his for her, and has conceived his
plan of escape and revenge : Aïda must draw from the young warrior
the name of the pass by which the Egyptian hosts, again on the move
to repel a new Ethiopian invasion, will cross the mountains, and induce
him to fly with her to live and reign in her native "balmy vales."
This exquisite duo is one of the most charming pieces in the opera.
Full of caressing memories of the past, golden dreams for the future,
horror of the deed she reluctantly consents to do, pity for her suffering
tribes, it is dramatic and lyric at the same moment, an idyl and a
tragedy.   Rhadamis, not knowing how to escape the abhorred marriage
with Amneris, consents to fly, and unconsciously confides the fatal secret,
which is overheard by Amonasro in his hiding-place with a yell of savage
joy.   Amneris, issuing in that moment from the temple, surprises and
denounces the trio.   Rhadamis covers the flight of Aïda and her father,
and surrenders himself prisoner.

The fourth and last act opens in a hall of the palace.   Below are
the subterranean dungeons, where the priests of Isis are already assembled in judgment.   The deep voice of the high priest is heard :
" Rhamadis, Rhamadis, Rhamadis ! thou hast betrayed to the stranger!"
The priests join in : "Defend thyself!" and then a dull distant roll of
drums sweeps by like a wintry gust, expressing wonderfully the gloomy
silence of the accused ; it dies away, and the whole chorus take up the
anathema, " Traitor !"   The music resembles the chant of priests in all
countries, except where its melancholy monotonies are broken by the
sobs of Amneris, who listens above.   This dramatic point recalls the
tower scene in *Trovatore.*

In the last scene the stage is divided into two floors.   Above, the
illuminated temple of Vulcan, glittering with gold and gems ; below,
the massive dungeons, wrapped in gloom.   Rhadamis is condemned
to death in his living tomb.   The priests are closing the heavy
stone over his head; the flute and clarionet, an octave apart, exhale
a sort of sighing moan; Rhadamis perceives that he is not alone
in the dungeon.   Aïda, foreseeing his fate, has found means to
enter and hide there, where for three days she has awaited him.
The maestro has poured all the mournful sweetness of his genius
into the despairing farewells of the dying lovers.   The drama passes
like that of life, without noise or tumult.   The orchestra murmurs some vaporous notes on their last regrets; here and there a
celestial harp-note cleaves the sphere of their lost heaven with faint pro-

phecies of other worlds ; above this gloom shines the glittering temple ; once more the solemn hymn of Thermuthis, the slowly-waving chain-laden arms of the priestesses, the dreamy dance, the curling smoke of the incense return to weave their mystic threads, to twine and inter-twine around the despairing death-song below, and around the sobbing prayer of Amneris, who kneels upon the stone that seals her lover's tomb; and once more, as if drawn by invisible spirits, the curtain slowly falls, and this great and eloquent poem is finished.

For a moment no one stirs ; a sort of spell binds the audience, but it soon gives way to that wild enthusiasm of which only an Italian public is capable. The maestro is called out twelve times, and brings with him the artists, director of orchestra, master of the chorus, designer of the scenes, *e tutti quanti,* which means "the whole lot of 'em " (liberal translation). In all, the calls the first evening numbered thirty-four, the second twenty-seven. By this work Verdi, discarding his old conventionalities, has placed himself at once in the position of the greatest of living composers—the true union of Italian genius and German study.

Aïda is a unit. There is scarcely an air you could detach from the opera as a concert-piece. The master has presented a complete and perfect poem, a musical picture, a character, an epoch, a civilisation, a drama. With *Aïda,* Verdi enters fairly what is called his latest manner. As samples of his continued progress the Italians cite, first style, *Nebucodonosor, Ernani,* &c.; second, *Rigoletto, La Traviata, Il Trovatore ;* third, *The Masked Ball, Luisa Miller ;* fourth, *Don Carlos, Aïda.* The opera passed smoothly and perfectly the first evening. The second, a moment of genuine fright was experienced when the veil of Amneris, in the last act, took fire as she passed the lamps. The singer extinguished it, however, with great presence of mind, and the opera concluded without further disturbance.

The Italians have the right to be proud of this great and splendid offspring of their ancient traditions, which, in connection with the numerous dramatic works presented for the first time this year, seems to prove that the return of political liberty and unity in their country has brought with it a corresponding reawakening of thought and genius. B. S. A.

(Special Correspondent *C. T.*)

CHAPTER XIV.

I HERE interpolate my first criticism on any of Verdi's works, written to the *Chicago Times* after the performance of the *Messa di Requiem* in Paris :

Paris, June 12.

I had a faint idea that I was going to write this week about pictures, but I feel that neither mind nor body can rest until I tell you of Verdi's *Messe*, and its performance, which I have just listened to at the Opéra Comique. The world over, we all like Verdi. There is something in his music that every one can appreciate; and who will not say that the man who has shown so much genius even in poor works, if the right opportunity offered, could not rise to sublimest heights? To write opera music is one thing, to compose sacred music is another. Giuseppe Verdi has now shown the world that he can do both. Had he never written but this one requiem mass his name should be sounded throughout the length and breadth of the land as a great composer. Now an acknowledged author, this last effort only adds to his former greatness. If we liked his operas, we must now adore his masses, because we can recognise in the latter that absolute perfection to which he never seemed to reach in the former. By that, I mean to say that in all his operas we feel that the composer starts out with grand intentions, but so far as fulfilling them is concerned he has never succeeded as well as in this last work. It is so different, in fact, from his general style, that one's recognition of him, the composer Verdi, is very slight; and only that it is so fine, and worthy of a man of genius, can one say, " O, no one but Verdi could write music like that !" It is true he is great ; but the world over, when we like any one, everything that person does seems right. In this instance, where genuine merit arouses enthusiasm, it is bound sooner or later to receive genuine recognition.

The idea of any man's writing forty or fifty operas, and in his old age composing a mass that, from its wondrous beauty, threatens to cast into oblivion the works that have made his reputation, is a wonderful thing! It is from this one standpoint that Verdi may be viewed as the greatest living composer. To think of Verdi's age, and that this is the first sacred music that he has attempted ; and also to think that it took the musical world by storm on its first hearing, with no straggling growth, no pushing its way into public favour, but with one grand leap it cleared the heads of all that is known in classical music and has taken a position at once that will endure for ever. An evidence of Verdi's greatness is his constant improvement. In the case of some writers their first efforts are their best, but with him one can never say that. Still, with the heaven-woven fibre of genius running through and through the score, every new touch of melody shows greater finish in the science of harmony and yet retains a purity of style that is perfectly irresistible. For sacred music, it is divine ; and as a whole, is, indeed, the most wonderful composition of its kind ever listened to. Verdi conducting it in person was an added charm, and it was a pleasure to realise that the man before us was the author of such a work : that slender gray-headed man who stood up and wielded the baton with such decision ; who watched with such anxious eyes the movements of the solo artistes, and whose white-gloved hand fairly spoke in its quick, gliding motions. I think now one of the ambitions of my life has been realised : to have seen Verdi conduct in person ; to have seen in Paris a new work brought out under the direction and sole leadership of the composer himself. Then to hear the cries of " Verdi ! Verdi !" and witness such enthusiasm as I never saw before displayed on any occasion in France ; to see the dignified old man come again and again, bow profoundly, and to know that it was really he, and to feel how his heart must have been touched by so many expressions of appreciation ! To compose music to the memory of a great man in this case was to immortalise oneself; for who that ever thinks of the greatest modern Italian poet will not think in the same moment of the greatest modern Italian composer ? Were Alessandro Manzoni known but as Verdi's friend, this work would immortalise him. We would say, " The memory that could so inspire genius must be the memory of a great man and of great deeds." What Verdi has accomplished in his years of labour may not be laid aside and forgotten; but I do say that one never can compare any of his other works with this. It is entirely different in every respect. Broader and deeper, it shows a strength in certain parts that one never supposed him capable of possessing, and especially so in fugue, a style that is as unlike Verdi as Offenbach is unlike Wagner. As to originality, it is originality's very soul. I believe Verdi has been accused of copying Wagner in some parts of *Aïda ;* but never can any such thing be said of him in this his last work. One would think that a first effort in a style so new to him would have savoured more of imitation than originality; but it is utterly devoid of even Verdi mannerisms, and stands out in bold relief —a revelation in classical music—something so new and masterly that it is simply a wonder how any man that has never written anything but operas could possibly start out and compose in an entirely different style, and have the first effort a complete success in every sense: and this, too, in a city where a new piece has to stand wholly on its merits. Several French journals have attempted a comparison with their pet composer, Ambroise Thomas; but one might as well compare the machine with the brain that originated its mechanism as Thomas with Verdi. The one is all passion, soul, and sentiment; the other all science, mechanism, and art. It is the pure gold compared with " French gilt," or a waxen flower beside a natural one. One cannot find fault with the author of *Hamlet*, as what his music lacks in soul it makes up in science, if such a thing could ever take the place of inspiration. Verdi certainly was inspired when he composed this last and greatest of all Masses, and the French people may well be jealous of their neighbouring Italy, and most particularly of her musical geniuses. In the case of Verdi, his *entrée* into Paris with his Mass has been *Veni, vidi, vici ;* and, as he might say to the French " in his sleeve " with the purest Italian, *Come si fa?* (" What's to be done about it?"), and a quiet laugh all to himself. But now for the Mass.

The opening number is a " Requiem et Kyrie " in four parts, with chorus, sung by soprano, tenor, mezzo-soprano, and bass, and a chorus of about two hundred voices. It was magnificent. There was a freshness even about the grouping of the instruments in the orchestra that gave a new life to the " Kyrie;" and the artists—was there ever heard such blending of voices, or was there ever heard before such voices to blend? I think not. Certainly I have never listened to such matchless singing in my life as I heard to-day; and I begin to fear that I never heard anything in music before to-day, either artists or compositions. However, when one speaks of artists, one must prepare oneself to talk in an undiminished strain of most extravagant language, in order to do justice to those two wonders, Theresa Stoltz and Maria Waldmann. Being a woman myself, I ought to rave over the men—the tenor from principle, and the basso from habit; but I am absolutely incapable of thinking of any one in the artistic line while I see these two noble-looking women standing before my eyes, and while I hear their superb voices ringing in my ears. Let me speak first of the Mass, as I dare not begin with Stoltz and Waldmann, lest everything else be neglected.

"Dies Iræ, à quatre parties," with solos and choruses, constituted the commencement of the second number. I have already mentioned the first part, the "Kyrie," so I will speak of the grand *tuba mirum*, or trumpet-chorus, although it is utterly impossible for one to give any thing like an idea of its real magnificence in writing; still, I wish to try and tell you of the enthusiasm it created. There have been many trumpet-choruses; but when old theatre-goers of Paris stand up and say there never was anything like it before in music, one may gain some slight idea of how great a composition it is. Verdi reaches a grandeur in this that places him head and shoulders above anything else he has ever written. The orchestra at the Comique is usually very fine, and on this occasion it was not even up to its usual standard of excellence. Had it been, I do not know what the people would have done. As it was, the house rang with applause, and cries of "Verdi!" "Verdi!" "Bravo!" "Bravo!" fairly rent the air. It is certainly a revelation in that style of music. Such superb crescendos! And it is not so much the inspiration I speak of as the harmony. The melody glides in and out in a serpentine movement with the deepest bass of the trumpets, while the chorus sings a minor accompaniment.

It is not Wagner. It is greater than anything he has ever written, and is something so masterly that we can only bow in admiration before the genius of a man that could not only imagine, but bring forth, such a world of divine music! Next we have a chorus with fugue that is almost equally good, especially the fugue. It is strange that Verdi should now show such great power in instrumentation—a something he never has done before, and a something never expected of him. Now, one would think it his specialty; the effect is something overwhelming — so much so that one can never imagine greater perfection in this direction than he has now attained. After comes a trio, "Quid sum miser," that was exquisitely sung by Mesdames Stoltz and Waldmann, and Signor Capproni, the tenor. It was also so thoroughly original that a new beauty in concerted music was, for the first time. heard; and immediately following came a quartette with chorus that was simply indescribable. Each successive piece showed something more beautiful than the preceding one; and the audience was kept on the *qui vive* of excitement during the whole performance. Want of space compels me to hurry through the description of the first duet, " Recordare," for the mezzo-soprano and soprano, saying only that each number is worthy of high praise. The solo for tenor, " Inge-misco," is very fine. Signor Capproni is not only a very excellent musician and a cultivated singer, but his voice, when compared with the others, is quite inferior He seemed indisposed, and perhaps the heat affected him, as he was evidently labouring under some slight difficulties in using his voice. He gave a magnificent high C in pure chest tone, and which was most enthusiastically applauded, and sustained it longer than any tenor I ever heard. He held it firmly and with great ease, and I do not wonder that he " brought down the house." His style is good, and he is a very acceptable artist. The "Confutatis" solo for bass created a less agreeable impression, as the rapid changes from one key to another made most intricate harmony. But it was indeed glorious! Signor Maini has one of the grandest of bass voices, and the tones rolled out in perfect waves of sound. His head-notes ran sharply up to *sol* with a volume that was intense. He was rapturously received, and an encore demanded, but gracious nods and a smiling countenance were the only response. It was delightful once more to hear a bass voice with notes high and low—like the deepest tones of an organ—and to see a man stand up and make the best use of every tone, and sing with an ease that showed perfect control of every breath and sound. The " Lacrymosa " quartette and chorus finished Part I., and the " Domini Jesu," offertoire for four voices, commenced the second. I do not think that four singers can be found who absolutely breathe together as these artists do, and there was no liberty taken with the score. Verdi just stood there beside them, and they watched his every motion. It is hard to sing with-out any accompaniment, and be in perfect tune at the end, so that when the orchestra commence they seem to have taken their note from the singers; but they were perfectly true, and to such a nicety that the instruments seemed a continuation of the sound long after they had finished.

The " Sanctus,"fugue, with two choruses, followed, and was well ren-dered. I have spoken of Verdi's fugues before, so will turn to the gem of the Mass—the " Agnus Dei," duet and chorus—sung by Mesdames Stoltz and Waldmann, and the chorus of female voices. This is a quaint ingenious composition, of splendid finish, written in unison for two female

voices, and most difficult for any two women to sing without the detec-
tion of some weak points, either on the part of the artist or the composer.
In the duet, "Agnus Dei," the soprano sings an octave above the contralto, and each had such perfect intonation that one seemed to hear a
third voice ! Waldmann's organ is so much like a tenor's that you can
hardly realise that a woman is singing. And then, when she would
commence in *re*, and creep slowly up to *sol*, with tones like an organ,
there was the soprano, just an octave above her, singing and soaring up
with a voice like a heavenly harp, and so perfectly did they sing together
that it was like one voice. Their styles are as near alike as it is possible
for a contralto and soprano to be; and when they commenced the second
phrase, singing the octaves as a sort of fugue, with the flutes and clarionets
mean time playing the melody, it was simply superb. The enthusiasm
of the audience knew no bounds. Before the last notes died away the
public broke into a perfect whirlwind of bravas, and the singers were
obliged to repeat the number. A third repetition was demanded, but
the demand could not be complied with. It is utterly impossible for
me to give you any idea of this duet. There never was such an one written
before. Imagine two voices singing in fugue, an octave apart, fugue
style, every note accompanied by flutes and clarionets, with occasionally
a few pianissimo notes breathed out as assistant accompaniment by a
perfect chorus of female voices. There is only one word to express
what it is as a composition, and that word is, Revelation ! When you see
selfish Parisians rushing breathlessly towards the Opéra Comique with
a copy of Verdi's *Messe* under their arms, you may know that I only
echo the sentiments of the whole musical world of Paris. All have to
acknowledge that it is one of the cleverest compositions known in modern
or ancient music ; and if you could have witnessed the enthusiasm, as I
did, inside the walls of a French opera-house, in behalf of an Italian
composer and rival, you would be amazed. The Parisians lost themselves completely, and nothing is talked of in the streets and music-
stores but Verdi's *Messe*. But to return to the performance.

A trio followed, sung by Madame Waldmann and Messrs. Capproni
and Maini. It was, like all of the rest, beautiful ; but the "Fugue Finale
Solo," for soprano, with chorus, was the climax of greatness for
Madame Stoltz and Verdi. I will now tell you of the voice of this lady.
Madame Stoltz's voice is a pure soprano, with immense compass and
of the most perfectly beautiful quality one ever listened to, from the
lowest note to the highest. Her phrasing is the most superb I ever
heard, and her intonation something faultless. She takes a tone and

sustains it until it seems that her respiration is quite exhausted, and then she has only commenced to hold it. The tones are as fine and clearly cut as a diamond, and sweet as a silver bell; but the power she gives a high C is something amazing. She is said to be the greatest singer in the world; and I presume it is true, as I cannot possibly imagine any one greater than she. Her cultivation is absolute perfection in every way. Where nature has done everything, and art has done even more than nature, what more can you ever expect to hear? One is completely satisfied after listening to her. There is nothing more to be desired. She opens her mouth slightly when she takes a note, without any perceptible effort, and the tone swells out bigger and fuller, always retaining that exquisite purity of intonation, and the air seems actually heavy with great passionate waves of melody, that entrance the hearer and hold him spell-bound. She is a fine appearing woman, and dressed simply in white, with a veil of black lace falling from a shapely head. She had more grace and dignity than is usually seen in one of her years, and her manners were charming. But Madame Maria Waldmann, if possible, has a grander voice for a contralto than Madame Stoltz has for a soprano. It certainly is rare to hear such quality of tone in any female voice. Many times one would think it the tenor, and only when one would look at her and see some slight quiver of the otherwise motionless form, could he realise that it was a woman singing. It is wonderful beyond anything I ever heard of, for a contralto, and she has as perfect cultivation in every way as Madame Stoltz. She is a very lovely person, with golden hair and sweet oval face. She was also dressed in white, with great elegance and taste; but the dress didn't amount to anything—it was the singing. Both Stoltz and Waldmann could stand up muffled in Indian blankets, and, after a few notes, have a world at their feet. The " Libera me " is a fitting finale to such a composition. The power that Verdi evinces in the instrumentation in fugue would appeal to the heart of every worshipper even of Bach; but not every composer can bring out a work for the first time with such artists, and under such favourable auspices. He came to Paris, and has, after one representation, established anew a reputation and a fame that recognises in this last effort its crowning glory. May his remaining years see, if possible, greater successes, and the last hours of his life be blessed with even a few moments of such happiness as he gave the world in the production of this sublime Mass! May his name and memory in the hearts of all be not only Verdi, but Verdissimo !

CHAPTER XV.

Paris, June 5, 1875.

THE second season of Verdi's Mass at Paris, one morning the thought struck me, "I'll call on the great composer, and see what he looks like face to face." Learning that he was stopping at the Hôtel de Bade, I carefully noted down the address, fully intending to avail myself of a kind invitation, received a little time before from the maestro himself, to call on him some day at his residence.

A hurried rush into the director's room after performance is never very satisfactory, and compliments, however earnest, must be very ingenious to be well said in a hurry; so, after the *au revoir* at the stage-door, I made up my mind to see the great master before he went to London.

The Hôtel de Bade is always graced by any amount of professionals, and we were not surprised in coming up before the entrance door to see a number of the stars lounging about in the sun. No. 79 is on the second floor, and after the *concierge* sent us up I fell to wondering whether Verdi would look like an ordinary man or not. A very smiling waiter elbowed his way past with a tray, and somehow it looked as though we ought to follow him, which we did, and we stopped before a door numbered 79. He went in, and we gave our cards to a smart-looking servant who came out of an inner room. Mamma and I sat down, waiting until we should be shown into the presence of the author of *Il Trovatore*.

The anteroom was rather large. At one side was a table, at which was seated a woman busily writing. She didn't look up, and I am sure she was not very interesting. I stared hard at her and then hard at the wall, which almost seemed to touch her left elbow. The wall was perfectly blank and dark-coloured, but some way I saw scores of music all over it; then it gradually became a stage, where musicians, chorus, and artists all seemed jumbled together in one confused mass. I looked harder, and they began to shape themselves. There was the orchestra at the back of the stage, and the chorus-singers, all dressed in white, with graceful drapery of black lace falling over head and shoulders. There was a murmur, and two dark gentlemen came forward with a look that said, "Behold the tenor and bass solo artists." They took two seats in front. Then there was a slight rustle, another murmur, and two queenly women, in long trailing robes of white satin, came forward, their faces lighted with pride and pleasure. Following them closely was Verdi himself. The three stepped forward to the footlights, and my imaginary stage seemed to tremble with the shouts and cries of welcome that rang on every side. The ladies sat down. Verdi took up the bâton; there was a hush, and the music was about to begin. I seemed in dreamland; I could hear the first soft notes of the instruments as they commenced the opening number; I could hear the melody wind in and out, like the clear waters of a mountain brooklet. I looked at Madame Stolz, then at Madame Waldmann, and I wondered if there ever could be such lovely golden hair as she had, unless in a picture. The threads seemed to shimmer and glow under the black Venetian veil she wore, like summer sunlight falling on a gilded harp. The music grew sweeter and louder; the wave of the bâton was more vigorous, and the chorus was just about to come in, when I heard a decidedly waiterish voice say, in pure French,

"Have the goodness to come into the large salon; M. Verdi will come in directly." I started and looked at my wall, but the musicians had faded away, leaving it blank as before. Evidently I had only been dreaming. The waiter's voice brought me to my senses. Imagination was very tame compared with the reality that was soon to be before me. I got up, but vouchsafed a last look at the *nonchalante* who sat at the table. She was still writing, and, as she never turned her head, we went into the grand salon.

Did you ever hear of a woman before who had so little curiosity? I thought she'd look up once at least; but no, she never moved, and we were allowed to enter the parlour, feeling that there was one person in that hotel totally unaware of the great importance and honour of making a morning call on Verdi.

The door closed, and we found ourselves in a richly-furnished room, with a square table containing a coffee-service on one side and an Erard piano on the other. Of course the piano took my eye first, and after that the china. I was wondering whether the one was up to concert pitch, and how *Traviata* would sound played by the master's fingers; then next, if the china was Sèvres or Dresden, when I heard as near by, " *Buon giorno, signorina*," and the maestro stood before us.

Yes, he looked just exactly the same as when he stood on the stage of the Opéra Comique.

His personal appearance is not striking; he is small but very broad-shouldered, with a full, generous chest, and well-built body. He has large, laughing gray eyes, eyes that flash and change colour every instant. The face is strong, and shows very few lines for a man of his years. The features are large, the cheek-bones high, and the lower part of the jaw rather sunken; the chin and side of the face are covered with a short heavy beard, once black, but now slightly mixed with gray.

The mouth is large and pleasant, but it is almost totally concealed by a dark moustache, which gives the face a very young look. The forehead is very broad and high, denoting great character and quickness of perception ; the eyebrows are heavy, also gray and black. The hair is very long, lying lightly on the forehead ; it, also, is slightly mixed with gray. There are a wonderful firmness and hidden strength in Verdi's countenance, which made me think of a picture I had once seen of Samson.

In one way I was disappointed in his looks. He has the air and figure of anything but an ideal composer. I do not know what I expected to find, but certainly he has the frank, social manners of an ordinary individual rather than the exclusive and sometimes painful diffidence characteristic of men of great talent. I cannot say he lacks dignity, but there was so utter an absence of self-consciousness in his bearing, and such a happy, gracious smile on his face, that I was charmed with his whole manner.

We arose as soon as he entered the room. He came forward with outstretched hands and pleasant words to greet us, and then begged us to be seated. Smilingly looking at the breakfast service, he said, " I haven't taken my coffee yet ; will you excuse me, and perhaps you will also have a cup— you know one can always drink coffee in Paris."

We declined the proffered nectar, but looked at the god.

Verdi, looking quickly up, said, " Mademoiselle, how do you like Paris ?"

" Paris ! Why, dear maestro, it's the most beautiful city in the world. Don't you think so ?"

" Yes ; it's too beautiful," said Verdi. " My time is always wasted here. I do nothing, and find that some way the hours fly while I am even thinking of work. Yes, it is far too beautiful for anything but pleasure. I never could compose

here. I am very fond of the city, but, strange to saý, I am
more fond of the country—agriculture, roaming about the fields,
through lone forests, where I can be quiet and admire nature
with all its many beauties undisturbed. I do all my writing
in the country; somehow there everything comes at once, quite
without effort, and I am more contented."

"But," I interrupted, "you go soon to London; how do
you like that great city?"

Verdi groaned. "Don't mention it," he said. "It's as
much too sad as Paris is too gay. I think were I to live there
more than three weeks that I should die."

Then he stirred his coffee vigorously, and I sympathised
with him in his opinion of London, only I persisted that during
"the season," for a time, it was very agreeable.

"O! I was speaking of 'the season,' also," said Verdi;
"but London is a sad, dreary place at all times."

"Aren't you pleased with the reception given you by the
Parisians?"

"O, yes," said Verdi; "the French people are an amiable
race, and I am sorry I cannot stay longer in Paris, but must
go soon to London, as the rehearsals must begin in the Royal
Albert Hall for the *Messa di Requiem.*"

"Ah, that Mass," said I, "how beautiful it is! And then,
too, maestro, you are fortunate in being accompanied by such
artists."

"You are right," said Verdi. "I am every day more thankful that the score is in such hands. But how do you find the
male singers—the new tenor Masini, for instance?"

"I think I like him much better than the man who sang
last year."

"O, yes," interrupted Verdi; "I think he has the divinest
voice I ever heard: it is just like velvet. Then, too, he is
very young, and he is not quite at his ease; but this is his

first public appearance, and I think he does very well considering. I find his tenor, from the highest key to the lowest, simply perfect, and he has great talent. And the basso—how do you find his voice ?"

" O, it's magnificent ! I particularly like the effect in the concerted pieces. It carries very well."

" Ah !" said Verdi, smiling; "so you have discovered it ; that is the great thing in which he excels. I like him for that better than the artist of last year.* How do you compare this performance with those of the last season ?"

" If possible, it is more perfect than the first representations were. I find the last trio faultless ; and as for the ladies, well, Signor Verdi, I am sure they were never equalled before, and how divinely they sing !"

Verdi looked upward, and the look said much more than I can ever tell you. " Have you met them ?" he said finally. " I think I heard them speak of you ?"

" O, yes !" I said quickly. " I had a delightful call on Madame Waldmann,† and she seems sweeter off the stage even than on. How modest she is, and so young ! Mamma and I were talking with her sister, and she told us so many things about her : how she first studied in Vienna, where she was born, and how, after three years, she made her début in Milan at La Scala in *La Favorita ;* but she said that she never would have her picture taken, and that she detested publicity of any sort, but she was very fond of singing, and she was truly pleased with her first success in Paris."

" O, yes," said Verdi, " it's all true ; she is extremely retiring, but she cannot hide her voice and her great talents. You ought to see her in opera."

* Masini, the celebrated tenor, and Medini, the basso, replaced Messrs. Capproni and Maini, who first sang the *Messa* in Paris.

† Madame Waldmann retired from the stage on her marriage with the rich Count Massari of Ferrara.

" Yes, indeed; I am most anxious to see her in *Trovatore*. She must be a superb Azucena. Madame Viardot thinks her wonderful. By the way, madame sent her compliments to you, and I will deliver them now.".

" Madame Viardot ?" said Verdi. " Ah, yes, my old friend. Did she ever tell you how she once sang for me ? Well, I must mention it. It was during one of my first visits to Paris, and *Il Trovatore* was to be given at Les Italiens. Alboni was suddenly taken ill, and the next day being billed for the performance, I was in despair and really worried at the idea of putting it off. It was in the morning, and I happened to think of Madame Pauline Viardot, and hoping to find her at home, I rushed off at once to see her and beg her to undertake the part. I found her in her music-room at the piano, and I said : ' You must sing this for me. Madame Alboni is ill.' ' *Il Trovatore !*' screamed Madame Viardot ; 'impossible! I never even saw the score, and I am very busy.' ' Let's look it over,' I said soothingly. ' Perhaps you can do it. And think of me.' Then madame laughed, took up the book, and—"

" And thought of you," I added.

Verdi smiled and said : " Yes ; the same day, after having learnt the whole score in a few hours, she sang it after one rehearsal superbly, and I never can forget it. She's a woman of great talent and altogether remarkable."

" She expects you this evening," I said, " at her grand farewell reception. Shall we see you?"

" O, yes," replied Verdi ; " I look forward to this evening. But you study with her, I believe you said?"

" Yes," I answered proudly. " She is my teacher, and some day, Signor Verdi, I will sing your opera for you."

" Good!" said the maestro, laughing ; " but it's such a child (*fanciulla*). When am I to hear you?"

" Not for some time. I am not yet ready to sing, and I

G

never should have the heart to attempt *your* music until I could do it justice in some way at least."

After quoting an Italian proverb, Verdi said : " You have time in years from now ; do not be in a hurry. Americans are so ambitious."

I felt my heart throb when he spoke of my compatriots, and said excitedly, " Who would not be ambitious to want to sing such music as yours ? And they are very fond of you in America. When are you going there ?"

" Now, don't mention that," replied Verdi ; " I hate the water, and one is so long at sea ; besides, I am getting too old now. I must rest. I shall give up composing and travelling. I think the *Messa di Requiem* my last work."

" Please don't say that. We will allow you to stay where you will. Only never give up writing."

" Suppose I am tired," he interrupted ; " don't you really think I ought to stop now after so much—" (leaving the word unsaid, and indicating with one slender finger a pile of music near the piano).

" No, I don't," said I stoutly. " You are not a bit old, and you look as if you did not mean what you say. Isn't it true that you love composing and you will never give it up ?"

Verdi sighed, and thoughtfully said, with a tiny French shrug of the shoulders : " *Que voulez-vous ?* I suppose you are right. I am like the others."

" Dear me," said I, glancing at the clock, " maestro, you are too kind ; think how much of your time we are taking up. Much as we would like it, I dare not trespass longer on your amiability."

We were sitting around the table most socially. Verdi had finished his coffee, the tray had been pushed on one side, and I had never even noticed that the time had passed so quickly, as the call and conversation had been delightful, to say the least. We arose, and Verdi insisted that we need not be in a hurry ; but he got up and added that he had nothing to do except to go to the box-office of the Opéra Comique, and he had plenty of time before twelve. Yes, it was twelve. Where had the hour gone to? Hastily saying *au revoir* to the great composer, we shook hands and parted. He smilingly invited us to come any time, assuring us that we would not disturb him. We then left our compliments for Madame Verdi and the artists of the *Messa*, and saying " good-day," walked out.

" He's a dear," said I, when we had reached the boulevard. " Just think of seeing so great a man, and finding him so simple, unaffected, and yet so kind l I have met many people, but never any person more agreeable than Giuseppe Verdi."

Then I reviewed his life in my mind: how he had commenced by writing comic operas, and how little hope of success he had in his young days. He was born in 1813, and now he looks scarcely as old as most men of fifty do. He lives in the country most of the time, in his beautiful country seat, " Sant' Agata ;" there he writes all his operas. It is only when conducting an orchestra that Verdi seems possessed of unnatural power, and then his face looks as might that of Moses when he smote the rock with his rod. There is an inspiration in every move, in every look, and in the leader's chair one understands the completeness of Verdi's genius.

Of twenty-six operas that he has composed, the familiar ones of *La Traviata, Rigoletto, Il Trovatore*, and *Ernani* will never be forgotten. They say he will write soon a new mass to the memory of Donizetti, to be performed at the cathedral of Bergamo, but he told me he would compose nothing new, so I cannot credit the *on dit*.

What words of mine can add to Verdi's greatness ? He is known throughout the length and breadth of the land, and should we never meet again, I shall ever retain most pleasant recollections of my call on him in Paris. To my mind, had he never written anything else, the introduction to the last act of *La Traviata* would immortalise him as an operatic composer. He has given more to the world than it ever can give to him; and while his name ever will be an inspiration to the young composer, his music cannot fail to awaken the same ambitious feelings in the heart of the singer.

That same evening my happiness was complete when I stood in Madame Viardot's parlour, and saw and heard what one hears and sees once in a lifetime: Gounod, Ambroise Thomas, Verdi, and Lamouroux listening in rapt attention to one of Mendelssohn's trios. Rubinstein sat at the piano, Madame Viardot turned the leaves, and her son, the young genius, Paul Viardot, a youth of fifteen, played the first violin.*

"I think the *Messa di Requiem* my last work." Verdi's words as I said adieu to him in Paris so long ago, and yet even he did not know himself. This is the year of our Lord 1887, and he has written another—who shall say a last?— opera called *Othello*. This time poor Piave is no longer the librettist, but one of the most gifted men of the day, Arrigo Boïto, the celebrated author of *Mefistofele*. This latest work has been talked of for the last three years or more, and the world shall soon see of what the maestro Verdi is capable.

Othello is to be brought out at La Scala on or about February 1st, and if prediction proves true, we shall assist at Verdi's crowning triumph.

* Special correspondence, *Chicago Times*, 1875.

CHAPTER XVI.

AFTER the success of *Rigoletto, Il Trovatore,* and *Traviata,* Verdi's worldly prosperity may be said to have commenced. He commanded at that time a very high price for his operas, and began again to think of settling in life. He shortly married Signorina Giuseppina Strepponi, the first to sing in his operas of *Count Oberto, Nabucco, Traviata,* &c., in which latter rôles she had been one of the first to make a success of Violetta. Signorina Strepponi was the daughter of the choirmaster of Monza Cathedral. Monza is the Royal residence near Milan, and boasts a very good conservatory of music. Signorina Strepponi had not only a magnificent voice of very musical range, but she was a veritable lyrical tragedian, endowed with splendid dramatic sentiment and talents and taste. Without doubt this lady contributed greatly to the success of Verdi's early operas, and it is not strange that the maestro, who had found in this young cantatrice so devoted a colleague and so warm a friend, should have thought of asking her to unite her fortunes to his. They were married at Collange in Savoy by Mgr. Mermillod, the famous divine whose career has since been so marked, and whose name is to-day celebrated throughout the episcopal world.

Verdi lived in Milan for many years, but conceived the idea of establishing himself in Genoa, rightly named " the city of palaces." In a flat of the magnificent Palazzo Doria, where

Carlo Quinto had banqueted, and the Genoese nobles had held high revels, maestro Verdi took up his future home.

One day, several years ago, after the usual tourist expeditions in this palace, after looking at the broad terrace and fountain, said to be by Michael Angelo's pupil, Montorsi, I was idly gazing at the neck of land which runs like a silver thread into the sea, when the island of white masts and shipping that covers the port of Genoa suddenly lost their attraction for me, and I was drawn towards a slender man, dressed in fustian, with dark eyes and bearded face. At that moment he lifted his hat, and, in the most natural way in the world, said,

"A beautiful sight, is it not? You are a stranger in Genoa?"

"I am a stranger to the city," I said, "but not to Genoa. I find it very beautiful."

"Youth finds everything beautiful," he interrupted, smiling; "but this is really worthy of admiration. Good-day; may you enjoy your sightseeing!"

Then he saluted me, and turning, walked under the loggia, and began ascending a lofty flight of stairs leading to the upper apartments of the palace.

They say we sometimes entertain angels unawares; so it was that I saw the great Verdi for the first time, and did not know it was he. I was then a melomaniac, and would have given a year of my life but to have looked upon the face of my idol. How often since I have bemoaned the Fates that no word of warning came to tell me, to discover to me, who the man was! I still say, what would I not have given to have known and spoken, perhaps have shaken hands, with my idol, Verdi! When I met him in Paris, strange to say, I did not recognise in him the man whom I had met in the Doria Palace. Verdi purchased a country seat not far from Genoa, which he named Sant' Agata. This place is several miles outside of the City of Palaces,

and is remarkable for nothing beyond being the favourite home
of the composer. Sant' Agata is set in a plain, about ten
miles from Busseto, and is in an almost isolated position: if we
except the cathedral and a few houses built up here and there,
there is little that lends life and being to the property of
Giuseppe Verdi.

Villa Verdi, where the master has composed his finest
operas, and lastly *Othello*, is a square house, Italian in form,
absolutely denuded of exterior decoration. It is placed in the
midst of a beautiful garden, however, where trees, flowers,
and flowering vines, shadow some beauty on the bare structure. Verdi's pride, I am told, is not in operatic composition,
but in agriculture. I presume he might feel badly if you were
to tell him that an aria or a concerted number were not a success, but he certainly would be heart-broken if you were to
reflect aught on his flowers, fruits, or various kinds of vegetables. Verdi's farms are immense, and extend from the
Busseto valley to the waters of the Po. The generous fertility
of these plains is somewhat broken by magnificent forests,
planted by the maestro's own hand, which, during the many
years that he has inhabited this spot, have grown, as it were,
under his very eyes and care. Near the river, Verdi has also
attempted vine-growing; the first years without success, but
at present, in spite of the terrible inundations with which
this stream, the Po, has so frequently overflowed the land, the
vines have not only done well, but have begun to yield fair
and fruitful crops.

Verdi's life is a very simple one: in summer-time he rises at
five o'clock, he potters about the garden, goes into a secluded
library, writes, and writes, and writes; at ten o'clock he
breakfasts, and after the midday coffee, of which, by the way,
he is very fond, some neighbour or passing stranger may
gain an entrance to say good-day, and talk harvests, but never

harmony. Signora Verdi is usually present at all interviews; she has a great deal to say, and in some questions the master does not even allow his soul is his own. At five o'clock comes dinner, and after that a stroll in the pretty garden. Verdi and his wife live, so to speak, week in and week out, alone. On Sunday the maestro's niece, married to a merchant in Busseto, comes thence to pay a visit to her uncle, bringing with her her little children, the delight of the famous composer and the Signora Verdi. The solitude of Sant' Agata is something strange, almost lugubrious. You can scarcely imagine that within the thick, deathlike walls of the villa lives, year in and year out, the writer of such passionate, exuberant music. One can scarcely realise that a composer, and such a composer, can have spent so many years of his life in such a spot.

I must not forget two dogs, watch-dogs, "Top" and "Jenna," who guard the villa with the watchfulness of an entire army. When I saw Verdi in Paris after his Mass of Requiem in 1875, he said to me,

"Paris is too gay, too bright, too noisy; I cannot work here; but I can work at Sant' Agata. Here I should be completely upset; there the solitude encourages and inspires me."

Now that I know what Sant' Agata is like, I can understand that he would prefer solitude, but the pleasure of inhabiting such a place as he has chosen seems to me like the acquired taste for caviare or olives.

In personal appearance Verdi was never what we call a fine-looking man. In pictures of him in early youth we see the clear eyes, intelligent brow, and sober cast of countenance which have been his lifelike characteristics. The mobile mouth has been covered by a heavy beard and moustache for more than half a century.

In every man of genius whom I have known it has always pleased me to find that Nature had bestowed some distinct

VILLA VERDI, AT SANT' AGATA,

The Composer's Summer Residence.

THE NEW YORK
PUBLIC LIBRARY

ASTOR. LENOX
TILDEN FOUNDATIONS

mark to demonstrate, or even suggest, that he had been cut in a different clay, and belonged to a different class of being from the ordinary mortal. Verdi is the one great man absolutely the antithesis of any special mould idea. He is absolutely the ordinary Italian borghese, wearing a look of shrewdness rather than intelligence ; a look of good-nature rather than heart. Taken altogether, a man one would never turn a second time to look at. Duncan (*Macbeth*) says,

"There is no art to find the mind's construction in the face," and the words seem a prophecy in this special instance.

Verdi looked in youth as he does now, like a very good-natured peasant, or shopkeeper, or perhaps a commercial traveller. Beyond a certain pontifical dignity of manner, acquired from the conqueror's position and long habit of the ermine of success, Verdi is anything but a striking man. He has perfectly acquired his rôle of human superiority, which, like the part played by kings and queens prior to the invention of dynamite, was in itself a model of perfect ease and grace.

On looking at Verdi, I defy any human being to think him a man either of genius or any uncommon talent. His face is pleasant but rather stolid, his smile develops a certain cunning, faithful replica of what you have previously remarked in the eyes : that gleam you often see on the face of a peasant bargaining on market-days, or perhaps Shylock when he referred to his ducats and his daughter. I can very readily imagine the maestro Verdi selling his wares, calling in his farmers to expostulate with them; Verdi deciding on the price of corn or cabbage; but I cannot imagine Verdi the man I have studied and repeatedly seen—the genius writing the adorable " Parigi o cara " of the *Traviata*, or the touching, even more refined, measures of " Ah, inseparabile," in *Rigoletto*.

Verdi lives in such quiet at Sant' Agata that he is rarely disturbed. In fact, the only persons whom he ever allows

to interrupt him are his farmers or tenants; and any day he
would stop in the midst of the divinest phrase to see if one
of his men had sharpened the second scythe; if another
had mowed a meadow-patch, or another had planted early
seed for an early harvest. Verdi's nature is absolutely
inexpansive, and without effusion; even from his earliest youth
his character was the very diamond of honesty and uprightness, and we have seen that when he was living near the
Porta Ticinese that he not only worried, but was absolutely ill,
several days beforehand, fearing that on the hour when his
rent-money fell due he should be unable to meet the quarterly
payment. The same foreshadowing persistency, and taking
time by the forelock habit, have followed Verdi throughout
life. He is the one composer who has nothing of the Bohemian in his nature, and with the single exception of one
dangerous illness which disabled him from meeting his contracts, we have never heard of his not having fulfilled to the
smallest iota the most difficult and pressing of his engage-
ments; an irreproachable model in virtue, and yet what is it
that jars on our nature? There is no reason why a man of
genius should not be upright; but, alas! there is a great deal
of precedent to the contrary, and we poor creatures of education
and observation have inherited the old traditions with the
old idea. We laugh at the story of Rossini under lock and
key until a certain opera was completed. We sigh a sigh of
naturalness at the tale of Donizetti's impecuniousness or lavish-
ness; we follow Bellini to midnight supper, masque, or revel,
and perfectly comprehend the creature cut out of other than
Nature's ordinary stuff scorning the level line of law laid down
for the masses; we mentally recall the spontaneous, generous, and
supple natures wherein genius had been pleased to drop her
spark; we think of them, of Verdi, and wonder if this latter
really be cast in the same mould and clay of which were cast

so many men of greatness. Those unfailing rent-days, those
sharpened scythes, and remarkable vegetables speak with a loud
voice. We believe Verdi would have been choked in that special
atmosphere mentioned by Baudelaire as genius-oxygen. Such
moral rectitude frightens us; habit causes us to doubt the
hexameters of a godly man, but rarely question those of
a Bohemian. We should hate to be awakened, but laugh at
genius " roaring for punch at four A.M."

Verdi was as strict with others as he was strict for himself,
and seems all through life to have had an ancient idea of justice
in his mind : to quote Scripture, " an eye for an eye, and a tooth
for a tooth."

With all this stern rigidity and moral equilibrium, the master
has been not alone one of the most generous of men, but one of
the most loyal friends and protectors. With the same austerity
he has never let his right hand know what his left has done.

One instance we can mention—that to his librettist Piave,
who for many years was ill, and incapacitated from working,
and would have been on the verge of starvation had Verdi not
come in opportunely and extended a helping hand. He not
only aided Piave in the first of his malady, but during fifteen
years gave the poet an annual allowance from his own earn-
ings, not only enough to keep him above want, but to enable
him to live in content and comfort.

Theatrical directors in Italy and elsewhere have complained
a great deal about Verdi's hardness, and even this year there
was a great scene among the box-holders at La Scala because
Verdi and the Ricordis together insisted that if the new opera
of *Othello* were to be brought out at this theatre, another of
Verdi's operas should also be included in the grand Carnival
repertory. The screw thus having been put on for the new
work, the subscribers found themselves obliged to listen for
the twelfth consecutive season to *Aïda*. There is no reason

why Verdi should not work in his own interest, and there is every reason why the Ricordis should work in theirs; but when we look at the matter closely the whole affair seems rather exacting. Verdi simply said, " If you don't give *Aïda* you shall not give *Othello*," and that settled it. Perhaps he remembered when, in that same theatre, his *Nabucco* came last on the big playbill, and in that same town his talents were not considered worthy of tuition in the great Milanese Conservatory. He may be excused if, knowing his powers, he occasionally makes a show of them.

Verdi is at present the possessor of very great wealth, and beyond his niece and little niece and nephew, there is no one to inherit the vast estate of Sant' Agata, or his other extensive properties; yet we have been told of a still greater charity which he has in his mind, and one which will put to shame his generosity to even poor Piave. Beyond a suitable remembrance to his niece and her children, the whole of Verdi's estate, amounting to something like two or three millions of francs, perhaps more, is to be devoted to the building of a hospital at Busseto, in which asylum all sorts and conditions of indigent or suffering creatures of all nations and classes may find a permanent refuge. This is Verdi's one ambition, and the pride of his life is in thinking that when he is gone the money which he has earned by his own hands and talent will be the means of doing some good in the world, and specially benefit the poor. You will see that Verdi will give away millions, yet he would not yield an inch when the box-holders of La Scala proposed, instead of *Aïda*, to bring out the opera of perhaps some poor and struggling composer. These are strange anomalies in a man's character which I, for my part, shall never attempt to explain, and I do not know that any one is called upon to explain. Verdi's talent may belong to the world, but his private affairs certainly concern no one but himself.

Verdi's name is world-wide, yet he has few friends and fewer acquaintances. No one knows Verdi. The extraordinary secretiveness of his nature, so to speak, the vein of suspicion, and a strange want of demonstrativeness, are his chief characteristics. Perhaps a remembrance of his early youth and early vicissitudes have sealed his nature with the royal seal of impassibility. As I have said, Verdi has not many friends : he can count them on his fingers. He has never made himself common. I do not suppose there is a person living who can recall any "good times" with Verdi ; no human being ever spoke of him as "such a good fellow," or referred to any Bohemian revelry, midnight suppers, or, in fact, any letting himself go of any sort. Verdi would never give himself up to any of the pettinesses with which the career abounds. He is worshipped in Italy for the simple reason that he is a myth or a 'god ; but he is not a man whom the people know. He has received titles, distinctions, and decorations without number. He is a senator of Italy's united kingdom ; his ribbons and stars would be enough to set up any modest duchy in hereditary honours for centuries to come ; and yet when you see Verdi, he is the plain, unassuming man who might be your poorest neighbour in any land. But never by word or deed could you imagine him a famous or great person in his own country. Perhaps he is great in his way ; if simplicity be greatness, then Verdi is the model of all greatness. He never speaks of himself, and is absolutely unpretentious in manner and personality.

And yet Verdi is adored in Italy. I still think that, as every Italian is an Orsini at heart, patriotism has been a chief link between the composer and his compatriots.

The strange fatality of war always followed the announcement of any of Verdi's operas, and it seems almost enough for him to refer to a new piece for a simultaneous reference to war in some country or other. It was the same at Milan and Naples, when *Rigoletto* was brought out ; at Cairo, when *Aïda* was produced ; and they were bargaining at the Grand Opéra in Paris for this last work, when Paris was being besieged, and the German Emperor followed and stood under their great Arc de Triomphe, victor and conqueror of France. Some way Verdi's name brings to mind all these things, and it is not strange if people in Italy, who are essentially patriotic, should associate his name in music with political and patriotic events. Most of his operas will be dropped out of the Italian repertory, and years hence certain airs sound even to Italian ears like words pronounced in a strange tongue ; but in the smallest hovels of Piedmont or Parma the peasant tending his silkworms or gathering his vine in the fruitful vineyard will hum some patriotic stanza of the long ago, some measure from *I Lombardi* or *Nabucco*, and repeat Verdi's name, as when a Cæsar went to battle the legionaries proudly shouted the name of king and conqueror.

And *Othello ?* I am going to Milan to see and hear for myself—once more to see Verdi, and once more to hear his name ring triumphant through the streets of the old cathedral city.

Book the Second.

CHAPTER I.

January 30th, 1887.

MY DEAR FRIEND,—You asked me to write you from Milan all about my trip and all about the city, especially about Verdi and his latest opera, *Othello*. We left Paris last night by the new St. Gothard route to Italy. The weather was cold in France, but warm compared to Switzerland. Have you ever travelled over the Alps in the winter-time? if you have, you can imagine Bâle at six in the morning. The wind was bitter cold, and plenty of frozen travellers poured out of a long train into a frigid coffee-room, where frigid breezes rushed madly through the door and window. The sound of this winter symphony was enough in itself to freeze the very marrow in one's bones. My teeth chattered an accompaniment to some very cold crockery, some very bad cookery, and some equally bad coffee. To put it plainly, I found Bâle—Greenland. Here we changed our train for the direct to Milan. The cold became even more intense, our voices died in our throats, and the breath floated off to form frost-flowers on the window-panes. I began to fear I should be frozen to death. I longed to do something desperate, but finished by mildly scratching some circles on the glass: it was impossible to look out. While I was yet scratching, the air congealed and the frost again covered the window. After three hours of arctic cold the temperature gradually became warmer, the ice thawed, and we could at least glance outside.

The scene was indeed one of passing beauty. Enthusiasts rave over the Alps in the summer, but who that has ever seen the superb mountain range in the winter will not add an epilogue of amazement and delight? The great summits, which lie in bronze and purple against a June sky, lie in white festoons against the January horizon. Forests rich in the combined wealth of the northern pine and the Mediterranean olive now wear the toga of an eternal frost. The supple trees are weighted with a chain armour of ice, the tiny leaves and branches droop in long fringes of patriarchal gray : the wayside shrubs bend under their weight of diamond sleet, and the frail hedges guarding the roadway stand like waxen sentinels presenting eternal arms to his majesty the frost-king. In some places the fields of snow were transformed by the brilliant sun into fields of amber ; the ravine's sides sparkle with the dew of a thousand waterfalls, and clasp the mountain's base in a necklace of glittering opal. The mountain torrent that rushes on in its heedless course still continues its way, and one sees a water-line gliding like quicksilver underneath the frozen surface, the ice freezing it over in transparent folds, one over the other, like rose-leaves over the heart of the rose. The earth was shrouded in one long winding sheet of white ; mountain, valley, hill, and dale, crag and rock, were motionless beneath this ridged shroud: only the breath of a gentle spring, if it ever comes, can flutter these pallid cerements and tear away the winding-sheet from this winter of death. Can you imagine the stillness of the mountain and valley, the stillness of those dumb waterfalls, the stillness of the trees, and the stillness of those unending plains of snow ? Switzerland is sad enough in summer-time, but at this season it is a picture of phenomenal desolation. We travelled miles and miles without one sign of life. Just before nearing

some little canton, a dim habitation here and there peeped
forth from the wayside, but even these wore the general
aspect of muteness ; no forms appeared at the window, no
gray smoke from the silent chimneys curled up into the gray
sky, no birds or fowls were picking in the sterile garden, and
no watch-dog's form appeared at the threshold ; the sight of
this abandonment, instead of enlivening, added to the sadness
of the scene, and the effect of this vast mid-winter necropolis.
was something beyond words.

After hours of those endless wastes I felt as if I might grow
into some fixed image, as if my body were slowly petrifying,.
congealing into some unearthly substance which could no longer
reëcho to any sound of life ; no longer talk or laugh, or cry or
scream, no longer rejoice, and no longer weep. I thought I
should never leave these plains, where everything was immut-
able, nevermore play my part on the stage of life, never.
commune with friends or foes, never see home or country
again : however I should come back in spirit. The first bird
you hear in the spring-time, calling at your window with its
faint voice, will be me—open the casement ; a body lies under
the alpine snows, but a soul has returned to sing anew the
joyous song of being.

At last the cold grew less intense, and patches of earth
showed here and there through the drifts ; the trees were no
longer dripping branches of frost, and now and then the off-
shoot of some tender pine lifted its verdant head to the horizon.
We were coming into Lucerne, and an air of living, if not
wholly of life, began to loosen the awful chills which had
crept around my heart. Lucerne is charming, and very different from what we had left behind ; it looked gay, bright, even
cheerful. A brilliant sun was still high in the heaven, and a
crowd of happy peasants filled the streets with an ever going
and coming throng. We were gradually escaping those end-

H

less mountains and seemingly endless heights. By the time
we reached Lake Lucerne the temperature had so changed
that a vagrant breath of spring-time rippled its waters. We
finally touched at Lugano, the loveliest spot of the Italian
Alps. Lake Lugano is always beautiful, but I have never
seen it as it appeared yesterday. The first rays of the setting
sun had changed its sapphire to rose, and sweeping veils of
amber filleted the valley from hill to mountain-side. Of all
the Swiss lakes, Lugano has always seemed the most enchanting: however, I must not describe it to you, when such a
portrayal exists as in Meredith's *Diana of the Crossways.* If
you have not read it, do so; the page on Lugano alone is
worth every other description : especially true that part about
the bells. Bells are always ringing here. We had long missed
the Angelus, but swung around the little lake just as the mellow
vespers sent their echoes to join the herdsman's jodle.

From Lugano we reached Chiasso, the station just before
the Italian frontier. Here hand-luggage was examined, the
usual bore of Continental travelling, which reminds me you
must have enjoyed your trip in America. No dragging you
out in the dead of the night, no stumbling out in wet or cold,
no overhauling of trunks or boxes by the sacrilegious fingers
of the dirty revenue officer; even a sight of the blue sky of
Italy can scarcely atone for these governmental indiscretions.
After Chiasso we came to Como. Como, to quote Bulwer,
whose " Marble palaces were lifting to eternal "—what are the
lines? I always forget—well, the palaces were visible only to
the mind's eye, for not only had night fallen, but it was pitch
dark. We finally reached Monza, the royal summer residence,
where Italy's blond queen, a child, used to sit on the knees of
grandpapa Victor Emmanuel, and a maiden walked in the
forest, where she is said to have plighted her troth to her
cousin, Humbert of Savoy. At last, at last, we reach Milan.

It was so changed, I hardly recognised it. The great station lit up with electricity seemed twice the old size, and the way leading thence to the city was one blaze : it was as bright as noonday. When we got to Via Alessandro Manzoni, a line of white lights from one end of the street to the other look like so many stars dropped from the heaven. We finally reached a palace hotel which would not disgrace America, and here the changes were indeed remarkable. The vile-smelling lamp and green tallow dip that used to stifle us a decade since have been replaced by electric wires under alabaster shades. French waiters stand about the antechamber, lifts whirl you up to the highest *piano nobile*—about the sixth floor in English—and carpets, real carpets, cover the wide old stair-cases. When I recollect how that musty marble in days gone by used to freeze the very marrow of my bones, used to chill me from the soles of my feet upwards, I still shudder ; but no, Milan is changed, wonderfully changed.

After a comfortable dinner we strolled out, and found that it had indeed become a modern city. As usual, at night the streets are filled with " all sorts and conditions of men," and the fact of Verdi giving his new opera has completely over-flowed the town with strangers. There is only one topic in the city, Verdi and *Othello.*

I looked with surprise at the people, the Milanese, who, with the city, certainly have not stood still. I had thought the Italians always Italians, but in Milan they are now become cosmopolitans. There were representatives of every race in the streets, few bearing resemblance to the monkeyish Sicilian or broad-browed Roman. You hear every modern language spoken ; in fact, Lombardy has become so modern that we laugh at tales of Belloveso, we doubt Marcello's consulship, and even the name of Julius Cæsar has become a fantastic legend. Walking down this nineteenth-century Mediolanum

749952

we found no footprints of the gallant legionary, and could
scarcely realise that those pert cobble-stones hid the dust of
Sallust. The individuals themselves, the Italians, have lost
their national look. The picturesque cap, close curling hair,
and cutaway of velvet are replaced by modern hat, modern
cropped locks, and modern fustian. The women's pretty picturesque heads are rarely covered with the graceful black veil
which used to be their winter and summer adornment. We no
longer saw the old-fashioned Milanese walking down the once
Italian streets, but a troop of modern men and women swarm-
ing in and out the modern shop-lined thoroughfares. I could
scarcely realise that such a change could have come with one
decade, and cannot say the change quite pleases me. In
looking about I felt that something was missing, I looked in
vain for some shadow of the past. Why could not progress
spare us Italy? We all have our idols ; Italy was one where
the blue sky and time-stained houses, fragrant air and picturesque happy people, together suggested an earthly paradise.
Italy was once artistic, it is now commercial ; the ghost of an
Attila or a Charlemagne no longer visits houses lit by gas or con-
densed lightning. The demon 'Progress' has ventilated antique
niches, it has caught and imprisoned the stars that once shone
from heaven, it has defaced monuments, and dragged aside the
curtain which veiled a charmed and poetic past. Naturally the
denizens of this new world have imbibed the spirit of the time ;
the prince no longer talks, masks, and revels ; the soldier no
longer dreams of the tented field, the poet no longer breathes his
sonnets, and the singer no longer dreams of music and art. The
one discusses selling his castle where Barbarossa saw visions
of glory, the other wishes a change of garrison to the newest
capital, the poet lays his sonnet, not at the feet of the muse,
but of the millionaire, and the singer no longer dreams of
triumph in art on the stage, but in the world and society.

As I say, I received my first shock when I saw the city lighted with electricity, the next when I overheard the tenor of the street conversation, my next when I saw the Milanese women wearing bonnets instead of veils, and my last when I saw the graceful Italian transformed into the Cook tourist. Intelligence says plainly that the new order of things is the best, and yet we are so used to associating poetry, and not prose, with this ideal land, that innovation comes hard. We wish all the world to move on, but this adorable country to stand still. I imagine I hear you say, "O, this is nonsense! Italy is always Italy, there is the blue sky—" Yes, but how long will it be the blue sky? If this progress keeps on, Italy will catch the nineteenth-century epidemic, and, like an intellect developed late, make more rapid strides in a year of serious effort than in a lifetime of premature and indifferent application. She will let out the blue heaven by contract to some advertising company, and where we once saw a Dante's prophecy, or dreamed a Guido's Aurora, we will see visions of angels running patent sewing-machines, and modern Messalinas lauding the latest designs in patent soaps.

I walked home in a state of semi-comatose; the streets with their noonday glare, the hum of un-Italian voices irritated me. It was all very strange. I scarcely wanted to sleep; in fact, I could not have slept if I had tried, it was all so unnatural. Before I retired I wanted to see my old Milan, and determined if there was a bit left in the city, to hunt it up that very night. I wanted to see the centuries of dust and darkness, the high houses looming on quaint corners, and the miles of cobwebs stretching their immemorial fillets across the trecento windows. I walked on and on and on, and finally came to a low panelled arch where all was silent and gloomy. In a rude niche cut in the dark stone, a Madonna and babe in the pinkest of flesh and bluest of vestures smiled under a lamp placed as a light to the Virgin. Under a low vaulted doorway, a Raphael-like child was sleeping in her mother's arms; another was tearing at her nurse's neckerchief and threading her tiny fingers in and out the silver braided hair. In these old haunts I gradually found the old Milan. Amongst those shadows I saw again the shadows of the past, those sleepless phantoms of ages who eternally wend their nightly round. We passed the old church Santa Maria della Grazia, the old Dominican convent, and the old canal. I felt a chill creep over me, I thought I saw something or some one hiding in the shadow of an angle: a man with a long beard which fell over a long cloak—you know they say his spirit watches over his great work, and as long as we see a ghost hovering about the sainted convent, so long will the beauty of Leonardo da Vinci's "Last Supper" endure.

After seemingly interminable wanderings I was satisfied. I had found my old cathedral city, and could retire with a clearer conscience. There were no shadows as we got back in the Via Manzoni, only the same crowd of modern-dressed people, the same brilliancy, the same glare from the new lighting system. We passed the Grand Hôtel de Milan, and saw maestro Verdi's windows lit up like day. The hotel wore such a festive appearance that it was transformed. Magnificent plants and flowers made the entrance-door a bower of beauty, and a red stair-cloth ran like a crimson thread straight to the upper floors: quite like a wedding, only instead of broken hearts in perspective, there will be broken heads for those who crush into the piazza on the first night of *Othello*. We finally reached our hotel, once a palace, always a palace, and now a palace hotel. However, had it been a hovel, I should have been glad to get back, as I was beginning to feel rather tired. As I reached the entrance-hall, a modern valet asked me in French if I would like to take a lift. I nearly fainted. What, after

seeing shadows of Da Vinci and walking with visions of the
trencento, to have a chance to place my feet where Dante
and Silvio Pellico have trod, to ask me to take a lift! it was
too cruel—I mean too modern. I bestowed a look of scorn
on the waiting-man, and wended my way where, in spite of
carpeting, I felt the footsteps of the hallowed deadhad still
left a faint impress on the antique staircase. I stopped a
moment at a landing, and looked forth from a gilded terrace
to where San Carlo Borromeo had once walked, carrying comfort and prayers to the pest-stricken Milanese. I stopped to
glance into a chamber, where a beautiful young princess had
died of love for a prince, and—and—a voice behind me suddenly said, "This is the number."

I entered the open door. "Give me a light," I said—" a
candle."

My attendant smiled, and scornfully touched a white button.

" There is not a candle in the whole of Milan," she said ;
" certainly not in this hotel."

In spite of this triumph of electricity, I remarked that she
still spoke in dialect. I think I shuddered, and I certainly
determined to try on the morrow to buy a humble packet of
tallow dips. I was about to compromise and mention a lamp.
She read my thoughts, probably because, like her words, they
were also in dialect. She began arranging my room.

" It is too late," she said. " Madam is tired, without
doubt—and—they say the tenor is ill."

" Tenor ill ! good heavens !"

" Ah, madam may well exclaim ' good heavens !' The town
is full, the opera has been put off three times, the Scala has
been one long disaster this year, the opera *Flora Mirabilis*—"

" Ah ! *Flora Mirabilis !* have you heard it ?"

" Sainted heaven, yes ! It is charming, but too light for
La Scala. It was a great success at the Carcano Theatre, but

in that big place it has the effect—well, you might as well put
a miniature on the steeple of the Duomo, and expect it to be
seen by the crowd below."

"Ah!"

"Yes. But I have heard some of—"

"No. Now, don't tell me you have heard some of *Othello.*"

"Yes, indeed I have; my brother is a chorus-singer at La
Scala, and he says the music is divine. Verdi has outdone
himself. Madam will be there ?"

"Naturally; as you will be, I presume." I added this
politely, not even doubtingly. Remember, this is a land of song.

"I would rather lose my place," she replied, shaking the
pillows, "than miss that performance; all the house is going."

You see how the opera is supported in Italy. Nice for
art, but rather hard on the stranger within the hotel gates.
Should I by any chance not go, I hope I won't have an in-
auspicious cramp on that auspicious occasion.

Whilst Gianneta was arranging my bed for the night I
strolled idly to the window, the way I always used to do in
Italy before I went to sleep. I was tired in mind, in body,
and still thinking about everything: the glare in the room, if
I could only subdue it, but with electricity you can't turn the
light up and down as you can the humble gas, or even the oil
lamp. I hinted as much as I opened my casement and looked
out. The sky even had changed. In spite of myself I cried,

"Heavens! where are the stars—the moon ?"

Then Giannetta, turning down my bedclothes, murmured,
"We are just out; the demand has been so great; perhaps
to-morrow—the hotel has been so full." A brusque "good-
night!" followed, and wonderingly I heard the door close on her
retreating form. But this is not all. I remember when I used
to be in Milan, calm in the solitude of my chamber, one of my
special delights was to look at the quaint old walls, study the

frescoes which ran around the panels; and stare at the quaint mythological divinities who used to soar over my head in the star-studded ceiling. The walls are just as rich now in frescoes and shadows, and divinities and cupids, but—they are not the same lit up with electricity as they were by candle-light. My eyes wandered idly up and down the once familiar room. The Veronese greens in spirals of eglantine now looked like serpentines of young chickory. The delicate roses, which had suggested the perfume of a thousand-fold attar, waved their leaves in faded brick-colour poppies. The vines looked as if touched with phylloxera; the divinities were monstrosities, and the sporting cupids dropsical fat boys, fit only for Islington, or a dime museum on the Bowery! And I had once thought those crude creatures beautiful! O, progress, what hast thou done for Italy? How long must I stay here? It is true I came to see *Othello,* but also—sainted heaven, and the tenor ill! The vines grew greener, the monstrosities bigger, and the cupids fatter. " Surely," I said, " the god Morpheus is seeking me." But I could not go to sleep in that terrible glare. I arose, groped about, and nearly broke my collar-bone trying to find the electric button. Finally, after evolutions that will not bear description, I replaced myself in my conch and fell asleep, praying for myself, that is to say—the singer. The anxiety felt for the dove's return was poor compared to that which we all feel whilst thinking about this ill-starred artist. Is he ill? Is it hoarseness? Is it temper? Or is it only tenor?—Yours ever.

P.S.—I am a wretch—are you better? How is London, and don't you wish you had come on to see *Othello ?* The excitement is so great, that a clever Italian critic, Signor Caponi, has renamed the town Otellopolis. Significant, is it not? I wish it had been *me* to have thought of it.—Yours ever, &c.

CHAPTER II.

MILAN.

January 31st, 1887.

DEAR FRIEND,—You ask me to tell you about my Milan. I take you at your word, and enclose a leaf from my diary, but I am too lazy to rewrite anything. However, I warn you there is little in it about Verdi, and nothing anent *Othello;* but le voici. Milan always has been, and always will be, one of the most interesting of Italian cities. It is neither musty nor time-stained, but is old enough to be both. The situation, geographically speaking, is one of the finest in the peninsula. It lies in the heart of the great Lombard plain, whose boundaries are broad rivers and high mountains, fertile valleys and smiling landscapes. Milan proper is situated on the banks of the Olona, whose waters mingle with those of the Grand Canal, derived from Ticino, Martesano, from the Adda, and the Canal of Pavia—Milan's neighbour remarkable for great battles, arts, and sciences. My Milan is at present so gay, so young, so cheerful that it requires a vast stretch of imagination to take me from the present back to the remote past, to realise that Miolano was once called Mittland of Celtic origin, and that long before the Star of the East appeared at Bethlehem, Miolano was the Latin Mediolanum, inhabited by thousands of Gauls and those Legions famous before the anti-Christian era. Milan's real history, however, may be recalled since the time of the gallant Gaul, Belleveso, who, six hundred years B.C., founded the present city, which was then known as the capital of the Insubri or Lombards. Following Belleveso and his victories come those of Marcellas, who in the year 222 B.C. with his Roman army entered and took possession of the city, thence onward to the immortal Julius Cæsar, under whose dictatorship Milan acquired the right of Roman citizenship. From these hollows of antiquity float upward glorious spirits, visions whose names alone thrill the soul, heroes whose deeds one by one gleam bright on the azure of history's panoramic past.

'The flower of the peninsula,' as Sallust called Milan, was again overrun with a barbarous horde. Maxmiliano Herculaneum girded her with massive walls, named her the capital of Italy Septrional, and the sound of Pagan revels and barbarous tongues rang throughout the length and breadth of the Lombard city; this lasted until Great Constantine planted the cross at Mediolanum's portals, sang anew the song of the Saviour's birth, and told anew the story of the vision he had seen hovering in the skies of ancient Rome.

" After Constantine the waters of memory ripple over those tideless seas, on whose glorious bosom float the names of an Atilla or a Charlemagne. Milan becomes engulfed in blood and fire. Death, destruction and rebellion succeeds the uprising of the nobles. Milan is dominated by priests or devastated by military adventurers. The heart beats anew at mention of Legnano's victory, and the peace of Constance in the early due-cento; of the reign of the great Italian ducal houses of Sforza, Visconti, and Della Torre; of the rich cinque and seicento, when the language of Dante was beginning to be appreciated, when arts, letters, professions, and sciences made Italy the spiritual flower-garden of the world; that epoch when Raphael put his sweet saints in their immortal niches—when Leonardo da Vinci spread the divine 'Last Supper' on the walls of the old Dominican convent; when Michael Angelo put life into the cold senseless marbles, and Benvenuto Cellini scattered the roses of his genius broadcast amongst the flowering plains of Tuscany.

"The eighteenth century my Milan is rich, prosperous, and powerful. The city echoes to the sounds of revels in Venice, routs in France, and masks in Andalusia. The proud houses of Anjou and Austria succeed each other successively and alternately in the city's government; coins bear effigies of the French King Louis, and Francis I. upholds Louis XIII.'s sceptre; gallant Carlo Quinto is a prisoner, and until the peace of Utrecht little else reverberates along the Alpine hills, than rapine, carnage, pest, and death; the fair Austrian's head, dissevered by the fatal guillotine, has long been cold, the end of the French Revolution is near, and the daring Corsican makes a triumphant entry into the second Lombard capital. All this seems but yesterday—Josephine's tears, Napoleon's fall, and the black and yellow flag waving over Milan's walls. The wars of '48 and '59 are not even yesterday but to-day. Austria is conquered, Milan is free from the hated dominion, and the Italian tricolour waves over the ramparts, won, and how gallantly won, by the great and illustrious house of Savoy.

"Milan, with its grand edifices, its people, its arts, its sciences, its wealth—of these alone remain to her the first and last named: her magnificent churches, her noble palaces, and palatial homes are still Milan's aristocracy, but her wealth belongs to the city. It was once in possession of the nobles, but now belongs to the *borghese*, or commoners, or Israelites. Everything, with a few exceptions, is changed and has changed hands. Society is changed, the middle classes are changed, and the lower classes are changed.

"Milan is and always has been the musical centre of the world. The love of song and arts remains, but their worship is fainter, and their public recognition still more faint. The nobles no longer have money to protect arts and letters, great

names without money are to-day without influence; and money
in the hands of the vulgar and low-minded—alas! we know
but too well what that means, and have sad enough example
of what that creature of to-day, the parvenu, really is. As to
Milan's commercial and industrial prosperity, the improvement is most remarkable. The International Exhibition held
here in 1879 was a startling surprise to me. Such progress
in modern design, in utility and . comfort! There were
machines and machinery whose power and mechanism might
well challenge England's or America's brightest inventors.
Such fabrics in iron and wood, such stuffs in silk and wool,
such patent inventions and contrivances in bric-à-brac as would
make the hair of the most ingenious Yankee stand on end.
I do not speak of the laces, mosaics, or glasses; of the Venetian, Florentine, or Roman specialties, heretofore thought
perfection. Even these had gained in richness, variety, and
device; but the general whole presented such forward strides in
progress and practicability, that, confronted with these ocular
proofs, one speaks less of Italy's past and poetry, soft skies
and *dolce-far niente*, to descant on her industries and ripened
industrial powers, her newly - dawned common sense and
awakened interest in the practical culture of the peninsula's
commercial resources.

" But I am not so surprised with this forward march in the
utilities; it is but natural, and had to come. Even the Italian
begins to travel, to visit other countries. He sees the younger
sons of the noblest houses engaged in selling tea or turnips; he
learns that it is less disgraceful to work than it used to be, and
although the old leopard cannot change his spots, the young
leopard born in captivity by his tameness makes you forget them.
Some old families in Milan, however, still guard the air and
habit of the jungle; I fear, however, they are powerless to check
the tide of innovation that the new distribution of wealth has

brought about. Above all, Milanese society is completely
changed. Industry and commerce dominate the once proud
capital. Henceforth—perhaps for ever—the gilded halls and
splendid chambers of the patrician are closed to the first-born,
leaving to those families enriched in commerce and chemicals
the care of hanging the Christmas myrtle, of relighting the
taper in the glittering chandelier, and dusting Time's powder
from the brocaded sandal; the care of giving balls to princes
whose escutcheons record struggles and victories : battles won
in the crusades of—the Stock Exchange.

"In past years, the great theatre La Scala was a typical
place of reunion for Milan's high life. Descendants of the
Sforza or Della Torre adjusted their robes and reflected the light
of eye and aristocatic feature in the Venetian mirrors. To-day
the boxes are no longer tenanted by noble beauties, they have
left the place to beauties of the middle class ; women, perhaps,
not less beautiful, but their lineaments are carved in the nineteenth - century cameo. The borghese's robes, jewels, and
vesture are equally, even more rich than those of the ancient
Milanese nobility ; but lines of the face have no patrician
stamp; the high-bred look, that insignia of race, remains faithful only to the great lady, its ancestor. O rich people, think,
reflect, how sad that money cannot buy everything. The
marriage of money with the most ancient title has not spared
the first-born's outlines ; plebeian wrists and ankles grace baby
extremities, and remind me of Voltaire's words: 'Surely, if
as much attention were paid to the coupling of the human
races as to dogs or horses, a finer specimen of men and
women would be the result.'

"Hence money bids fair to rule Milan. Blazonry of silk, of
cotton, or chemicals bids fair to efface the serpent of the Visconti, the golden balls of the Medici, and the legendary wings
of the Borromeo. Happily for those families who are left, and

have not been able to accustom themselves to this commercial
invasion—alas, more fatal than all barbaric hosts—Italy has
other cities, especially Rome and Naples, where still remains
a vestige of ancient class, and where society is still composed
of the oldest and most illustrious families; those people have
conserved, so to speak, the ancient customs and traditions of
the elegance and education obligatory to a noble race. I do
not speak of the titles who have married American fortunes:
these are many, but few and far between, compared with the
great mass which throngs the gardens of the Pincio, visits the
Queen at the Quirinale, or pays court to his Holiness Leo
XIII. at the Vatican. Some noble representants remain, but
noble traditions are rapidly disappearing, and—for ever.

"As to individuals, the women are backward, but the men,
of whom Italy may well be proud, fortunately have not followed this modern tide. At the play, in the drawing-room, on
the street I am confronted by a masculine change which is
as agreeable as surprising. The Milanese youth are become
London men about town, even Beau Brummells. The spirit of
modern Anglomania seems infused into every male individual;
their elegance and fastidiousness have stolen the gardenia from
proud Westminster to transplant it on the portals of the Duomo;
they talk horses and stocks, and yachts and shooting-boxes in
the language of Dante—O, no, in the language of Musset—
perhaps of Bret Harte. I am sure they would be incapable of
singing a Laura's charms; but they will descant with fervour
on the latest goddess at the Gaiety.

"And the women, who still dress badly, dream and look love,
roll languid eyes into indifferent ones, think of sonnets and
serenades, flowering walls, sleeping duennas, rope-ladders, and
back staircases—alas! these vain dreams belong to centuries
agone. The newest volume of De Maupassant or Paul Bourget
must fill the soul which once fed on Tasso or Petrarch.

They put their hearts away in the rose and lavender of their grandmothers' conquests, drape their romance-sick bodies in modern garments, and put modern bonnets over their once love-sung Venetian-veiled tresses; and the children—ah, this time our sex first. The little girls no longer learn to work tapestry, dance, or embroider altar-cloths; they are early instructed in mathematics, foreign languages, and the sciences; the little boys—

"And this is the nineteenth century in Italy! poetic Italia!

"Yesterday I paid a visit to a charming and accomplished Marchese F—, who lives in the superb palace known as Casa Busca, and renowned as having been the head-quarters of the Great Napoleon during his stay in Milan. Her only son, aged five, the little Marchesino, after showing me with great pride the N and Imperial eagle, and the gilded fire-board surrounded by the wreath of imperial laurel, after showing the room hung in gray satin, where Napoleon slept, and the little bedstead he slept on, suddenly went to his mamma and whispered something. She shook her head and reddened, he stamped his foot and cried. I wondered if he wanted a cake or candy, a doll or a locomotive: nothing of the kind. He wanted his horse, his groom, and to go out on the Bastioni.* Three minutes later he was mounted, and galloped like a second Archer under the peristyle: he lifted his cap to me as he passed down the Corso, crying, 'Good-bye; if not in Milan, we shall meet in London.'"

A visitor is come, I must close my letter. The excitement is growing anent *Othello*, and the tenor is growing better to sing *Othello*. One word more: Maestro Verdi is getting nervous about the opera. Last night Vergil walked from the Café Martini to Grand Hôtel di Milan with one of the Ricordis, and he—R.—declared the rehearsal had gone very badly. Verdi had actually said, "I am in doubt; I am not sure. Give

* The public gardens and promenade of Milan.

me back my opera, and we will put it *in the fire* and say no more about it." There's tranquillity for you—or nervousness. I don't believe he would burn it, and yet he is so unstrung, he is capable of anything. If it only comes off, I shall be grateful. Even I am beginning to feel anxious. Boïto is as cool as a cucumber. That man has no nerves.—Yours ever.

I

CHAPTER III.

Otellopolis, February 1st.

DEAR FRIEND,—Another month begun—how time flies! The weather is lovely, but cold, and the brightest of bright sunlight pouring into my window, like the May Queen, "waked me early." After devouring the morning papers—the tenor is better, and the opera positively announced for the 5th—I had as good a cup of tea as I could get in London, and began to wonder what I should do with my day. I dressed and strolled out. Via Alessandro Manzoni, unusually alive, was filled with reporters, floating about like clouds in heaven: there were hundreds of strange faces which said plainly, "We are the critics come to hear *Othello*." These individuals wore anything but happy expressions, explained by the reason that as Verdi will permit no one to attend rehearsals, and the opera having been again retarded, correspondents who have put off important work and come thousands of miles to write up this opera, find themselves shut up in Milan wasting time in prowling and growling. Milan is a delightful town; but critics know it, as they know everything, by rote. Travel and sight of new cities has often been recommended for broken hearts—broken for love, I mean; but how about hearts broken in the fine-art cause? Sightseeing is only possible to people who are morally and physically unbroken, and Milan's foreign visitors present a deplorable colony, ill, anxious, and out of employment. Vergil and I decided to breakfast at a café in the Galleria, and going thence ran across our old friend Malvern, come to write up *Othello*—Heaven knows for what paper. I have forgotten. He complained bitterly of what he called Verdi's inconsiderate, brutal treatment. He says he has been in Milan a whole week, with nothing, absolutely nothing, to do. I suggested sight-seeing. He looked woebegone. In vain I tried to cheer him, and said that any reasonable human being, even if he had seen everything, could spend days and days in this city with great profit. I then began the usual rigmarole, " Have you seen—etcetera—etcetera?" To every question he returned a dismal "Yes." I finally caught him.

An advertisement for some miraculous hair-oil directed my thoughts. Following Edgar Poe's theory, you will see how simple it was. Hair-oil suggested pomade; thinking of pomade, I recalled a certain ambrosian liquid said to be inval-uable in cases of baldness; ambrosia suggested the Bibliotheca Ambrosiana, and before I could speak my critic cried,

" Yes, so I have heard. Her hair was yellow, and they say a lock of it is in the Bibliotheca Ambrosiana, with a letter she wrote to the gallant Cardinal Bembo, that facetious priest, whose love affairs and love letters were the talk of not alone the whole Venetian province, but Italy and the Two Sicilies."

" Exactly. And these letters are signed in full—Lucrezia Borgia."

He smiled. Isn't it odd what a difference the sound of a name has, pronounced in daylight or in darkness? With a blue sky and strong sunlight those fatal words have something almost cheery in their accent.

" O wicked critic !" I cried; " I know what you are think-ing about. Whom do you want to poison? Let us go to breakfast." I indicated a neighbouring café. Vergil smiled, knowing the country; but my critic cried, looking at the one indicated,

" To poison? Not myself, surely."

Vergil added, " Let us retrace our steps, I know a better one " (*sic*) ; and we went towards it.

This restaurant, called Café Cova, was a sight to see. First, you go into a cake-shop, where ices, fruits, wines, and quanti-ties of enormous panatones, or fruited, spiced, sweet Christmas bread, are spread out. An old man and two smiling women back of a counter wish you the compliments of the day, inquire if your family is well, and ask if you would like something. Of course you answer " yes, you would like something," and immediately take something, a Vermouth de Torino—the best, by the way, and a most delicious cordial. Vermouth is an Italian liquor that must be healthy, as it is drunk in Milan more freely than water—that would not be a reason, however, as one is good, and the other is not so good. I do not know what Vermouth is, but it contains quantities of Peruvian bark, which plant, since its discovery, seems to have cured every ill under the sun. Vermouth may be especially qualified by the American distinction of a " pick-me-up," or a drink which gives " an appetite." Instantly after a sherry-glass of this inimitable draught, hunger-pangs seized us, and we made our way into the restaurant proper.

The rooms were lofty and Italian, the colonnades Italian, the cornices Italian, the ceilings Italian, the surroundings were Italian, the playbills on the walls were Italian, and over our heads all kinds of people talking all kinds of Italian ; for you know there are as many dialects in Italy as provinces or people. A strong odour of tobacco scented the middle room, and the bare tables were occupied by the most varied set of human beings it has ever been my lot to look upon. Besides the natives from Venice, Piedmont, Tuscany, Rome, and Sicily there were representatives from every part of the world Russians, Poles, Teutons, English, Americans, Turks, all eat-ing, drinking, and smoking, all talking in their national tongues, and of course all talking *Othello*. I never before had seen so many interesting people, and would have been delighted to sit there and watch the play of these varied cosmopolitan physiognomies. They expressed everything with such vigour. Every gesture, every tone, every look, was heart-whole, likewise their appetites, for each one was intent on his breakfast, and eating for dear life. As I saw all this my inward soul broke into Dante, and I turned to Vergil, crying,

" *O anime affamate*, it makes me hungry but to look at them !" We then made our way to an oblong apartment where the marble tables were graced by damask, and where the scent of tobacco was mingled with an odour of rose and violet; numbers of handsome women and distinguished men plainly announced the ladies' coffee-room. Every available nook and corner was full; but we finally found one vacant place and seated ourselves.

The room positively rang with voices—talking, of course, the eternal theme—Verdi-Boïto-*Otello* Tamagno. Italians are enthusiastic, and I had prepared myself for enthusiasm, but not for such an overwhelming excitement as prevailed. The confusion was such that it was some time before a waiter came to us. The Italian breakfast usually consists of transparent slices of raw ham—Italians always eat it raw—cured near Florence and consumed from the head to the heel of the boot; a *risotto*, the famous Milanese dish, rice not too much boiled, coloured with saffron and seasoned with mushrooms, tomato-sauce and cheese—Parmeggiano cheese, as they say, " to uplift it "—a fry called *frittura mista*, brains, liver, &c., wafer-like slices or ragout of veal hammered into tenderness, or, perhaps, a roast of the same flesh. By the way, it has just struck me Italians consume more veal than any other nation : it is the staple meat aliment, and their *panera* or cream is the most delicious in the world. How can you reconcile these facts?

not that there are cream and calves, but where on earth do
the cows come from? To continue : the wines are Barola,
Barbera, ordinary claret, and the Chianti, already so great a
favourite abroad. For dessert that wonderful Gorgonzola or
Grana cheese, fresh figs, and those horrid little yellow berries
called Japonaise nèfle; fruits of the season, and the usual
coffee and liquors finish this Italian repast.

Our waiter having departed, we began to look about, and
saw at one table sat two of Queen Margherita's ladies of
honour, the dark-eyed lovely Princess of N—— and the fascinating Duchess of X——, with attendant cavaliers; at another,
Panzacchi of Bologna, the distinguished poet who has just
translated Ernest Renan's *Abbesse de—* No, I must tell
you this. Alexandre Dumas met Renan and said, " Ah, *cher
maitre*, how is your *Abbesse aux Camé—*I beg your pardon—
Abbesse de Jouarre coming on ?" and seeing Panzacchi I thought
of the story—by the way, the latest I had heard before leaving
Paris. Near Panzacchi the eminent critic and writer, Giacosa;
to his right the great musical critic, Fillippi, despair stamped
on his face because even he could not go to the *Othello*
rehearsals; in another corner a dark-eyed woman chattering,
eating, smiling, laughing, lifting eyebrows and shoulders—
moving head and hands, the quintessence of liveliness and
vivacity—none other than Mathilde de Serao, the brilliant
novelist and brightest talent amongst Italian writers of to-day;
in an opposite direction the singer, Fidès Devriès, come up
from Nice with a party of friends to hear Desdemona, Signora
Romilda Pantaleone, and to say in her heart, as, of course,
she would say : " She is a good singer, but—I—I was cut out for
Desdemona ;" another table attracted my attention, Professor
Erlick of Berlin was looking very wise, and talking to Dr.
H——, both having an air of the Fatherland on their face,
and I judged from the latter's that he was not speaking—yes,

he was—not Wagner, but Verdi. I could tell by the way his lips moved. It is, then, a mania? Good heavens!

The waiter placed something before us—food? O no, not yet, only napkins, plates, glasses, &c. Vergil sighed, sighed, and would have yawned, but a familiar face at that instant came brightly into the room. The would-be yawn developed into a smile. It was Tosti, the song-writer. Of course, if you ever see that man stop to speak to any one you can make up your mind on the spot that that one is at least a princess. Tosti's face lit up as he went towards his friends, in voice and in gesture one heard the tinkle of Trevi and the murmur of Tiber. A tall man got up to shake hands with him : it was Marchetti, who wrote *Ruy Blas*, the opera whose adorable love-duet I remember from the moment I first heard it, it will haunt me until my dying day. Tosti then came up to us. He did not even say good-day, but his greeting was perfectly intelligible.

"*E una splendore, cara amica*—you have heard nothing to equal it—wait, wait."

A few more frantic words and he passed on. "Wait?" I am afraid we shall have to. Vergil smiled. It is unnecessary, I suppose, to say to what Tosti had referred. Vergil poured out a glass of wine and drained it off.

"I am beginning to have an indigestion of the whole affair," he muttered, "and wish it were well over. Ah, who knows if this is his last work?—I beg your pardon, this is very good ham."

"Excellent," I reply ; "he says it is the last—confess, are you not curious?"

"No, I am upset. I've lost my head. I have heard the thing talked up so much." A friend appeared at his elbow and said :

"Tamagno is really better," the friend murmured ; "have

you ever heard him? No? Splendid voice. He has only been
singing a few years, is rich, and after this season is going to
retire from the stage. His father was a poor hotel-keeper in
Turin until—he died. Heaven rest his soul!—but Tamagno
so loved him that when offered his first great *scrittura*, and
reading that it was not for his native city, refused to leave the
old man."

"An improvement on Jean of Leyden," I interrupted.

"The moral of denying one's own mother seems to have
had a salutary family effect on tenors," Vergil added.

"Yes; still, Tamagno is a prophet, not alone in his own,
but every country."

Our breakfast ceased, but Mr. X. continued. I spare you
the detail. Vergil put his hands before his eyes.

"Heavens!" Mr. X. continued, "something has gone to
your brain; what is it?"

At that moment the waiter reappeared with dessert.

"What," said X., "you don't eat cheese? Like fish, it is
brain-food!" Vergil looked at him and smiled. "O, I have
not taken any lately," Mr. X. continued, "but, waiter—"

Vergil pronounced the word "Gorgonzola." It proved
talismanic.

"Certo, Signore; which will you have, bianca or Verdi?"

"Verdi," he replied. I nearly fell off my chair. Vergil
looked up, the waiter's mouth was stretched from ear to ear.

"Va bene," the latter cried, "sicuro e il migliore?"

Vergil's face grew a dull red, an Italian oath parted his
lips. "Stop," he commanded, "I don't want any. I've
changed my mind." Mr. X. was smoothing out his countenance. "My brains do not require nourishment."

At that moment an itinerant band struck up outside
the door. The players were in the celebrated restaurant
garden of Café Cova, a really charming resort, where in mid-

summer tables groan under flowers and fruit, where an orchestra plays twice a day, where "widows" and matrons flirt, and maidens looking at comely youths tell off their daisy leaves, and wish they might : at that instant preliminary chords took form, and became suddenly familiar.

Vergil turned as suddenly paler. "Waiter," he said faintly, "the bill."

Mr. X. smiled. "Ah—the perennial—that strain again, to quote my friend ' The Bandit.' " *

" Se non e Verdi e ben trovatore."

* My old nickname for Mr. William Beatty-Kingston, author of the delightful work, *Music and Manners.*

CHAPTER IV.

Milan, Feb. 2nd.

DON'T ask me what I have been doing this afternoon—everything, nothing : I am resigned to the inevitable. I only hope that the opera will come off on Saturday, otherwise the town will certainly collapse. After our nearly fatal breakfast, Vergil and I started out to do Milan—O no, to see something we hadn't seen before, and—we succeeded. As we passed through the Galleria—by the way, have you been here since it was built? If not, I may say that it is the Duomo or cathedral's most powerful rival, and is the modern marrow of Milan's bones. Picture to yourself a long cruciform gallery running from Piazza del Duomo to Piazza della Scala. It is of enormous height, while a dome and nave, intercepting the centre, form an admirable rotunda. The roof is vaulted and decorated in marvellous stone stucco, while the gallery proper is lined with brilliant shops, quite as brilliant at night as the Palais Royal of olden times. But to look upon this passage, one dreams dreams of a Richelieu strolling under graceful arcades, or some Louis XIV. *grisette* making signs to her noble lover across a green palace garden. Had this gallery been built a long time ago, history would doubtless have lent it many classic recollections ; but, alas, no Marcellus or Charlemagne has trod its classic pavement, and the only story connected with it will doubtless become a legend. It is sad enough. Giuseppe Mengoni, the poor architect who planned and built it, in the act of placing the last ornament on the façade to crown his work,

THE NEW YORK
PUBLIC LIBRARY

ASTOR, LENOX
TILDEN FOUNDATIONS

TITO RICORDI,
Present head of Ricordi & Co., Publishers.

fell from the supremest height, and to-day a memorial tablet marks the spot where he lost his life. Some say it was accidental, some design, that his work did not please him, the front elevation not having the grand result he had intended ; I fear we shall never know the truth. However grand his ideas may have been, the reality certainly is a magnificent one, and he has raised a great monument to utility and art. It is true that from the Piazza della Scala the effect is not striking, but the fault is not with the architect. The Gothic cathedral kills everything near it, and any pretentious structure, no matter how grand, must appear an architectural failure. Of course I refer only to Milan, as the wildest imagination cannot calculate the possible effect of a San Marco, Certosa, San Pietro, or the Strasburg Cathedral all fronting in Piazza della Duomo. At present the interest in this Gallery may be said to be world-wide. The original façade made in stucco or plaster is to be torn down, and a new one erected. Plans and architectural designs have been pouring in from the uttermost parts of the earth, and the latest come from some remote regions in Asia, and latest, Teheran, Persia's adorable capital. I suppose some tender memories are connected with this peculiar interest in the Galleria ; students who have walked under the comely arches murmuring words of love to the picturesque contadina, recall the hours in whose cycle swung golden dreams of wealth and fame : those phantoms of youthful desire so readily evoked in memory's horoscope.

In the Galleria we paid a visit to several shops, but stopped to look in at Ricordi's windows, where admirable portraits of Verdi and Boïto were exposed. I had an idea, and communicated it to Vergil. It was to visit the Ricordi printing establishment, and in an instant we started for Via Omenone, the wholesale house where tons of musical scores are waiting for delivery, and where I had been told a great many precious autographs lay under the Ricordi lock and key. The foreman was rather surprised when I told him what I wanted to see. I had no permit, but I think after taking me in he decided that I could not well run off with anything, and ordered a most amiable personage to show us everything we desired to look at.

Then commenced a perfect feast of musical reminiscences. Of course, the chief thing I wanted to see was the very first work written by the maestro Verdi.

My conductor smiled.

"The *Conte di San Bonifazio,*" he cried, then pompously opened the sacred bookcase. From dozens, maybe hundreds, of large volumes bound alike in red calf, he extracted one thin work, dusted it, and laid it tenderly down before us.

I opened it softly, softly, this book of the past where every page spoke of some ambition, some hope, some desire, some illusion of the young composer. "And his first success? you ask —ah, no, his first failure."

The hand was a characteristic one, and I knew on studying it I should comprehend the character of the writer. Every line, every note was reticent, cold, and scrupulous. There were passion, but not sentiment, prose, but not poetry, uprightness, but not exaggeration, in these fine outlines, fine to aggravation. The strokes were slender and spider-like, and precise but firm, so firm that on reading you immediately said to yourself: "The man who wrote this is a man of character, a man of energy, coldness, enormous volition, enormous obstinacy, but scarcely a man of genius—there was no fire of youthful ambition in those precise notes, no hint of those vibrating melodies which have stirred and held spellbound the senses of half a century. I think, I knew I was disappointed; but I remarked something else which partially consoled me. It was a strange aroma which stole from the leaves : where had they borrowed, how imprisoned this scent? I wondered if Verdi had locked his book up, this his first opera, as a woman does her first love-letter; in a drawer scented with lavender, in a box of sandal, in a sachet of satin or a paper of tissue perfumed in violet: the packet tied with a ribbon, rose-coloured, naturally neither too thick nor too thin, too wide, too long, nor too short: how many times had he looked it over lovingly, how many smiles had it cost him, how many tears—how many?

I heard a sigh.

My guide was studying me.

"It was not a success," I said. "No? but it reads very nice all the same: there are scarcely any erasures, and he seems to have written straight off."

"No, it took him three years to write; there is some charming music in it. It was given at La Scala in 1839. I was there, but you—you were nowhere."

My eyes went heavenward. "I would willingly have been anywhere to have been—somewhere," I said; "but let me hear about it."

He then told me that the opera was not a great success. Marini, soprano; Salvi, tenor, and the basso, Marini, sang in it: there was one magnificent quartette, and a grand aria with a cabaletta—"splendid," he added; then instinctively, being an Italian, waved his arms with metronomic exactitude, and began vigorously:

"Sotto il tetto paterno—sot-to il tet-to pa—"

I was enchanted, but Vergil didn't seem so. The singer observed his evident signs of annoyance. The second or third "paterno" died on his lips—he waved his hands as does an orchestra leader when he dismisses his band, and concluded.

"This air is frequently introduced in *Luisa Miller*, all sopranos dote on it. I myself think it a masterpiece."

"Thanks." I offered him *Oberto di San Bonifazio*, at the

same time saying to myself : "I leave this door and buy ' Sotto il Tetto Paterno,' or die in the attempt." Our musical Barnum went on, " Can I show you something else ?" Then he took a mysterious catalogue from somewhere and opened it.

" Of course," I cried, and made a quick selection, the next being the maestro's last works, *Aïda* and the *Requiem*. There were the same clear pages, the same handwriting—the same, but slightly changed. The slender lines were now and then wavering and zigzag, the faint notes, perhaps too faint, but the whole, as in the first work, characteristic of the man. Here no odour of violet stole from the pages, but the ambrosia of fifty years of success, half a century of glory : and yet I missed the early perfume, that " rose of youth," once so sweetly expanded in the foglios of *Oberto di San Bonifazio*.

Next I asked for *La Sonnambula*, and as I read the inspired pages, what a crowd of Aminas stood trembling or faltering or trilling before me !

Bellini wrote also a fine hand. The notes were small, precise, and elegant, but not so upright as Verdi's. There were a simplicity and tenderness in the Sicilian master's caligraphy which demonstrated the totally different character of the man. I noticed one thing. The former's pages wore a professional look, that look of handicraft which Verdi's first opera had not, but which I noticed in all his recent works. I suppose it is the same technique which is betrayed by the practical hand in any profession. I looked well over the *Sonnambula*. It was yellow, faded, and dainty. There were few or no erasures. The whole first act and final were written with dash and energy which showed a man writing in a highly nervous but determined state. The soprano parts were in the soprano key, and would puzzle many of the best artists of to-day to read as you must read it, three notes lower than it is written. In act second I turned naturally to " Ah, non credea " and the famous

" Ah, non giunge." I arrived at the word " fiore "—here was the first erasure. " Fiore " was blotted and rewritten, the notes changed, and finally the notes as they stand now, re-written under the line. Before the word " spergiura," half a page was cancelled. I tried hard to make out a few notes. Then our guide spoke. I was finding still more erasures. He said,

" Who knows what he did not cut !"

I added : " If some modern composers only had a few of these cancelled notes just to go on with ; in the mean time one could return home after listening to a new opera without a throbbing head and exhausted body, fatal result of an unequal struggle between public to understand and writer to make himself understood."

He lifted eyebrows, shoulders, hands.

" I believe you," he cried ; " between public and composer, the one to fabricate a melody, the other to retain it, a week of neuralgia or toothache is far less wearing. Sainted heaven ! if they only had !"

There were scores of Rossini's, in quantity. The original *Gazza Ladra, Gli Italani in Algieri, Il Turco in Italia, La Pietra de Paragona, Sigismundo, Bianco Fallerio,* and *L'Inganno Felice.* These were the earlier operas of whose existence the melomaniac is perfectly cognisant, but the outside world is generally ignorant.

Rossini's handwriting was large, jovial, generous, and natural. His first works were signed G. Rossini simply, and the later ones Mr. Cavaliere G. Rossini. The Swan of Pisaro's character was admirably depicted by his pen. Scanning Bohe-mian notes and liberal measures, it seemed as if one saw him at work shut up in prison to complete a long promised, never delivered score, trapped to dine and locked up in his impresario's house after dinner, in order, under compromise, to filch a few vagrant measures; Rossini, tormented, adored, dogged, or maltreated by the poor wretches who paid him any sum for an opera, and yet were never sure of their composer until the curtain had fallen on the last act at the dress rehearsal. O Rossini, Rossini, what a fertile, generous, but wholly Bohemian nature was thine! I could not help laughing as I took up the score of *Tancredi*, and remembered the history of one number of that opera. Rossini at nine A.M. in a garret-chamber without fire; Rossini, well bolstered up, swearing loudly, freezing inwardly, but writing interminably. One ill-calculated shiver sent the sheet of a precious solo flying from his fingers. It sailed aloft, then fell at the foot of the couch. He tried to seize it, to reach it with his stick, to get at it any way without leaving his bed, but in vain.

"Diavolo," he screamed, "let it go! I will write another solo instead."

The generous inspiration continued. The sheet, with its half-completed measures, lay a long time unheeded on the floor. Rossini wrote and wrote, when hunger compelled him to lay down his pen. He jumped up and was dressing, when the vagrant leaf caught his eye. He snatched at it, and a gratified look crept over his face.

"Ah!" he murmured, re-reading eagerly, "that is not so bad, I will make a duo of it;" and forgetting his hunger, sat down and wrote the adorable, memorable "Mi rivedrai ti rivedro."

Only to run over the pages of these immortal works was to see the man himself as everybody knows him. Strange to say, as posterity has set him down, for rarely have I seen a manuscript so thoroughly imprinted, so thoroughly impermeated with the character of the man who wrote it.

There were the originals of poor Ponchielli's works, *I Lituani* and *I Promessi Sposi*; the handwriting resembled Verdi's

to an extraordinary degree, but was less characteristic than
the others. I should say that it would have been difficult to
read this composer's mind from his penmanship. Next came
Gomez, author of a delightful opera called *Il Guarany*. The
frontispiece was one series of dashes, blots, and sprawling
letters. Ah! Signor Gomez. I wondered what kind of man
he was. I looked up at my guide, his face was impassive.

"Is he alive or dead?" I asked; "have you ever seen him?"

"O, he's alive. I've seen him often—here."

"Is he in Milan now?"

"No; I think he is in Brazil."

"Ah! floating about Brazil. Brazil is far away."

He looked as if he were about to say, "It is near enough,"
then—then we changed the subject.

I found another score. It was written in a dainty style,
there were frequent erasures, frequent hesitations, frequent
corrections. It was none other than *Lucrezia Borgia* and the
original of Donizetti's inspired work. Poor Donizetti! Again
I saw a fine Italian hand, sensitive and uncertain, proud yet
confident, a handwriting steeped in that mysterious language
of hidden senses, of emotions which vibrate when expression
finds neither verbal nor written utterance: creatures of our
fancy and soul who live in, and with, and about us, who
alternately dominate, delight, and destroy : beings who pre-
serve towards us an eternal incognito, yet pass their lives
in our extremest intimacy : phantoms who cast their prophetic
shadows over our page of life; perhaps to harm, certainly
to disturb, never to tranquillise. Aurora announcing the
dawn, to abandon the daybreak she heralds : robed in her
golden glory of day, yet trailing her garments in the dust of
night. Can we not read Donizetti's life in these poor charac-
ter3; his life of struggle, poverty, despair, glory, and final
madness? Madness, that awful death which precedes death,

K

that hideous nightmare which keeps pace with the fairest
visions in the spirit's realm, and, gliding side by side with
the mind's most glorious creations, one by one reveals the fatal
outlines of an implacable doom. So, in turning these old
pages, I re-lived Donizetti's miserable existence; in one of
Gennaro's divine phrases, heard again the strain of an undying
despair.

Our guide handed me a tiny sheet, a small folio covered with
miraculous characters, a very obelisk of operatic hieroglyph.

He said :

"This is considered the most remarkable musical autograph extant. It is Donizetti's original complete symphony and
overture to *Fausta*. The opera was to be brought out at the
Carcano, most charming of Milanese opera-houses, the theatre
where Rubini and Grisi first sang *La Straniera*, and Malibran
thrilled all hearts in the *Sonnambula*. Well, as I said, at the
Carcano, the master was worked to death and longed for the
country; so after the last rehearsal he just slipped off, and, for
the time being, utterly forgot his opera. He had barely got
to his destination when he remembered it, and remembered
also that he had written no overture. He sat down, and on
some sheets of note-paper, in a few hours, composed what you
have in your hand, posted it in an ordinary envelope that
same night, and the next morning it arrived at the theatre : at
eleven o'clock the band were rehearsing it. That is what one
may call quick work—inspiration."

"Yes, quick work; but is it good work?"

"Good? Sainted heaven! it is not alone one of the best
things he ever wrote, but one of the most beautiful and splendid compositions ever written by anybody. It is now completely detached from the opera, which was not a success, and
is often played with our classics in the Philharmonic symphony
concerts. Ah, it is indeed great !"

Then, as on a previous occasion, my informant waved his arms in an orchestral *larghando*, and in deep tones began "bom, bom, bom;" whether to give me an idea of the music, or merely as an escape - valve to his pent-up feelings, I never knew, and I fear history never will know. The melo-maniacal pantomime of *Sott-o il tet-to pater-no* was about being repeated in full, when my eye caught sight of another red-bound score. His quick glance followed mine, and his uplifted hand waved towards this latter instead of towards heaven.

"Ah," he cried, "that is but right, signora. The book before you is *Mefistofele*—Arrigo Boïto."

"Ah," I cried, "Boïto's opera—the original? Let me see it, quick!"

It was faithfully—did I imagine tenderly?—dusted, and placed before me.

Mefistofele is one of the most remarkable works that our nineteenth century has ever seen. Vergil came forward. "Me too," he said simply; "that is something I have long desired to look at."

We turned over the pages together.

"Boïto is unlike the *Fausta's* author in his manner of working," said Vergil, "but he resembles him in mind. He was years writing and rewriting this opera; but it will last. Methods, you see, are not all the same. Boïto is a conscientious worker; he never writes for money, he writes for love, for conviction, for art. He would spend his lifetime on one idea, one opera; but that one must be well done."

"He is writing another now," joyfully interrupted our informant, "it will be ready in two years." Then he sighed, and looked out over his glasses, took them off, and dusted them. "Two years," he continued, "he's been saying that for the past ten, and—and *Nerone*, the promised work isn't ready yet. Perhaps we shall be again made to wait: in the mean time, *Mefistofele* will make the tour of the world entire."

" Let us hope it," I said, and returned to my pages.

Not alone Boïto's music had always interested me, but having mutual friends we had been a dozen times on the point of meeting; some way the meeting had never come about. However, I may add that on that very evening Vergil and I were expected to dine at the Contessa D—'s, and hoped to have the pleasure of dining with the poet, for Boïto is poet as well as composer, and gifted in all arts. Next to having seen the great man was to have seen his original score of *Mefistofele.* I confess to a great, perhaps a most unreasonable, curiosity, as I took up the heavy red-bound volume, and eagerly turned over the closely-written pages.

What was it that disappointed me? I was first surprised at the handwriting, which was so uniformly like the other Italian hands, notably Verdi's, Bellini's, and Donizetti's. I suppose operatic writers get into a routine of writing which betrays them, as the professional copyist is always betrayed by his copy. Boïto's characters were concise, clear, calm, and inscrutable; you may read that handwriting for ever, I defy you to learn much from it concerning the man. There were plenty of cancelled measures, cancelled deliberately, clearly, calculatingly, and indelibly. I tried in vain to make out a few notes and phrases here and there, a measure, a strain. I understood nothing—it was perfect Greek—as dumb to me as Sanscrit.

" We expect great things of *Nerone*," proffered our guide; " but who knows when it will be ready?"

Vergil's voice interrupted,

" Who knows? He writes, and writes, and writes, and they say tears up as fast as he writes. He is never pleased with himself: he has one great ideal and idea in his head, and

he sacrifices everything to that unique ambition : everything
—beginning with what he writes, everybody—beginning with
himself."

A clock on the old San Carlo church chimed the hour
of four. Dear me ! could it be so late ? and I had not yet seen
the Ricordi establishment in person. I closed the book. Our
cicerone took it up with the same tender hands that had touched
the other scores. We bade him a hasty farewell ; yet I turned
yet again to him.

" I ask you a favour now," I said. " When we come the
next time you must promise—I sha'n't go away without that—
you must show me the original of *Nerone*."

His face beamed. "I will," he said delightedly ;
" unless—"

There are no unlesses; of course he will. Boïto has
given his word, and Boïto being a gentleman—if for no other
reason—will not break his promise.

P.S.—There must be a P.S. to every woman's letter. Of
course, being interested in music publishers, you will want to
know all about the great house of Ricordi. I would have
waited until my next, but being on the subject, may as well
tell you now as at any time.

CHAPTER V.

P.P.S.—The Ricordis owe their present fortune to Verdi, as Verdi in one sense owes his fortune to the Ricordis. This publishing house, like all great firms, had its being in the humblest of ways. Giovanni Ricordi, the founder of the establishment, was a poor violinist, and sometime director of the little theatre Fiando in Milan—a modest Punch and Judy show, to-day celebrated in the city's theatrical archives. Ricordi also occasionally copied music for the Scala musicians, receiving from twenty to thirty centimes a page for his work. When an opera at La Scala was a great success he sometimes copied as many as twenty or thirty numbers a day, which he quickly sold to enthusiastic passers-by, making from the sale the most infinitesimal of profits. His shop was a doorway under the old Palazzo dei Archivi in the Piazza dei Mercanti, where seemingly at any hour of the day or night he indefatigably worked and vended. He racked his brains to think of a plan to copy his music more quickly, and finally scraped enough money together to take him to Lispia, and there he entered the house of Briethof & Haertel, where he learned a new method, the art of engraving music. He returned to Milan, and set up a small shop in Via Pescheria Vichia No. 4023, a little street near the Duomo, and there published the first sheet of music engraven in Italy with the new system. This was in 1808. The piece was called "Le Stagioni dell' Anno," and was dedicated to

THE NEW YORK
PUBLIC LIBRARY

ASTOR, LENOX
TILDEN FOUNDATIONS

SIGNOR GIULIO RICORDI,
Acting head, Ricordi Publishing Establishment, Milan.

the Cavaliero Ferd. Satiranno di Breme, Chamberlain to his Imperial Majesty the great Napoleon. In 1812 Ricordi made Rossini's acquaintance, and published some operas for him. They became the warmest friends. Not alone Rossini, but Donizetti, Bellini, Rici, and Mercadanti employed Ricordi to publish their work, as at that time his was the only house in Italy which engraved music, the present Milanese musical publishers (although they do not care to admit the fact), Lucca Canti, Giudici, and Strada, all learned their art from the humble copyist, former director of Milan's Punch and Judy marionettes, now become the greatest publisher in Italy. Ricordi was the first to believe in Verdi's genius, the first and last in Italy who has ever published his operas. In 1853 Giovanni quitted this life, his son Tito, who since 1825 had been his faithful co-helper, succeeded to the business, and to-day Tito's son Giulio is in turn head of the mammoth establishment. I need say nothing of the personal qualities of the Dynasty Ricordi. Success, in this case, not alone bespeaks honesty, but so great a result from so humble a beginning attests to the legitimacy of their united labours and to the steady growth of public confidence in this house : it has not leapt into notoriety, but little by little, one by one, has laid the foundation-stones of its great wealth and importance.

I was thinking over all these things as we passed old Piazza dei Mercanti, but looked in vain for a Ricordi shadow under the old palace portico. The Ricordi ghosts, father and son, haunt many classical spots, but at present their living representatives do not stand under any porticos other than those of La Scala : do not live without, but within a very palatial Milanese palace called—home.

At last I arrived at Porta Vittoria. The wholesale house and printing-house proper is as large as Novello's, I should say, and occupies a splendid structure on the Milanese canal, which reminds me of one of those famed palaces on a Venetian lagoon. At sight of it I defy any human being to imagine that he or she were going to see a real publishing office and printing establishment, with printers, presses, printer's ink, and printer's devils standing about in alarming array. But so it was— a smiling individual opened two palatial bronze gates. We entered a square Italian doorway, and in an instant found ourselves in the office, a very lofty apartment where desks were ranged, chairs stood about, and richly tapestried walls betrayed an air of comfortable elegance! a life-sized portrait of Verdi stared down upon us, the only picture of any kind, I think, in the room. In a few moments I had taken in the whole place. Nine great presses were at work, and dozens of picturesque Italians with Raphael-like heads were bent over folds, folios, and single sheets of paper. There was the sound of rolling, stamping, and setting type : voices heard in soft murmurs, and a peculiar lazy hum which was as musical as it was Italian. In other similar places you know there is usually a vulgar uproar, but here it was so different. Had I been dropped from a balloon, although previously in complete ignorance of my terrestrial whereabouts, after one glance I should have said, " This is Italy."

They were printing—will you believe it?—the libretto of *Don Pasquale.*

"Tell me," I said, as a wet sheet of " Come gentil " was rolled off into my hand, " tell me, are there still human beings who read *Don Pasquale*, is there a human being in Italy who doesn't know *Don Pasquale* by heart? do you mean to say that you have any sale for *Don Pasquale ?* and have they not done with fifty years of *Don Pasquale ?*"

He smiled an inimitable, an inscrutable, an official, an Italian smile. I watched it; happily I did, for it was my answer long before he spoke, and when he did speak he rubbed his hands together and said what they always say here: " Come si fa ?'' (What's to be done about it ?)

I must tell you now that " Come si fa ?'' is the encyclopædia of the Italian language, the one phrase which serves for every question, answer, and explanation under the Italian sun. Civil, military, religious, artistic, commercial talk is prefaced, prepared, continued, concluded, like the one strain which constitutes a modern opera as the one refrain, " Come si fa ?'' A lady friend in a rage once said, " There are only ten words in the Italian language— nine are ' bene ' and one is ' grazia.' One universal exclamation, and that exclamation is—I will not keep you in suspense—' Come si fa ?' "

I saw some splendid title-pages for Tosti's songs, of which several millions—not the title-pages, but the songs—are annually sold. Do you know Tosti? By the way, he is a good fellow, and such a celebrity that I shall tell you about him, perhaps, in my next : in the mean time my guide explained a host of things about printing on stone or no longer printing on stone. He showed me the plaster stereotypes, and made an impression—on, as well as for me. I read something about " Sempre amare," naturally—in Italy. He explained the *modus operandi* of the presses, &c. I said " yes " to everything, and told him I understood ; of course, I had not understood a word, but happily he presumed on my intelligence : thence we went to see the binders at work. My eye fell on piles of folded sheets. Don't ask me what they were. He took up one.

" This," he exclaimed, " is the long - ardently - desired *Othello.*''

" Of course," I interrupted. I took up a cover ready for the binder. It was in cardinal-ribbed linen, which at first appeared like ribbed silk. The name G. Verdi was stamped at the top, the word *Otello* crossed the page, while at the bottom was the name of Ricordi's establishment. The reverse

cover bore a curious monogram of three interlaced rings—the
whole in dead-gold on this background of red. I had rarely
or never seen a more attractive binding, and I said as much
to my guide ; he smiled and replied :

" Ricordi wanted to outdo himself on this occasion. Verdi
says it is his last opera—who knows ? The gold lettering is real
leaf-gold, and on each book there is the value of nearly two
francs. He thought also it would serve as a memorable souve-
nir of a memorable date. We have never bound an ordinary
opera so richly before; but Verdi is Verdi, and "—will you
believe it ?—he added, " *come si fa ?*"

From the binders we crossed a small court to the ware-
house, another low Italian structure entirely devoted to books,
music, and music proof in every stage. The interior was
arranged with bins just as in a wine-cellar, only the bottles
were closely-packed scores, and the atmosphere was not
Bacchus, but Apollo. Never before had I seen so many books,
and on looking at them a wild idea came into my head.
What if a band and invisible chorus were to start up and
all at the same time sing one of these different operas? The
Tower of Babel or the purest Wagner gone wrong would be
nothing compared to it. My thoughts must have shown
through my face. The cicerone spoke : " There are over
seven hundred thousand complete scores here all arranged as
you see," he pointed to them. They, were labelled, numbered, and lettered with most consummate skill. After running over the Roman alphabet, after remembering the Paris
obelisk and its hieroglyphics, after mentally murmuring twice
two are four, like the man in the " One Hoss Shay," I stopped
perplexed " at what the Dickens was coming next." An individual whom I had not before noticed loomed out from one
of the classical bins. Shades of Eugene Aram, was it he in
person? He doffed his hat. My senses gradually revived,

and I asked, "But who is the guardian of these seven hundred thousand volumes, who can read those wonderful tickets, who—" Eugene Aram bowed low and smiled.

"I am," he replied, "I—"

"Yes," interrupted the cicerone, "yes, he can find any work at an instant's notice. He knows them all by heart, and well he may after forty-three years that he has been here. If he were to forget—*come si fa?*"

Eugene here begged to remonstrate, his eye glittered strangely, a withered hand clutched the serpentine handle of a covered lantern, and his face took an injured look. "You always forget," he said huskily—"not forty-three years, but forty-seven. There is a difference."

"Yes," I said cheerily, "a difference of four years, a mere nothing: myself—four years before I was born."

"We will not discuss the matter," the cicerone said, "but to my knowledge you have been here—" Eugene raised his eyes and hands mutely to heaven. Decidedly, thought I, I must change the subject. I will say I am going. "This is a delightful spot," I began, "so sequestered, so secluded, so—so musical; but if I don't take my leave soon I shall stop not only forty-seven years, but like most things in Italy, forty-seven centuries." I then said good-day to Aram, at the same time envying him the custody of so much glory. He was pensive, evidently still thinking about my taking root, but he referred to my taking leave. The cicerone motioned me to go before and "he would precede me," which I did. He spoke:

"Forty-seven—"

"O, really, is it forty-three or forty-seven?"

"Forty-three, but he forgets: he is so old—*come si fa?*"

We reached the outer peristyle, a golden sun was sinking back of Mont Blanc, a myriad of golden rays lit up the waters of the canal—all the gold, in fact, not on the backs of *Othello* illuminated Ricordi's establishment. Thinking of one I thought of the other.

The cicerone let me out. He ventured to say :

" And perhaps the Signorina will go on the first night of—"

" Perhaps ? I have come two thousand miles for that purpose ; but you—are you going?"

" Going ! I—me ? Why, we are all going ! Not a man in this establishment—we are over three hundred—has ever missed a Verdi first night " (" A reasonable *claque*," I muttered), "and on this occasion I ask you, would it be possible not to go ? No, the idea is not even questionable ; one must go—*come si fa ?*"

But I felt I must get home. I was tired with my long day, and a dinner on hand that I could not miss ; alive or dead, *I* must go, yet—*come si fa ?* I reached the hotel and found a note from the D—s, with one enclosed. Will you believe, after all my counting on seeing maestro Boïto, he is not coming, and through a stupid error? No one in Milan has any head. Countess D— had written on a card the day before, forgetting to date it, ' We expect you to dinner to-morrow.' Boïto received the card this morning. He answers: " Thanks, with pleasure." To-morrow—and to-morrow ! Who knows where we shall be, or what doing, to-morrow ? Boïto in turn did not date his card. At such a time he would be excusable for having no head, but the fact remains : the innocent, as usual, are punished for the guilty. I have plenty of head, but am not to meet the maestro this evening, that is sure.

You say, tell me all about La Scala itself. " It is years since I have seen it." I will to-morrow. Now, another line before I finish. When we got to the hotel I found that a Paris friend, the lovely Madame B—i, who has an equally lovely voice, was stopping at our house. I determined to say a little ' how do you do?' The waiter took me to her apartment—

sounds from *La Traviata* were heard ; I was for going in at
once, but Paolo stopped me with a very severe gesture, and his
face assumed a still severer look.

" Not while she is singing," he said. " We cannot interrupt. *In five more* bars she will have reached her cadenza,
and then—"

And then—and there are still human beings who deny that
Italy is a land of song ! Forget all I have written about progress—forget everything but that I am yours humbly and
convincedly, even musically.—Always the same, &c.

CHAPTER VI.

Milan, Feb. 2nd, 1882.

THE weather still continues beautiful and cold, clear as an iceberg, but cold as an iceberg. I never remember to have seen Milan so delightful in the winter. Usually at this season bitter winds sweep down from the neighbouring Alps, tempests of snow, hail, and rain are not infrequent, and the climate all in all from November till April is one of the most purely perfidious that I have ever known. The blue sky of Italy, the warm sun of Italy—all humbug, my friend, especially the winter-time. To tell the truth, I have never suffered with the cold in my life as I have here. The houses of massive stone are cold as barns, and it is almost impossible to warm them. You ask, how do Italians stand it? I answer, —I don't know. Perhaps, were my accent a purer Roman, I might suffer less from the cold; but take my advice, never come to Italy in the winter without an ample provision of warm wraps and—southern Italian accent.

Last night we went to La Scala to hear an opera by a young composer, Samara, called *Flora Mirabilis*, but which had little effect in that great house. As to the opera's success, you may judge from this: the scenes were something extraordinary; one phrase was applauded, another hissed; an artist applauded one moment, hissed the next; one stage picture applauded, another hissed ; and so on till the end of the chapter. I can't say till the end of the opera, for—poor opera—the public wouldn't allow it to end. The curtain was

ordered after the second act, and the public roared "Ballet!
ballet! *Now, at once!*" &c. An Italian audience is not an
easy one to manage. It is composed of artists, ex-artists,
musicians, composers, amateurs, and, above all, connoisseurs.
These people know not only what is good, but exactly what
they want, and more than all, always bear in mind what they
have been accustomed to. "Nessun maggior dolore" here
holds good, for the most renowned artist in the world is
treated like the beginner, absolutely according to his merits,
and no amount of patronage, advertising, or any kind of puff-
ing can uphold a singer in Italy : if he be not up to his reputation, on the contrary, so much the worse for him. If he sing
well, he is applauded; if he sing badly, hissed; if execrably,
ordered, even made to leave the stage. The sense of gratitude
applied to art does not exist here, and why should it anywhere?
In every profession artisans before the public are required to
do their work well. You would not excuse an architect who
would build you a bad or unsafe house, you would not accept
a portrait if badly painted, you would not wear an ill-made
coat or a pair of badly made boots, but by a mistaken idea of
politeness you will treat bad artists with leniency, and you
will be wrong—there is no politeness in art. Opera-singing
is a public profession, and opera singers accept money to
perform a public trust : if performed badly, dishonestly, one
should not overlook the failing : above all, to sacrifice art to
individuals is in itself little short of criminal. The parasite
indifference is a yesterday's plant, yet see what bitter fruit
it has borne. There are no more artists, there are even
no more singers. Why? Because they have been spoiled;
they have sung out of Italy, and find that no matter how
they perform, they are applauded just the same. Where
there is no discrimination in the public, there is no reason
for consideration or delicacy in the artist, and conscien-

tiousness no longer exists amongst singers.   If an Italian sing
in Milan or Rome and is hissed, he now laughs and says, " I will
go to London or America.   There I can do as I like, and make ten
times the money beside."   He used to say, " The fault is mine;"
he now says, " It is that of the public."   He will not do as
Pasta did after a failure—retire to the country and study five
consecutive years before thinking or daring to re-appear before
the people he has outraged.

     The Italian will permit no trifling.   His artistic accounts
are settled on the spot.   He neither bargains nor cheats, but
he will neither be sold nor cheated.   It is undoubtedly this
rigour which has made Italy the only school for singers in the
world ; a school which to-day, although in its decline, is certainly a long way ahead of any other country, and the only one
where a vestige of old-time perfection remains.   Paris theatres
have a claque, but I should like to see any claque succeed at
La Scala.   The massacre at Massowah would be a joke compared with that.   But speaking of theatres, I remember I promised to tell you about this renowned opera-house, this
temple which has echoed to a century of never-to-be-forgotten
sounds, whose very walls are sacred, whose memories are one
pearl chain of names in art, purer and more priceless even
than that famous necklace which clasps Queen Margherita's
gracious throat.   The old Teatro Reale, built in 1717, was
burned down in 1776, and the authorities ordered a new playhouse : this was built on the site of the celebrated Chiesa
della Scala, founded by Regina della Scala, wife of Bernabo
Visconti.   Piermarini designed the plans for the theatre, and
in August of 1778 it was opened with a melodrama, *Europa
Riconosciuta*, and a grand ballet called the *Prigionieri di Cypro*.
In 1814 the adjoining monastery of St. Joseph was demolished,
and the stage and theatre were enlarged to their present proportions.   You may imagine what they are when I tell you

that the auditorium contains seven hundred stalls, and standing-room for several hundred people. There are one hundred and ninety-four boxes distributed in five galleries, tier upon tier, and the seating capacity is nearly four thousand. The boxes are mostly private property, and are spoken of by their owners' names, as in the olden time one spoke of Madame de Sévigné's or Madame de Rémusat's salon. The stage is of enormous depth and breadth, and holds from six hundred to a thousand persons without seeming crowded. La Scala always looked shabby to me, but in 1878 it was cleaned and redecorated, and last night I was amazed with the improvement. It is lit with electricity, thousands of lights run around the gilded galleries, the boxes are hung in red and gold, and the cornice and ceiling are marvels of taste and beauty. The auditorium is formed in a pure horse-shoe, and the stage perfectly visible from every part. It is so big, or rather so ample, that you could not recognise your dearest friend across the house without a glass, and from the rear centre of the platea the figures on the stage resemble puppets in a marionette show. This is a disagreeable feeling at first, but wears off as the performance advances. The greatest quality of La Scala, however, is its absolutely perfect acoustic. A whisper on the stage, like the loudest sound, is heard with the most perfect distinctness from one end of the theatre to the other. I know of no more delightful feeling at the opera than this sense of hearing perfectly. It is certainly the first requisite in a playhouse, and the quality, alas, whose absence is felt in most of the great opera-houses of Europe, notably the Paris Grand Opera House, the San Carlo at Naples, the Royal Albert Hall of London, &c.

I am not going to inflict a complete history of La Scala upon you, but will turn at once to the ballet. We see ballets all over the world, but you must know that a ballet at Milan and La Scala is really something out of the ordinary. It is

L

quite a performance in itself, and often lasts two hours without
the curtain once falling. The story is told in pantomime by
the *mime*, as they are called, and the dancing is interpolated
like the melodies in an opera. Words can but inadequately
describe the care and attention paid these representations.
They are certainly more magnificent than even I had dreamed,
and differ from Paris in this, that while they have all the luxury
and brilliancy of the latter, in the art of dancing and pantomime
they display a perfection unknown, not alone to the French
capital, but outside of Italy. I never could make head or tail
of the ordinary ballet, but here the dancers are so remarkable
that you understand what they mean as plainly as if they
were speaking. There is every reason why dancing in Milan
should attain such perfection : the most famous ballet school
the world is attached to La Scala, and is as much a part of
that theatre as an arm is part of the body.

In 1613 the school was regularly instituted, and since that
time its development has surpassed the most extravagant
expectations. To those who know nothing of ballet-dancing
or the necessary study obligatory to one learning the art, a
few words may not be without interest, and if you care to
know, I can do no better than to tell you of Milan and the
way this academy is conducted. I cannot say that the profession of dancing is a disgraceful one, as after experience in
this line I only see in dancers poor, hard-working creatures,
whose life must be anything but an easy one. Those belonging to the Milan corps have as much protection as virtue ever
should have, and their conduct on the stage is ever that of
irreproachable modesty and decorum.

In order to be admitted to the school, the aspirant is first
examined to see whether its limbs and feet are perfect, and
whether its health is correspondingly good. No child may be
admitted to the class under eight or above twelve years of

age. The first three years they not only work for nothing, but furnish even their studying clothes. After the third year they receive an annual stipend of two hundred lire and upwards, each succeeding year bringing a visible increase in their salary. The regular term lasts eight years, at the end of which there is an extra term called the " term of merit." This lasts three years, during which time the dancer receives something like four hundred lire (16*l*.) a year. The merit term is almost one in name only, as the student is usually pronounced finished after the eight years. It would be impossible to conceive a more carefully regulated institution than this : every consideration as regards health, merit, intelligence, and disposition being carefully and rigorously weighed. The first year is one of probation, at the end of which health, form, and aptitude being favourable, the pupil is considered acceptable. Those who at the end of the first year show no possible disposition for the art are sent away, and their place is but too quickly filled. Milan is full of poor children only too anxious to embrace this profession, who are brought up with this idea from the cradle, and who wait their turn to dance, as patiently as a Cabinet Minister waits audience in a king's antechamber.

There are two classes only, the first called primary, and lasting four years, the last being called the finishing class, which completes the eight years above-mentioned. The school commences in winter at nine A.M., finishing at twelve, and in summer one hour earlier; one hour is then devoted to pantomime, after which the day's studies are supposed to be concluded. The strictest regulations as to health are laid down for one and all, in spite of which consumption claims many and many a victim. It is strange that ballet-dancers usually fall a prey to this insidious disease. If they survive the first years, they sometimes live to a green old age, and, like Fanny Ellsler at seventy, walk serenely in the Vienna Prater, or the once fairy-limbed Taglioni, bent, doubled, and gray, sun her decrepitude and eighty years in the Acacia walk of the Bois de Boulogne; but young, many fall, not like autumn leaves, ripe after a rich season, but like blasted June roses, cut by an untimely storm of midsummer hail. We also think of dancers, and imagine that because they expose their forms they cannot be virtuous. This is one of the most unjust of ideas. In the Milan school good deportment is as strictly cultivated and looked after as heel-and-toe practice. Likewise during study hours their morals are vigorously attended to, and while in active dancing every precaution is taken to protect these children of misfortune—for I can consider them nothing else—to guard them from the slightest breath of scandal or harm. As soon as their studies are sufficiently advanced, they are required to perform at La Scala always for the grand Carnival and Quaresima, or Lenten season, and if there be an extra opera, oftentimes in the early autumn. The theatre-carriage calls for them and deposits them at the stage-door, and at the close of a performance again comes and takes them to the doors of their own domiciles. There is a duenna, and such a duenna! a tutor, and such a tutor! to stay by and keep them in order. They have as safe and sound an escort as it is possible to have, not, as is often supposed, the recreant youth or more frequently bald-headed lover.

Everybody is interested in the school, the ladies and gentlemen of the nobility each season watch the progress of their favourite as one watches the training and cultivation of a choice flower. This interest is all the more commendable, invested as it is in poor creatures who live in the powder and paint, sham and tinsel of an utterly artificial life; and yet these plants flourish as healthy plants often will, in spite of obnoxious surroundings, live on in spite of a familiarity with vice which becomes to the nature what ivy does to the oak. At first I was

surprised at the remarks I heard in the boxes, and the comments
on certain dancers. Neither óne nor the other were of a lascivi-
ous kind; men as well as women speak of the artist's progress,
of her talent, of her aptitude, and not unfrequently of her goodness and virtue. There was one especial consideration, and that
was the question of lovers ; with Italian dancers it is a question
of sentiment, not position. Once floating on the world, freed
from the Argus-eyed duenna and prison-like theatre-carriage,
they marry or enter into liaisons, but nearly always listen only
to the heart—an Italian dancer who is rich or has made a fortune is almost unknown—she will take her butcher for better
or worse, as did a pretty Jewess called Gasseau, bright particular star of several seasons ago, or she will live in a mansard
with her dark-eyed Romeo, cooking, baking, stitching, and
cleaning, tending her bird, who, like herself, sings all day in
a sweet and accustomed capacity, dancing and mumming
at night, enjoying her poor life and never sighing for wealth
and station ; if she beg a smile, it must be of her beloved, and
if she dream of jewels, they will be the bright eyes of her
inamorato. This extraordinary disinterestedness is peculiarly
Italian; it is a fever amongst the lower classes, and simply
an epidemic amongst the ballerine.

The school is large this year, in splendid form, and the
ballet *Rolla* simply perfection. There are nearly six hundred
dancers in all, and amongst the prima assolute, ten second
stars who are really delightful—sirens born of Terpsichore and
Achelous ; these drive the Milanese youth to desperation, and
their battle-ground bids fair to be strewn with the titles and
coronets of many a too willing Hippomenes. These sirens have
a mischievousness in eye and form which make me almost doubt
the mansard and deny the canary ! In watching the graceful evolutions of these accomplished creatures, we can readily
think of dancing as art, can see La Scala of the past, where

the Taglioni couple danced in *Europa Riconosciuta* and *Bianca di Messina*. By the way, the first ballet at La Scala was in 1778, and was called the *Destruction of Troy*, and the first dancer was Caterina Curz. Who knows anything about Caterina Curz? Even the name sounds far away—no one remembers how she danced, what she looked like, and where she studied. Amongst the names familiar to our century were the Taglionis, husband and wife, who in 1824 were the Scala stars. Signora Taglioni, of course, did the prima parts, and Signor Taglioni those ancient, terrible, turn-round jumps and postures to-day unchanged, and to me as unnecessary now as they must have been a hundred years ago. Has it ever struck you how singularly uninteresting male dancers are? Well, to return to the Taglionis. Old Taglioni wrote the ballet himself, and after *Bianca* and *Messina* he presented a new one each season, always with increasing success, until the world-renowned *Flik and Flock* set the seal upon his choregraphic merits. In 1837 the beautiful Elisa Varin was the prima assoluta, and in 1838—memorable occasion—fascinating Fanny Ellsler appeared for the first time at La Scala, and took the old Lombard world by storm.

She and Varin alternated in the spring season. In 1848 Rosini Gusman captivated the Milanese youth, and in 1841 Maria Taglioni, famous daughter of a famous race, appeared on the scene and was announced as engaged "for eight nights only." The same season Jane King danced, but after that Taglioni for many years held undisputed sway. In 1844 Lucille Grahn appeared and speedily became a great favourite. I have seen her picture : a beautiful creature with a slender straight figure, dark eyes, sweet mouth, and black hair, dressed in the height of fashion : her dress was extremely rich, and, strange to say, was not theatrical ; her skirts were long, and frills of dainty lace fell over and half hid the most shapely hands ever given to mortal.

O, then were the days to see ballet - dancing. Think of season after season with Taglioni and Cerito, Ellsler and Grahn, each one differing from the other in grace and beauty, yet each one idolised by the most despotic adoring public in the world. The Milan school is still perfect, the public is unchanged, but where are the dancers? The same gulf stretches between past and present—between the artists of to-day and those before-named—as between the singers of to-day and yesterday—the Grisis and Malibrans of three decades since, and the poor fledglings our epoch calls cantatrice.

Of the dancers who are known to present fame, Rosita Mauri is charming, Sangalli the most perfect as regards school, and Signora A. Rossi, now prima assoluta at La Scala, a very clever ballerina, but not a great artist. Who from this school will ever become a second Fanny Ellsler? You must not think that the nine or ten years of study makes first-class dancers of all. How many never go beyond mediocrity, and each succeeding Carnival, washing their old tights, lounge over the tub and tinted water, add the flesh-colouring to the faded meshes, and wring in new illusions with the rose-colour, which, alas, dies the usual death before a new wash is required for practising-garments! What a hard life, what thankless labour, and how few ever become great like Taglioni! At the same time, we must admit that the poor girl who entered the school and left it earning two thousand francs a year must feel a proud moment when she returns to the stage where she was once the veriest slave, now acknowledged queen, fêted, feasted, and sonnetified ; envied by all the old companions, and receiving, instead of a few hundred lire, not only from thirty to fifty thousand francs, the usual sum given to the stars for the season at La Scala, but, more gratifying than all, the prouder recompense of success and unfading laurels.

The class-dancing here is marvellous, indeed nothing could

be more perfect: hundreds of young women make one shadow, hundreds of satin-shod feet, twinkling over the great stage, tap their pointed toes in a cadence as rhythmical as the murmur of a fountain. There is something inspiring in the elegance and grace with which these masses float about. The crash of lively music, the thousands of lights, the gorgeous costumes, and the lavish richness of the stage decorations make the scene one of positive enchantment   Dancing is dancing the world over; but I still hold the perfection of art alone gives that pleasurable feeling of security and satisfaction. In London, Paris, everywhere you see pretty women, pretty costumes, hear pretty music ; but the dancers pay little attention to time, almost none to sentiment, and constantly offend by not keeping a perfect line, being either too far forward or too far behind ; in short, dancing without school and a painful lack of technique. False steps in dancing shock as much as false notes in singing. The Scala public seems even more rigorous towards its dancers than its singers. I have often heard an artist yell gloriously out of tune without special admonishment; but I have never seen a dancer out of line or step without raising a perfect whirlwind of reproof. Since seeing the Milan corps, I understand why we are often shocked elsewhere by ballet-dancing. It is an art which requires absolute perfection in order not to fall into the rut of vulgarity. If a dancer does not dance with school she is apt to be indecent; the very motions and gestures which, performed after certain rules of art, are the embodiment of grace and etherealness, performed in a slovenly or unfinished manner have just the opposite tendency : they become vehicles of suggestiveness and immodesty. The action negatives the idea, and all the sentiment is lost in the performance.

But heavens ! what a long letter ! you will think me ballet-mad, and await my next appearance in parchment wings and rose-coloured fleshings—of course I shall come on to stirring music, and be accompanied by the usual paraphernalia of Terpsichorean satellites. What if I appear, not under a cloud, but on one near your very door, for instance? You might think me part of a very white fog which the *Telegraph* informs me is now hanging over London, and not even make me welcome. I confess, like the objectionable fog, I should be *en représentation* for nothing; and after vainly floating near your front-door in —in visions, heartbroken — would return to Milan singing, sadly singing,

"Multum incola fuit anima mea."

Good-bye: more anon. To-night we are going to the Manzoni Theatre. Will tell you about it in my next. *Othello* still keeps the town in an uproar. It is positively to come off on the 5th inst. There is not a seat to be had at La Scala for love or money. The Scala's portico, the public promenades, the Piazza della Scala are a sight to see. Where on earth will they house this crowd on the great night? And, of course, you have heard the awful news about the massacre at Massowah. The Ministry is fallen, and a demonstration, so called, is taking place : rosy-cheeked schoolboys and misses, on a holiday, are parading up and down the Corso, howling and singing—I doubt if they really know what for—and is it not strange? Verdi's name has something fatal in it. It suffices for him to give a new opera for disaster to break out somewhere. Signora Serao, the most celebrated writer in Italy, has telegraphed Verdi to request him to give the first performance of *Othello* for the benefit of the Massowah victims, &c. I see the Corti Brothers, La Scala's impresarii, smiling, and Verdi, the perennial, wrinkling his brow at such audacity. There is not a chance of such a thing happening, only the clubs have a new item to add to the opera budget.—Yours ever.

CHAPTER VII.

February 3rd, 1887.

TEATRO MANZONI, named after the great Alessandro Manzoni, is one of the most charming theatres in the world. It was built after designs by the architects Scala—you will think everything Scala in Milan—Scala and Canedi, and although I have frequently heard grand opera, here is chiefly devoted to tragedy and comedy. The interior is all white, red, and gold. There are several tiers of boxes, ranged, as at La Scala, almost to the ceiling; an ample parterre is filled with the most comfortable of seats, armchairs, called here by the singular name of " poltrone." The boxes are large and luxuriously furnished, with easy-chairs and mirrors, little drawing-rooms back give a sensation of space, most welcome to those accustomed to the cupboards called boxes, and the asphyxiating atmosphere of the Paris fire-traps. Here it is a pleasure to go to the theatre. Throughout Italy they are everywhere ample, spacious, commodious, and comfortable, and one may listen to a week of consecutive tragedy or comedy without the stiffened joints that we usually carry away from even one evening at the play.

The Manzoni is not only beautiful, clean, and comfortable, but it presents so pleasing an aspect under all circumstances that on entering the doors the exclamation " Simpatica !" springs instantly to the lips. Last night the scene was simply charming. The house is lit up with electricity, and showed off a most fashionable audience to perfection. The great attraction was a young Piedmontese, Eleonora Dusi, successor to the gifted Virgini Marini, and the one upon whose shoulders the great Ristori's mantle will certainly fall. I have seen Dusi twice, in *La Femme de Claude*, and—you will laugh when I tell you what the other play was, you will laugh still more when I tell you how it was; but let me finish first with La Dusi. She is young, pretty, graceful, delightful, and hers is the one name in dramatic art on Italy's lips; she was born in 1860, in the express going from Padua to Vicenza. She belongs to a family of histrionic celebrities who for more than a century have graced the Italian stage. Strange to say, she could imitate perfectly before she could articulate plainly, and at the age of five she played the usual infant prodigy. She was really one of the most precocious children the footlights have ever known, and before she could speak she began the theatrical career. She must have been a hardy plant, for instead of dying from premature nomadic blight, each succeeding year added to her vigour and grace. She led the usual wandering life and the existence usual to this profession—one day with plenty, the next day with nothing; one night sleeping in a palace, the next under the canopy of heaven; one day shown from the theatre in triumph, the next hooted at and sent off in secret. These vicissitudes continued until little Eleonora grew to big Eleonora. Children's parts were abandoned for those of adults, and one day La Dusi won her first laurels—suddenly, unexpectedly, decisively. She was playing in Rome, here, there, everywhere, when Fate threw her in immediate contact with Signora Pezzana Gualtieri, one of the most remarkable tragedians of Italy. One night in Naples they happened to appear in the same rôle, and the volcanic city awoke the next morning to the fact that Italy possessed two great dramatic stars: one already celebrated and no longer in the morning of life, the other almost a child, equally gifted, wearing the double " rose of youth " and talent. The play was Cossa's *Messalina,* work of that gifted poet who has added not a little to Italy's dramatic repertory of to-day, and in this trying study Eleonora Dusi carried off the most triumphant honours. She was frantically applauded and as frantically discussed; her failings were weighed in the balance with Pezzana's weaknesses, and those of the latter were found to bend the scale : even according to adverse critics the individual gifts of intellect, power, passion, and spontaneity were found in greatest force in the younger actress. Add to this a marked, almost irritating, personal originality, and it will readily be seen how sure a place in histrionic art La Dusi was bound to command. From this time forth her name reëchoed throughout Italy. She had not alone the Pezzana and Ristori's niece, Adelaide Tessero, for rivals, but Virgini Marini, one of the most delightful actresses I have ever seen. I remember this latter in *La Dame aux Camélias* at this same Theatre Manzoni, when Madame Eugénie Doche, the creatrice of Marguerite Gautier in Paris, wept with the rest of Milan over Marini as the sympathetic courtesan, and yet La Dusi in the same part supasses even Marini's splendid talent. This precocious excellence won as many backbiters as supporters—" thorns grow thickest on the flowers of fame "—but in spite of jealousy Dusi began and continued a triumphal career. She has been on the stage but a few years, yet her renown is national. Whenever, whatever, wherever she plays attracts; her name is the theme in drawing-room and club, and houses are packed to see her—packed at the highest of prices, and no one ever regrets his money. Boxes are bought, borrowed, begged, and I almost said stolen; stalls are booked months in advance, and standing-room alone without prcmiun. Of late I have been to Italy several times, but always missed her, and you may imagine my delight when I discovered that she was with her company in Milan. We procured seats with the greatest difficulty. We went to the play, and, writing this in cold blood, I am more than ever " under the charm " of her varied excellences.

Of course you will want to know what she looks like, and all about her. I will not keep you in suspense, but begin at once. She is rather slight in stature, her small and shapely head is crowned with masses of soft jetty hair, that black hair which has a silken look and bluish tinge, a seductive sort of hair—I half imagine Delilah's was something like it, and in my mind reverse the legend. Dusi's eyes are soft and of that peculiar gray-black which at times seems ebon and at others almost opal : one has a slight cast or turn which gives her face a strange look. Her mouth and teeth are charming, her skin a clear olive, and her whole person the very ideal of— again that word—" simpatica." She is a bad dresser, makes up even too little on the stage, and has not that grand air which celebrated actresses so soon acquire. La Dusi is sweet, simple, and positively the most natural, unaffected creation I have ever seen. She moves her hands rarely, but always well ; she walks with admirable motion ; she sits and stands with remarkable ease, and she knows how to listen as does no one ; in short, without the slightest effort, seems a part and parcel of every rôle she undertakes : I really don't know when I have seen an actress who has so pleased me. I have only told you of the personal detail of her physique, but add to these genuine pathos and a subtle, tragic fire, positively electrifying in their quickness, and you will have some idea of her natural gifts. She goes from one to the other, and effects these changes so quickly, that before one can realise how it has all come about she has thrown you into smiles or sighs, or tears or terror, and with the finest of magnetic chains has completely wound you round her little finger. They say Rachel possessed these qualities. I never saw Rachel, but certainly Dusi has the most remarkable histrionic gifts of any actress I have seen to-day. How far her art is nature, and her nature art, I am still unable to determine. After some seemingly most studied effort, I cried out, "That is the perfection of natural endowment," and after a most natural gesture as readily exclaimed, "That is the perfection of artistic culture." Dusi is a creature of sur-prises, and whatever her method may be, she is a woman of extreme dramatic temperament, dramatic to her very finger-tips, and an actress, if she lives long enough, destined to a great career. I say "if she lives"—she is so delicate that she can only play twice or three times a week. Her organisation, like that of most naturally gifted human beings, is one of such super-sensitiveness that a nothing unstrings and irritates her. She wears herself out when she plays, and is one of the few on the boards who throw their whole souls—a part of themselves— into their work, who never spare themselves,—in short, the old story of the blade using the sheath. I scarcely know how to compare Dusi. She has no paragon on the stage. Those who remember the famous French star say she is a second Desclée. I never saw that great actress but once, her last appearance in Paris. She recited a single scene, yet in that brief moment I felt her greatness, and as Dusi instantly reminded me of Desclée, I understood the comparison. Eleonora Dusi possesses those fine, nervous qualities which border on genius, yet often cross the frontier of hysteria. She is subtle, insinuating, catlike. There seems to be a constant something gnawing at her vitals, a constant struggle for a perfection which she never attains—will perhaps never attain. She makes you feel this inward effort, and it communicates itself to you by a per-sonal magnetism, which at first has something of the disagree-able effect of touching the cord of an electric battery. Her voice is rough, and at times feeble. This is her weakest point, and yet after a while you get accustomed to it, it becomes in turn a part of herself, of her distinct originality, her distinct personality. Her versatility is equally remarkable. Her repertory includes *Messalina, Femme de Claude, Fédora, Odette, Dame aux Camélias, Frou-Frou*, the heaviest tragedies of the old and new school, and the highest efforts of Goldoni, Meilhac, or a Sardou. I shall not tell you of the *Femme de Claude*. I don't like the play, although she is magnificent in it, audacious, disreputable, passionate, and vengeful ; but I will tell you of *Pamela Nubile*, Goldoni's delightful work.

Some of the greatest names and talents in Italy were patiently awaiting the curtain at least half an hour before its rise, jostled by the populace, crowded, elbowed, and crushed, standing head to head in the platea, as eager for the first word of their new prophetess as an Athenian student to drink in the words of Aspasia. The electric lights have not spoiled artistic Italy. As the play began, it did my heart good to listen to the comments, see the enthusiasm, which becomes oxygen in an Italian playhouse. A long experience of cold, cosmopolitan audiences, had almost unfitted me for the warmth of this volcanic public, but I soon re-accustomed myself, and found the murmur of disapprobation quite as easy to my lips as the outburst of applause. And the play ? I had nearly forgotten to mention it, and that would have been inexcusable. One may forget a Dumas or a Gilbert, but one may not forget a Goldoni. Goldoni then it was, and called *Pamela Nubile*. I shall not attempt to describe the comedy, the name alone of *Pamela* being sufficient to recall that classic virtue whose immortal luck has not only been the ruin of nearly every employer, but of every female who has since entered domestic service. I have never seen Richardson's play, if he wrote one, but the gifted Venetian's version sent me into fits of laughter. The

lord only weds the servant when he learns that she is a peeress
in her own right. With the single exception of Signorina Dusi,
the players were almost beneath contempt, their efforts to
appear English, or even half English, or British, or Scotch, or
Irish, or what you will, something quite unworthy the efforts
of supposably intelligent people, supposably capable of playing
a Goldonian comedy in one of the most critical and fastidious
cities of Europe; before one of the most critical, refined, and
fastidious of European audiences. La Dusi, as Pamela, displayed all the qualities I have before named. Of the other
actors I will not speak, but of the play I must. Ought one,
dare one, should one, criticise Goldoni? Yes, if you think he
is in the wrong, and behold in me the heretic who attempts
such an ungrateful task. Goldoni's interpretation or adaptation of Richardson's classic is certainly audacious, is mon-
strous viewed from our own or the English standpoint, curious
viewed from any standpoint not Italian, curious even viewed
from the European standpoint. Throughout the piece we are
pervaded by the noxious perfume of the coarsest Italian morals.
All the delicacy of feeling betrayed by the young lord for his
hireling is here changed into exactly the opposite sentiment.
This might pass, but the ending of the play is such that all
moral beauty is completely nullified. When Lord whatever-his-
name-is reflects on Pamela and marriage is suggested, he hems
and haws, and finds a way to insinuate the usual wedding on
the European plan, wherein license and marriage-ring play no
part. I stood this and similar hints with perfect equanimity
until the last act, when an individual, an exile—not *à la* Victor
Hugo—rushed in, and, after rare blood-curdling imbecilities,
announced that he was a certain Count d'Arco and the father
of Pamela. The nobleman's surprise, joy, and delight to find
in his beloved a peeress in her own right—perfectly legitimate
sentiments, I allow, ordinarily, but not here—were such that

I nearly had a convulsion; and when he calmly told his family
of his knowledge of the change in Pamela's fortunes, crying :
"Now I can legitimately marry her. She is a countess, a·
countess, a countess!" my hair simply pricked into my head
with astonishment. I said, "O shades of Richardson, what
has become of the admirable moral of your work ? What man·
in love would not marry·a countess in her own right, when
that countess is the woman he adores?" But the best part
of *Pamela Nubile* was the extremely laconic attitude of the
public. They found it quite right and natural that one well-
born should have behaved with such immaculate prudence,
for, with all their sentiment and due deference to the follies
of Romeo and Juliet, the Italians. are prudent. There are
more marriages of convenience than love, there are more
parchment-signed contracts done up in due form before the
mayor than kisses stolen on a Capulet's balcony, or vows
sealed before the inconstant moon. The enthusiasm of the
public was immense. Such applause, such recalls, such re-
echoing of "Brave, brave!" Everybody was called for, even
Goldoni. I need not say, however, this latter did not appear.
I wish he had. He would have received a piece of one
woman's mind. Although he did not die young, the gods are
evidently still protecting him.

I cannot begin to tell you of half the notabilities present :
one, however, I may mention. Several times I had noticed a
fair man in the stalls who did not listen to but was absorbed
in the play, and as to La Dusi, his enthusiasm simply
amounted to frenzy. Once he turned his head in our direction,
and a friend, the well-known Chevalier L—i, whose lovely
wife has the most charming, in fact the only, salon in Milan,
said directly, "Ah, there he is. I'll bring him here."

Before I could say a word the Chevalier had disappeared,
and in a few moments I found myself shaking hands with the

M

fair man—tall, eminently distinguished, and—and—can you not
imagine who he was? I can still hear the Chevalier's voice
saying, "Permit me to present you—Signor Arrigo Boïto."
Ah—at last! But my letter is already too long. I will tell you
of Boïto in my next, or in one of my future inflictions : you see,
I intend to write until you will telegraph me to cease, and you
may not do that with impunity. Telegraphing costs twopence
halfpenny a word from England to Italy—sèe what comes of
the simple request to send letters from the land of song.

I have always said, and insist upon it, that we lay the
foundation for more real mischief in a moment of thoughtless-
ness than in a year of premeditated crime.—Yours ever, &c.

CHAPTER VIII.

Feb. 3rd, 1887.

IT is really a pity you are not here : if nothing happens, the great event will surely take·place day after to-morrow, the 5th. You speak of changes. Ah ! Milan is indeed changed, and her growth in architectural elegance is truly remarkable. Ten years ago, Piazza del Duomo wore a different look from what it does to-day. By way of fine buildings there were the magnificent cathedral in the Piazza del Duomo, to the right the splendid columns of the new Galleria, and to the left the charming old Palazzo Reale ; but a mass of tumbledown houses and edifices in every sort of architecture disfigured a square which otherwise might have been a model of archi. tectural elegance. All this, however, is altered. On walking out, to my surprise I saw a number of symmetrical and elegant new structures had replaced the old and dilapidated ones. The Piazza, which once wore a ragged and deformed look, had become transformed into a magnificent modern quadrangle. Milan's pride, however, will ever be her Gothic cathedral, which stands out in beauty from other sainted temples, as do these new buildings which have replaced the ancient ones in the Piazza. For all this church has been so much talked about, I cannot forbear speaking of it, especially as some new facts anent its origin have been brought to light, which I think cannot fail to be of interest to your artistic soul. The original architect or designer had left no name to be handed down to posterity. All standard histories, guide-books, and authorities, without exception, have given various names as the founder of this unique temple and it was supposed that its real origin would ever remain one of the mysteries; but patient research has recently brought to light many facts concerning the epoch of its earliest fabrication, and some highly probable theories in relation to that epoch bid fair to rend the veil of inauthenticity which has so long clouded the construction of this great sanctuary.

The first date of this church's birth is 1386, when Giovanni Galeazzo Visconti was supposed to have been the originator and founder; at the same time its endowment was attributed to a concourse of Milanese citizens; again to the initiative and help of a celebrated engineer, one Marco da Frisone; but some very recent archæological studies have established beyond much doubt that the date of the cathedral's origin was anterior to 1386, and that the real designer was a certain Simon di Orsenigo, one of the remarkable men of the epoch, and one whom present calculation points to as the veritable architect. Marco da Frisone's long illness and death in 1389 or 1390 leaves but a slender margin to go upon as to any active part taken by him in the cathedral's construction, even admitting the church to have been commenced in 1386; and if begun later it is difficult to attribute a work to one whose name is so slightly connected at any anterior period with public affairs in Milan. It would be possible, but almost useless, to go into the detail by which this conclusion had been arrived at, viz. that Orsenigo was the architect of the Duomo; suffice it to say, however, that many documents brought forth by indefatigable research, and referred to in a late Milan journal (letters to Milan *Perseveranza*), are quite strong enough to leave to him the honour of having designed this immortal work. The present discoveries are the outcome of long and furious discussion as to the Duomo's character and style of architecture. The Italian nation naturally wished it to be considered purely Italian. The Latin cross dominates, and the five naves would have helped this delusion; but the interior chapels, and the form a half octagonal, absidiale poligonata, with the curious wings flanking the sacristy, are so uncommon, that students have unhesitatingly compared the Milanese Duomo with the Cologne Cathedral, and see in the priority of the latter's construction, 1248, the reason of the former's multiform designs. In the present state of political affection between the two countries, France and Italy, it adds little to the Italian's pleasure to reflect that the great Cologne temple was designed by a Frenchman, one Girard de Rile, a celebrated man, whose talents graced the world a century and a half before the Milan cathedral was ever fairly outlined. This is the present theory, and seems probable enough to hold good for the future. The only flattering discovery is that no matter where the draughtsman borrowed his design, he at least owned his birthright to Italy. The Milan Duomo is not absolutely a model of pure architecture in any school, and were it not for the miraculous exterior decorations, its form even would appear inelegant. It is supposed to be a pure Gothic, but the front portals, squarely cut, of old Italian design, lessen the artistic whole, and are the one blemish on an otherwise unique temple of Gothic art.

The Duomo was erected on the old site of Santa Maria Maggiore, a minster of the twelfth century, which was noted for the highest steeple in Lombardy, and remained the chief temple of worship in Milan until this edifice, its successor, although in a most imperfect state, appeared in 1486.

To my mind this' church is the most fantastically beautiful in the world. The shapely body is fashioned in white marble, scarcely less pure to-day than when it lay dreaming in Candoglia's virginal arms : little by little the finest sculptors

and most delicate chisels in Lombardy transformed their blocks
into a mass of white frost-work, intricate, fascinating, laby-
rinthine. What fane is a greater wilderness of ideal imagery,
of graven statues, and holy shrines—wilderness of carved and
fluted columns, of miniature temples and secluded chapels?
Terrestial habitation of the world's chosen and heaven's blest!
Like the Church itself, it has been the work of centuries. Little
by little faith has perfected her original model, little by little
completed her original design !   Mingled with the older mar-
.bles, the new ones seem timid and pale ; but since your visit
years ago, the cornice is become a strange surplice in white—
·dear me, no ! but many shades of white and gray, or yellow.
Already Time, inimitable softener, has mellowed the dainty
frieze. The ancient stones look like rich old lace, and the fine
dentils running around the roof proper are like a border of
Venetian point. Of the temple's inner beauty, what words can
describe its holy conceits ! The star-studded ceilings and graceful
naves, the quaint altars and incrusted canopies, the saints
in their solemn niches, and Madonnas in their still, cool aisles,
remind me of some miraculous entablature in ivory : so deli-
-cate, that an indiscreet hand might crush into powder; so
·strong, that the wear and tear of centuries has left no trace,
·beyond a more manifest fragility, a deeper harmony of tone on
the old background, and a richer yellow in the amber-hued fore.
I looked with awe, for the hundredth time, upon the vaulted
roofs, the mysterious naves, and the majestic rows of octagonal pillars, noble columns, rising to the vaguest heights, like
those lofty Pyramids, which loom on endless horizons, to lose
themselves in the blue of eternal skies.   I gazed fascinated on
the many glittering altars ; on the pale tapers, whose mystic
gleam lights up the visions of fair St. Agnes and Melchione
Gherardini's angels ; at the Virgin-Mother holding counsel with
the good saints Victor and Rocca. Those dear images in their

sacred niches, enshrined in gold, are framed in arabesques of
so fleeting and unreal a fantasy that they do not seem the work
of man's hand, but rather the prayers of good souls, surged up
from some dim vista of the past to beg for the salvation of
the poor, the sick, the lost, and the unhappy : dear thoughts,
which have taken shape and form in the flower-garden of the
heart to bloom perennial in the flower-garden of eternity. I
lost hours roaming from aisle to chapel and chapel to orifice ;
I was not alone, but surrounded by palpable forms ; I held
communion with that sainted band, who in the long ago have
come and gone in these sacred walks.   The sombre light, steal-
ing through the carved oriels, cast flickering shadows on the
trecento mosaic, and in each dark angle or obscure corner I
seemed to see the ghost of San Carlo Borromeo, or perhaps
one of the stern Medici, whose splendid tomb in the central
nave hides their mortal glories and remains.

Thence I wandered to the sacred vault of the church
treasure, where the wealth of accumulated centuries lies in
glowing banks of gold and precious stones—metals so richly
carved and jewel-studded that their shields might have served
for invulnerable Achilles armour ; the ivory vessels, cut in
rarest Greek friezes, might have served nectar to the gods ;
and the sacred tablets, on whose unspotted white are recorded
divine records, pure and lasting memory of good deeds and
glorious human achievement.

Like yourself, I have seen most of the world's cathedrals.
Their beauty is unusually the triumph of architecture and
material effect. They are divine edifices, which rarely suggest divine thoughts ; but the Milan Duomo has something
so unreal, so weird, and so supernatural, that I am more
inclined to think it the work of heavenly inspiration than the
great Strasburg cathedral, which, if we are to believe the legend,
was designed and even built by supernatural aid.   St. Peter's

space and gorgeousness remind me of a mammoth modern railway - station. The eager sightseer, not even Sundays excepted, with guide-books in hand, is not the religious enthusiast, but the frantic tourist, who awaits but the ringing of the station bell to take the first train on to Paradise *viâ*—Palermo. He must do Rome in a week, and his " latest improved" says, " Two hours at St. Peter's." I allow I was wonderstruck to look upon so much magnificence and cleverness, such a heaping up of this world's riches and capabilities; but I was not so much permeated by the idea of divinity as by the omnipotence of human power, the value of money, and the verification of Horace's words, " Nil mortalibus arduum est." No, there is little sanctity about St. Peter's. It is a colossal show-place, a museum of Golcondian wealth, but it is not a house of God.

St. Mark's goes to the head like a too subtle perfume or a too rich wine. Its gold and effulgence, barbaric wealth and splendour, overcome the senses, and intoxication is the only sentiment I have ever felt on entering or leaving this marvellously entrancing place of worship; intoxication not for religion nor for the joys of the world to come, but intoxication of this earth's material beauties, the joy and the gladness of living in the plentiful realisation thereof. Ah me! what sensations do not follow a visit to St. Mark's ! But the Milanese Duomo—that is another thing: when you first look upon its frost-like form and ethereal turrets, you may not at once realise its saintliness, or feel its supernatural charms; but the oftener you see it the oftener you will be filled with a sense which no language may describe ; you will attempt in some outburst to say just what it is like, but the moment you put your thoughts into words, like some painters who put oil to their charcoal, the picture is no longer the same : the simile remains, but the likeness has vanished. To-day I made my accustomed pilgrimage thither, to breathe again the sanctity which has ever brought peace to my soul.

How many times have I threaded these sacred mazes, how
many times descended into the perfumed crypt where San Carlo
for centuries has slept his long sleep; studied the glittering dome
above his sepulchre, and the incrusted jewels which light up the
vault, as good deeds light up a man's earthly record ; at the
sculptured panorama of lambent silver, which, like a pure stream,
bears on its bosom the lilies of an untarnished life ! I looked
again at the gorgeous priestly vesture, and the poor old head on
its sainted cushion: at the closed lids lit by a mysterious light,
and illuminated by the reflection of this gem-studded canopy;
the hands that did so much good folded and at rest for ever,
were folded on the withered breast, the fingers half closed over
Maria Theresa's princely gift, the arms lying lightly on the body,
the body lying peacefully on its hallowed bier.   Thence back-
wards, upwards, I retraced my steps through the mazes and
sombre aisles, past the rich columns and brightly-burning tapers,
past the dama murmuring her aves and the peasant murmuring her prayers : past the square doors and the shell basins
where the holy water shono like drops of crystal ; thence out
into the street.   Long after leaving the sainted spot there was
a sense, not of earth, but of heaven : of having communed with
angels, and having caught athwart the temple's open portals
a glimpse of that immortality which we are never so near to
as when living with the creations of genius, divine inspirations
which have gone to glorify the temples of the Most High.
Do you not think with me that the most truly beautiful object
on earth is the one which most appeals to the soul ? I repeat, the
Milan cathedral has never awakened in me other than holy
thoughts.   I never could reduce it to the modicum of sight-
seeing.   I do not know how many columns, how many altars,
or statues, or chapels it contains, the number of its saints,
or sinners, or martyrs : I only know that it seemed to me a
divine place, that it appealed to my best self.   I felt only the

longing, the restlessness, the desire for the unattainable, the
immortal, that we feel when we gaze upon the truest objects
of Nature : the limitless ether, majestic mountains, or the
sea swelling under tumultuous billows: we think of the life
.beyond this life, of space, depth, infinity, the wonders of the
deep, and the wonders of eternity. You will admit with me
that the unknowable alone has power to exalt, to charm, to
hold. As you look from afar upon this divine temple, it floats
above the sea of commonplace, as the foam floats above the
wave ;. it rises ever mysteriously before you, like a vision in a
dream : you stretch out your hand to touch, to hold,.but it
assumes a supernatural aspect, and slowly fades away: dis-
appears, as the foam scatters to lose itself in the wave, as your
dream vanishes before Aurora's advancing footsteps.

You have asked me about Da Vinci's "Last Supper :" although my letter is so long, I shall speak of it here, also one
other church of Milan.

You know, beside the Duomo, there are over fifty sacred
edifices, and of those fifty to me especially attractive is Santa
Maria della Grazie : a gray, old-fashioned structure, particularly
interesting, not alone in itself, but in its historical recollections.
I never come to Milan without paying it a visit. The exterior
is very pleasing, with quaint gables, gray towers and flying
buttresses which lend a rich, although rather promiscuous, effect
to the style ; the interior, however, is charming and harmonious.
There are the usual perfumed chapels and holy altars, and
some very good pictures : a Crucifixion by Vizentini, some
frescoes by Ferrari representing Christ's Passion, and in the
choir many elaborate and valuable medallions. The sacristy is a
quaint chamber, with some singular decorations of Da Vinci's
school. In a little chapel, reached from an outer door, called
Capella del Rosario, there is a canvas of peculiar interest,
by Cerano, depicting the pest in Milan, 1630. I cannot

look at this ancient picture without re-living Manzoni's great *Promessi Sposi*, and the awful horrors of that terrible epoch.

From a side-door of the Santa Maria della Grazie you enter a chamber, supposed by many to be a part of the church, but in reality the ancient Dominican convent immortalised by the marvellous Cenacolo or " Lord's Supper," which was painted in fresco on one of the chapel walls. It was in this monastery that victims were tried and tortured during the Inquisition under the Spanish Government and tribunal of 1555. The convent has long since fallen into religious disuse, but has been successively a barracks, fire head-quarters, and once was a granary. When the French were in Milan in '59, a regiment of vandals was quartered in the old church. One room will for ever attest to an act of their barbaric presence; for in order to have ingress and egress into an adjoining chamber, these *profanum vulgas* cut a door through the very limbs of the Saviour : an act of sacrilege which not alone seriously injured the base of the picture, but, I believe, ultimately precipitated the ruin of the whole. In looking again at this divine inspiration I was reminded of Keats' words,

" A thing of beauty is a joy for ever."

The walls are insecure and damp ; the cornice is mouldering, and a white fringe, like the fungus overhanging the city's vaults, is slowly weaving its gray cobweb over the doomed transept : yet this picture is still " a thing of beauty." It is pathetic in its helpless and inevitable decay; it is more beautiful in its sad dilapidation than the more solid plasters of perfectly preserved works of art ; it is a mute yet speaking voice from that great past, when artists were artisans in the true sense of the word, when perhaps their genius lay not so much in their inspiration as in their patient toil and oblivion to all existence not confined within the domain of art. Look at the

copyists who haunt every available space of the old chapel,
then turn away from their anatomical Christs and barbarous
disciples, cover your blinded eyes after sight of their violent
reds and purples, turn your back upon the too artistic pot-
boilers, and look thoughtfully and regretfully at the great
model and softened colours, thankful that your days have yet
beheld it, regretful at what those who come after you must
irrevocably miss.   This work is also more beautiful now
because it appeals to a double sense, a double loss—not alone
the loss of a work of art, but, in this renegade epoch, of the
disappearance of a great moral teacher.   We have only to look
upon the Salons and Royal Academies of to-day to understand
that Agnosticism grows with the century—that the disgusting
efforts called "realistic" show the result of too much progress in mathematics, and too little in ethics.   But I need not
preach : we all know had Leonardo da Vinci painted only the
" Last Supper" he would have well earned immortality.   The
greatest brushes in Italy have tried to restore it, but their
efforts, one and all, have been vain.   Indeed, it was feared
they would completely ruin it, and the authorities have
decided that henceforth no attempt shall be made towards its
restoration.   Da Vinci used his own preparations : soft, subtle,
enduring, and beautiful ; like his genius, they were a part of
himself ; none, alas! has inherited the one or ever divined the
secret of the other.

The fresco, you will remember, covers one entire side of the
chapel; some parts of it are absolutely untouched by the
march of time, others show the sure sign of approaching ruin.
I was surprised at the brilliancy and softness of some of the
colouring.   In the draperies the blue and rose are as tender
as the hue of a fresh flower.   You know Da Vinci always
studied from models.   Looking at this picture, I have often
asked myself if the master in his wandering had not run across

one of those intinerant companies which played, as they do at Oberammergau, the "Passionspiel." Perhaps he went there, and the "Last Supper" is a study from life. Would it not be strange, and can we ever learn the truth? You know that in southern Italy the natives in the long-ago played a sort of Passion-play; and it is barely possible the study was made there. However, to return to the picture.

The faces still beam with life, and that of the Saviour, besides its living expression, is to me the great model of divine inspiration. The poise of His head, the folds of His vesture, and one slender outstretched hand, give an almost startling sensation of life. That soft gentle palm and those rosy-tipped fingers seem flesh and blood—one almost expects to see them move, to see the disciples move, to hear the tinkling of sacred vessels, to hear the sound of saintly voices, to hear John speak, and even to see perfidious Judas imprint the kiss of betrayal on the divine brow. How great are works such as these, when old, shattered, even desecrated, they still have power to lift us from ourselves, to take us with one bound to that past when the star still shone bright in Bethlehem's sky, and the Child born in a manger was destined to change time, space, and the minds of men! Looking upon such a painting, one follows civilisation step by step from the first year of the Christian era, and, a second Constantine, we would fain see the Cross, not alone resplendent on the horizon of the past, but resplendent in the sky of our nineteenth century : it is sad to think that such a work must decay, pass into oblivion out from the sight and minds of men. Such a picture is a liberal, moral education. Look at it once a day. It will be worth more to one hereafter than to tell prayers on a gold-strung rosary, to read the Bible daily, to put one's name to the most public charity subscription, or to raise the loudest voice in congregational singing.

From seeing the Cenacolo I went to the Brera Palace, and

looked again at Canova's "Napoleon" fronting the great entrance doors. I saw Luini's lovely "Rose Madonna" and Da Vinci's "Head of Christ." People laugh and scout the Brera Collection, but it is really an admirable exhibition, just large enough to make picture-seeing agreeable, and just small enough to permit one to retain easily the names and works of the masters and their masterpieces. When you go there, look at "L'Annunziata" by Raphael's father, Sanzio, and Raphael's glorious "Lo Sposalizio della Vergine." There are splendid Caracci, Rubens, and Paris Bordones, and, irrespective of school, one or more originals belonging to all the great names in pictorial art.

This time it is really good-bye until to-morrow, and the day after, *Dio volendo* and the artists willing, the great opera is to be given. Are you better? I hope so. Yours, &c.

ALFRED EDEL,
Artist, and Costume Designer of La Scala.

CHAPTER IX.

Milan, February 4th, 1887.

YESTERDAY, after the Brera, I remembered that we were to go
to the artist Edel's studio to see some of his works, and as I
promised to tell you about this young man—he is the costume
designer of La Scala — as well now as at any time; I
also enclose his picture. You see he is quite a boy, and his
position is marvellous for one of his years, although not for
one of his talent. Madame X— called for me at the hotel
about three, and we went to his studio. I tugged up—well, I
do not know how many stairs—you may imagine somewhere
near the number when I say that we left the *piano nobile* far
behind: the *piano nobile* is notoriously the sixth floor in English.
At every new landing, in answer to my faint " Is it here?" came
back a fainter " N—no, not quite yet;" but after mounting and
mounting, we heard on the stone staircase the cheery voice and
ringing step of Edel himself, who had been out, and the jani-
tor had just told us that he was in. My! what purgatory is
reserved for the purification of the facile-tongued portinajo?
But to return. Edel, out and in fifty times a day, had just
rushed over to La Scala with some "props," and was off for
another commission, when he learned that two friends had
gone to pay him a visit. We were presented on the staircase—reminded me of America. Madame X— was valiant
enough, but the poor man fairly had to drag me to his abode.
When we finally arrived I did not even regret the stairs,

his studio was so well worth paying a visit to. The rooms
are lofty and decorated in exquisite taste, carved columns sup-
port some curiously-carved arches, and a mauresque style of
cornice makes the roof not alone look as if it were vaulted, but
adds to the richness of the ceiling decoration. This cornice is
fringed with quaint wood-carving, dentils such as you see on
the roofs of old Italian palaces. The hangings and furniture
were of Oriental stuffs and of Oriental luxury—such divans,
such chairs, such seats!

"Heavens!" I thought, glancing around, "it pays nowadays
to have talent to design, to paint, to—"

Alfred Edel, watching me, laughingly interrupted my
thoughts.

"The place isn't much," he said; "it was a granary, but
they let me arrange it to suit myself, and I arranged it as you
see. But the view is my pride. Come and look out; or will
you rest first?"

After having climbed all those stairs, I own I would have
liked to repose myself a moment, but it really was not civil to
appear so tired, and I accordingly announced my willingness
to "look out."

He threw open the casement, and I uttered a cry of
wonder. Of all the apartments in the Galleria facing the
square, Edel's is the one which commands perhaps the most
superb view. We went on to the balcony, and Milan lay at our
feet like a gem in an ancient medallion. Away to the north,
south, and west, the white-capped Alps rose from a misty
valley and seemed to soar into the very sky; the whole range
of mountains looked like an endless necklace of milky jewels—
those great pearls which King Humbert yearly gathers for his
queen's monile; the broad Lombard plain, stretching away into
endless sapphire valleys was a perspective of limpid, constantly
changing blue. Nearer and yet nearer gleamed the low-lying

horizon—houses upon houses, as thick as bits in a mosaic: with
many-coloured roofs and many-coloured walls, packed in quaint
precision : one dense mass close on to the Piazza which someway bursts upon us. In the midst of the new-fashioned buildings surrounding the square was set the lovely lonely Gothic
cathedral, to quote Edgar Allan Poe, rising like his fairy city
from the sea:

> " Up domes—up spires—up kingly halls ;
> Up fanes—up Bablyon-like walls,
> Up shadowy long-forgotten bowers
> Of sculptured ivy and stone flowers.
> Up many and many a marvellous shrine,
> Whose wreathed friezes intertwine
> The viol, the violet, and the vine."

We finally left the balcony; Signor Edel installed us on a
delightful Turkish sofa, and began a chat about—well, I am
ashamed to mention the theme, but, of course, it was *Othello*.

Poor Edel, he is nearly dead. He is only the costume
designer of La Scala, it is true, but it seems there is no stage-
manager, and nearly everything falls on his shoulders : not
only the scenic decorations and costumes, but the scenery
itself, the stage properties, and I don't know what beside. I
noticed and mentioned a quaint Venetian swinging lamp.

"O, that is not worth looking at," he said. "I had a
really magnificent specimen of antique metal; they borrowed
it as a model for La Scala ; sent for it—took it—it disappeared
—and not only we haven't got it for *Othello*, but no human being
can find it in all Milan. I have hunted high and low ; but the
lamp has disappeared—*come si fa?*"

While he was talking the bell rang, and the door was
opened : some message from the theatre ; then again a pro-
perty-man came to inquire about Iago's châtelaine. Edel was
about to show us some drawings—another ring at the bell.
He put his hand wildly to his head.

N

"You see how it is," he said. "This goes on, and has been going on at any hour of the day or night for two months. I don't eat, I can't sleep—I wonder how I live. I don't live, I exist—at least, I can't exist much longer."

The new-comer was B—y, the celebrated Milanese hosier. B—y furnishes everything in the clothing line—known as the basso vestario—worn on the stage in Italy. He appeared with Iago's tights : one leg in pansy purple and white stripes, the other in darker prune, embroidered in splendid (*sic*) jewels. But something was wrong : the gold threads had to be picked out ; there was about two days' work to be done in less than twenty-four hours—however, I need not go into detail,.you know what the stage is. No matter if a year is spent in preparing, mounting, and costuming an opera or play, everything is left to the last minute—no one is responsible— one shifts his work on to the other's shoulders, and on the night of performance the curtain always rises on—a dress rehearsal. There is no stage-manager at La Scala : Verdi's orders are peremptory. Ricordi is Verdi's mouthpiece. One Ricordi flits here, another Ricordi there. The impresarii Corti Brothers manage the theatre ; the Theatrical Commission "boss" the management ; the artists "boss" the managers ; fifty people have something to say about the way La Scala is to be run ; and so it goes on. The odd part of it all is that we out-siders are on the *qui vive*. The anxiety has communicated itself to the whole town ; even I—cool-blooded me, I, what does one say in this case ?—even I am nervous. The sound of a mouse in the rafters made me jump, and Edel's door-bell ringing simply sent my pulse up into the hundreds.

Whilst B—y was talking, another individual arrived—the theatrical wig-maker. He held a series of top-knots in his flexile hands, destined for poor Iago—the one chosen being the only one that would not fit on, or glue on, or stay on to Iago's head. Wigs, like the world, are not made in a day; but another has to be got ready for the Venetian Judas, and that before to-morrow's sun is mid-high. We looked at the refractory wig long and earnestly; tawny locks curling subtle—ping, ping, ping at the door. Edel turned a shade paler.

"This time," he said, "the wire must be broken."

Only a message from the costumer anent Desdemona's veil.

Edel had drawn and designed an ideal Desdemona, divinely tall, divinely fair. Her first dress was to be an exquisite brocade. She was to wear a coronet, from which depended a veil, a misty Venetian fabric like the gossamer on a butterfly's wing. Madame Pantaleone, the prima donna, is short and black-haired: this last defect is a trifling one, but the veil she would not wear: it spoiled her coiffure, it dragged her head down, etcetera; could not Edel suggest something else?

"But the costume is incomplete without it," groaned the poor artist. "Why didn't she say so before—two months ago, two weeks ago, two days ago—why, only two minutes ago? For the gauze was to be caught up here, to float away there, and was altogether destined to add to the general effect of the dress, but—" another ring at the bell. Edel rushed forward, a portfolio of drawings fell from my nerveless hand, a cold shudder ran down my back, and a man entered, carrying an enormous bundle.

Edel was about to say, "What is it?" when the new-comer saved him the trouble. He began a harangue in so high-pitched a dialect that the cornice seemed to rattle: more discontent—more costumes to be arranged—heaven knows what! I spare you the detail: the new-comer raged for ten minutes without stopping to breathe, and then, with a gasp like a gust from a storm-cloud, finished by screaming "Addio! I wash my hands of the whole affair." He flung the parcel on to a divan, and saluting us all wildly, rushed as wildly forth.

" When does this—this opera come off ?" I asked timidly.
" If not to-morrow, ah, ne'er shall sun that other morrow
see."

Edel seemed stunned. Madame X— laughed.

" Shut them all out," she said, " and show us the designs
for the new ballet *Narenta.* Let them ring until—until they
get tired."

He smiled faintly, and went towards his easel. Alfred
Edel is only three-and-twenty. He is one of the cleverest
young men of his time, and you, who know everybody, surely
ought to know all about him.

He was born in Milan in 1864, and at an early age evinced
a remarkable disposition for drawing. Has it ever struck you
how few words there are with which to describe the youth of
a man of talent? I find myself getting into a very rut of
commonplace, *vide* above, and—and it is a pity, for Edel is
quite out of ruts and commonplaces, and deserves some really
unusual terms to express his very unusual talent. But to
continue. He studied drawing for years, and is one of the
first draughtsmen of Europe. Rome, Paris, Vienna, Berlin,
every great capital, with its masters, museums, art collections,
and art associations, have combined to this youth's culture.
His friends, and even enemies, said, " Edel will become a great
painter, perhaps a Titian ;" but Alfred Edel, while he had
great regard for great names in art, laughed, and said to himself, " I shall become nothing of the sort ; I love to make
little figures " (called in Italian *figurine*) ; " I take little
interest in colossal canvases or colossal human beings," and
" I really feel my *forte* is in designing costumes, theatrical
decorations, theatrical human beings, what you will belonging
to the theatre, but no masterpieces in oil—nothing of the sort."

He kept to his word and his work. The result has been
brilliant : few young artists have attained either his position,

fortune, or renown. What a thing to understand at the outset
of life what one is specially fitted to do, and to do it!

One of the most curious things is the quickness with which
he sketches. In the brief space of fifteen minutes he can design
in colour the most elaborate figures—some with jewelled
armour and very rich draperies cost him *half an hour* of trouble.
Is he not a miraculous artist? And nothing is slovenly or badly
done. I have seen studies made by others, supposed to be
quick hands, in two or three hours, but none so perfect in
every way as his.

We looked at so many remarkable studies that my eye
became a perfect kaleidoscope of dancing images. These latter
are for the new ballet *Narenta*; an Oriental, or Greek, or
Assyrian, or Egyptian young woman, carried off by the usual
bandit, saved by the Prince, and preferred by the people.
How can I describe *Narenta* to you? I don't think I shall try.
Suffice it to say that it is to be gorgeous with all gorgeousness,
that, compared to it, *Rolla* will be a poor affair, that even
Taglioni's ancient shows will fade into insignificance, and the
fabled *Excelsior*, as we say in America, take a back seat for
evermore. Hence, see *Narenta* and—live.

I find I haven't told you half I had intended about Edel:
of his kindness to young artists, his patience and unflagging
perseverance, and a host of good qualities besides his talent;
but my letter is so long it really must draw to a close; however, if you are still interested, more anon when we meet.

To-morrow is the great day. In spite of my hour at Edel's
studio, I feel, of course, Iago's wig, Desdemona's veil, Othello's
belt will be all right for seven sharp, dressing-hour at La
Scala. By the way, speaking of dressing, the noble Moor
wears a curious dress; a sort of chain-armour breast-plate,
fitted into the front of his costume, gives it a very warrior-like
look, and adds immensely to the beauty of the tunic. Edel

found the model in some ancient Venetian archive, and has most happily utilised it for Tamagno. When I looked at the costume itself, and in my mind saw the Moor arrayed in all his toggery, I also said to myself, " Very nice for the Moor and his breast-plate, but fatal to Desdemona and her wig, should she chance to recline her head on his bosom, which of course no woman ever missed on the stage with the man she loves. I shall tremble for veil and flowing locks if these latter catch in the armour." But I desist. This is really borrowing trouble for the morrow at two hundred per cent. Your place is reserved if you can come. Love nor money can no longer procure even a peg near the great Lustro, but threats might bring forth a poltrone in the platea.—Yours ever.

CHAPTER X.

Otellopolis, February 5th, 1887.

AT last, at last the great day has come and gone, and Verdi has added the crown jewel to his diadem of triumphs. I cannot tell you the anxiety felt in the city before nightfall. As early as five A.M. every one was astir, and when Gianetta brought my tea she informed me that she had already been to La Scala : the posters were unchanged, the opera would surely come off, unless—you may imagine I sent her about her business with her "unlesses"—unless the tenor, or the soprano, or the wig-maker, or the some particular hinge of the cast, she explained, "did not 'run ill' before seven P.M." Speaking of wig-makers, she also reminds me that any number of ladies in the hotel were having their hair dressed even at that unearthly hour—not me—eight "an may it please you," making preparations exactly as if the occasion were a State ball or a Royal wedding. These ladies will sit all day with bejewelled and elaborately-dressed pates, and not dare to lie down, or sit back, or lean over, for fear of ruining their puffs, &c.

You may imagine the excitement was not lost on me. I hastily dressed, and before noon was in the streets. Streets? There were no streets—at least, no crossings—visible, and had the blocks of houses not divided the town architecturally, everything would have been run together, like honey, with human beings, human beings, human beings! I never knew how the day passed. Vergil ran up against the La Scala doctor, and actually turned

pale as the M.D. went to speak to him. "Don't tell me!" Vergil
cried. "All right," laughed Doctor L.; "he is not quite well, but
will sing, of course." The "he" meant, naturally, the tenor.
I met Madame M. leaning over the piazza. "And to think of
it!" she cried; "it is four o'clock. Iago's wig was brought
home, and fits so badly that not even *glue* will stick it on to
his head. He simply won't sing if—" "Don't," I cried; "I
will give him my hair, every inch of it, and sew it on to a pate
myself, rather than that." Just then the wig-maker came round
a corner. Madame M. gave him one look; I slipped into the
Galleria, and was busy staring at photographs. Poor wretch!
that look reminded me of legends of Sioux scalping their victims,
and the fitful dripping tress that decorates the successful warrior's belt, flashed before my eyes. "The end of this day will be
human gore," I muttered; then turned to look again into the
square. It was alive. An hour passed; men, women, children,
beggars and ballias, hand-organs pealing forth Verdi tunes, Ernani, "Fly with me," and Manrico, "Do not leave me;" pardon
the vernacular. Leonardo da Vinci's statue gleamed out of the
sea of faces like a white eaglet's plume drifting towards a storm-
swept sea. The windows of the tall houses looking out on the
quadrangle were a mass of shifting heads: balconies were
freighted with excited humanity, and the Italian-terraced roofs,
where people were eating and drinking and shouting, were literally black with moving forms. But the exteriors of these old
stone palaces was the most curious sight. The panels were a
perfect kaleidoscope of light and colour. You know the Italian
women are fond of bright raiment. When they have not covered
their heads with their pretty black veils, they wear veils in
cream-colour studded with artificial flowers; they wear hats
which would shame a hot-house for brilliancy, and their necks
are hung with gewgaws: their bodices glow like an Oriental
chasuble; then, too, these creatures looked so happy, laughing

eyes, glittering teeth, bodies swaying to the pantomime of anti-
cipated pleasure : all this made an impression on me I shall
not soon forget; and as to the others, their spirits were so
contagious that the crowd seemed charged with electricity.

The Piazza della Scala was a sight to see, and the cries
of " Viva Verdi ! viva Verdi !" were so deafening that I longed
for cotton in my ears. Poor Verdi ! had he been there, he
would certainly have been torn to pieces, as a crowd in its enthusiasm rarely distinguishes between glory and assassination.
You will ask what I was doing in the streets at such a time ;
and I will answer : I don't know; I merely obeyed the common
impulse — went where the others did : the truth is, I also
wanted to watch the Scala bill-board, to see that no change
would be made in the announcements. We all stood staring
at the old theatre, just as those idiots on the Paris boulevards
on a summer night watch the magic-lantern, to read the different advertisements for enterprising firms : and this, you say,
in dead of winter? O, an Italian does not feel the cold on an
occasion like this. But to return. In case there had been
any change of programme I need not say there would not
have been found a person in all Milan courageous enough to
have put up the notice. There was death in the eyes of some
of those men, waiting like hungry wolves since the night before
to be first to crowd into the pit and galleries. Well, at last—
after dinner—I didn't dine, I swallowed food—we started to
the theatre. The carriage had to be sent off long before we
reached the door, the horses could not make their way through
the crowd. At best, human beings one by one between a line
of police could struggle towards the entrance. I expected my
dress would be in rags ; however, I managed to get in whole,
and once there the sight was indescribable. La Scala has
never before held such an audience, and although it was fully
an hour before the time to commence, every seat was occupied.

The light murmur of expectant voices issuing from three thousand throats, audible, but discreetly indistinct, reminded me
of the sounds in an enchanted forest on a summer night. No
one was too exalted or too proud on this greatest of all solem-
nities to jostle the contadina on the doorstep, or the fruit-vendor
humming a Verdinian measure under the portico of La Scala :
all were frantic to be seated before the curtain rose. Only in
Italy could such a scene take place ; for here pride of birth, or
rank, or position gives way before the homage which a land of
song sows in perennial laurel at the feet of her great composers.

From pit to dome, the immense auditorium was one mass
of eager faces, sparkling eyes, brilliant toilettes, and splendid
jewels. The Italian Court was a rainbow of colours, and
Queen Margherita's ladies of honour like a hothouse bouquet
of rarest exotics. The first and second tiers of boxes were so
packed with the Milanese high-bred women, so covered with
dazzling jewels and filmy laces, that the house seemed spanned
with a river of light, up, up, up to where the last gallery
was lost in a dainty cornice of gold. The gleam of diamond
tiara and corsage bouquet shot oblong rays on the black-
coated background ; while the new electric lights, imprisoned
in their dead-white globes, shed so unearthly a radiance over
the auditorium that we all looked like spectres uprising
from some fantastic dead-and-gone rout. As to the platea or
" stalls," it was simply marvellous. I know of no city in the
world which could present a spectacle of similar brilliancy.
In the first place, it was packed with officers—certainly the
handsomest men in the world—gorgeous in the varied and
brilliant Italian uniform : staff-officers in full dress, and
scarred veterans with their whole record in speaking breast-
decorations ; and the women—such pretty women as one could
see only in Italy ; for the Italians are a decorative race when
seen in Italy, and picturesque, my dear friend, is the only

word possible to describe them. The men look well anywhere; the women may not shine on the Corso, but at the play they will put women of every other nation in the shade. They are a special embellishment, a part of the gorgeousness, the glitter, the performance. They know just how to dress, and just what jewels to wear; how to sit, how to stand, how to listen at the right moment, and to look bored at the right moment; in short, their princely boxes are packed with such a baggage of perfections that the universal playgoing world most unanimously acknowledge their rightful supremacy.

" And the other portions of the house ?" you say. That is a just question; for La Scala is not alone in its nobility, its platea and boxes. Besides the celebrities here and there, the romancer who has left his pen, the painter his brush, or the sculptor his chisel, La Scala's real public is in the upper tiers, in pit, or lobbione.* Besides the throng of strangers, there were present all the old theatre goers who never miss a first-night, and those who go but on such occasions were there in full force, conspicuous in their habitual places. They never need programmes, they know the names of every living and working artist; they have heard all the great singers since Catalani and Pasta ; have seen all the dancers since Taglioni, father and daughter. They have supped with Bellini after success and failure ; and they have seen Verdi† on the one occasion when he was at his conductor's place in the orchestra. They know La Scala and everything pertaining to it by heart; nine cases out of ten, they are better musicians than those in the band, better artists than those on the stage. They come to sit in judgment: to applaud or hiss, as they honestly feel ; to lend their presence to the event of what is to them the entire world: the annual opening of a new opera, or a first-

* Chapter vii. vol. ii. *Stage Struck.*
Second performance o Verdi's *Requiem Mass* at La Scala, 1874.

night at their renowned opera-house ; in short, they are a part
of it. They have not dined, perhaps not even breakfasted,
and their pockets are filled with chestnuts : grave, anxious,
preoccupied, they are at the theatre-doors hours before the
opening of the doors, waiting their chance to rush pell mell
into the roof-gallery, called the lobbione. There are many
amongst them who have not tasted food for a week : the body
may be starved, but never the soul. They consider no sacrifice too great to enable them to figure at a first-night at La
Scala : no king is prouder than this old and faithful person.
Can you not recognise him ? No detail of toilette is neglected :
hair is pomaded ; moustache waxed ; linen spotless ; cravat
tied in perfect knot ; habit guiltless of dust ; a flower in the
button-hole, a rose or garofano ; gloves of a sickly white, from
having seen the cleaner's too often. Can you not remember him
as, opera-glass in hand, his eye roams over the sea of faces,
calculating which tier is to have the honour of his first glance ?
Last night this ancient man stood in his place until he had
seen each member of the orchestra come in ; then he sat
down, unfolded a silk handkerchief, spread it on his knees,
and with a friendly wave of his hand saluted his brother fossils
right and left, as much as to say :

" You see me ; here I am. Do you think *Othello* could go
on were I not present ?"

When I saw him I knew that the opera was about to begin.
The habitué wore the same eager look he has assumed twice
or thrice a year for half a century of Carnivals ; he has forgotten the hours of waiting at the street-door, the scrimpy
dinner, the meagre lunch of polenta, and the long, uneventful
year. He is a part of the whole, and believes he is responsible
for this night's failure or success.

I saw the ancient man stir, saw the glass move and the
handkerchief flutter ; saw him reseat and settle himself more

FRANCO FACCIO,
Author of the Italian *Amleto* (Boïto's libretto), leader of *Othello*,
and chief conductor of La Scala orchestra.

comfortably; then I said to myself, " Ah, the opera is about to begin : now for *Othello*."

It is generally supposed that on a first-night Verdi conducts his operas, but the idea is an erroneous one. With very few exceptions, for forty years or more he has not taken his place in the orchestra-leader's chair. On this occasion he would have been too nervous to have attempted such a thing. The present incumbent of the leader's place at La Scala is Franco Faccio, an admirable musician and composer, one who knows his band as a flautist knows his stops, and who for years has directed Verdi's operas under the maestro's own eye and dictation. Faccio's appearance in the conductor's chair, which he has filled so long and so well, was a signal for thunders of applause. The orchestra at once struck up a few glorious chords representing a tempest, which were followed by an instantaneous rise of the curtain.

Boïto begins his libretto with the second act of Shakespeare's *Othello*. The scenes are laid in a maritime city of Cyprus, and afterwards in Venice. I must first speak of the Italian poet's work, to which Verdi has written such sublime measures. Arrigo Boïto is gifted in arts, music, and verse. He has laid a hand upon the immortal bard's work which, placed by another than he, might have been heavy with sacrilegious weight. Boïto has transposed, added to, and—do not start—in some ways adorned the play of *Othello*. He has done what no one else has yet done : he has made a study from our classic which, while not absolutely Shakespearean, puts the English poet in a still newer light. The enormous difficulty of making an operatic libretto from a play is in itself an almost insurmountable difficulty. What to retain, what to reject, what will lend itself to the confines of a musical space, what cannot be compressed within the limits of musical expression, are considerations weighty enough in themselves to paralyse the most facile pen or imagination.

Boïto began to think of his *Othello* fifteen years ago Six years ago he sat down, and, after a world of conflict and worry, in as many months wrote and completed his libretto. It flows with a limpidity which we see in the wave lately freed from the blackness of the hurricane. The opening scene on the island of Cyprus presents Iago, Roderigo, and Cassio. A chorus sings a hymn of victory, rejoicing that Othello and his ships have been saved from Turk and tempest; a brindisi by Iago represents the Moor's wish that the city rejoice. " Every man takes on a merry mood : some begin to dance, some to make bonfires, and each man goes to what sport and revels his addiction leads him." Cassio and Montana take these instructions literally, and the duel follows. Montana wounded, Othello arrives. Cassio delivers up his sword, and the people disperse. Desdemona appears, and a tender love-duet finishes the first act.

It will be seen that Boïto, in cutting the first act of Shakespeare's play, by suppressing Desdemona's appearance before the Senate, and transposing the duel scene, brings her on at the moment when calm must follow the storm. Instead of two almost nondescript apparitions, we have one, which, by its present arrangement, is the climax of the act, and, philosophically considered, the veritable situation for such a climax. As a piece of dramatic writing in opera, I have never seen its equal in intensity. One striking situation follows another with such headlong rush that I can only think of an arrow shot from a bow.

In the second act we have Iago's solo and great scene, with a short speaking duet for Cassio and Iago. Desdemona is seen at the back of the stage receiving gifts from women and children, who are singing a chorus that forms a most original accompaniment to a duet with Iago and Othello, both of whom stand well to the front. The chorus finished, Desdemona comes forward

SIGNORA ROMILDA PANTALEONE AS DESDEMONA,
Act ii. *Othello.*

THE NEW YORK
PUBLIC LIBRARY

ASTOR, LENOX
TILDEN FOUNDATIONS

to solicit Cassio's return to the Moor's favour ; a quartette follows, and the act ends with a grand duet between Othello and Iago.

Act third is where we have most of Boïto's changes from the original text. He has interpolated here a trio for Cassio, Othello, and Iago, called the handkerchief trio, so admirable in form and poetry that it fits the English bard's play as a glove fits the hand ; then follows a duet between Desdemona and her lord, and one, still more dramatic, for Iago and Othello ; then comes the finale of the third act, which, in spite of its force, cannot help shocking the Anglo-Saxon worshipper at Shakespeare's shrine. We know that Othello was a Moor and half-savage, but we cannot imagine that he would have done what Boïto makes him do. It is true the scene Boïto describes takes place in the original play, but before Ludovico only, and not before the Senate. In the libretto the senators arrive and announce new honours for Othello and also his required departure for Venice. Othello, worked up to the supremest heights of jealousy in the preceding duet with Iago, breaks forth into a paroxysm of passion unknown even to Shakespeare's hero. Desdemona comes forward and begs to be allowed to accompany her lord ; she again most imprudently pleads Cassio's cause, when before court, nobles, and populace, Othello flings her to the ground, screaming " To earth and weep," at the same time dealing her such a blow that the people rush forward with one commingled cry of shame and horror. While the chorus rages, the Moor, with bowed head, sits aside, and the number ended he starts up, and sends off people, court, and Senate : seemingly alone, in a terrible fury, he attempts a cry for vengeance, but his force forsakes him, he staggers, and falls insensible to the floor. At that instant, Iago, who had loitered behind a column of the peristyle, rushes forth, plants his heel on the Moor's breast, and, with accents of piteous scorn, sings, in contrast to the Senate's call for Othello and the people's acclamations to the Lion of Venice, "Look upon him, here! Here is your Lion of Venice!" The curtain falls.

This scene, as I have said, is Boïto's chief innovation, and it seems to me an unnecessary one. The original situation where Othello strikes Desdemona before Ludovico is itself terrible enough to give the world an idea of Othello's character. This added expression of brutality strikes the first really discordant note of exaggeration in an otherwise extraordinary libretto.

The. fourth act is fairly traditional. The Moor kills his wife, but spares Iago, for the traitor flees with a scornful "Never! Ah! ha!" on his perjured lips, and the Moor ends existence in a fairly traditional manner.

Verdi's music throughout the whole of the first act is of a majesty, nobility, power, and inspiration which he has never before surpassed, perhaps never before equalled. The orchestration for the tempest chorus, the chorus itself, the brindisi, and the *duetti parlanti* or vocal speaking, form one succession of sublime pages, rich, not alone in genius and style, but fraught with that superior excellence of technique which the mechanic's hand, after years of practice, alone knows how practically to illustrate. Verdi knows what the public wants; he knows how to touch the public heart; he knows every musical variety of light, shade, and effect to the nicety of a hair, and to the nicety of a hair weighs them. Perhaps in *Othello* he has shown less respect for the feelings of the public than ever before. Divine bars of melody are cut by so-called philosophical breaks; surprise follows delight, and incredulity succeeds surprise. Verdi has not sacrificed Verdi as he has so often done. Verdi remains Verdi; an Italian and a composer who, in spite of innovation, temptation, and revolution in modern music, has written a work intensely Italian, and an opera which only an Italian could write. I began by speaking of the first act, but

SCENE IN ACT III., "OTHELLO."

The Moor insults Desdemona before Court and Senate, crying, "To earth, and weep !"

the same power and inspiration is visible throughout the whole opera. It is as Italian as the blue sky of Italy or the Lake of Como, and as a work of art is as distinctly original as the Milan cathedral. Besides being an operatic it is an architectural composition, with massive foundations, strong graceful pillars, and fretwork of embellishment which adorns the whole. The one current expression has been, " I did not know Verdi had such power." " Is it not wonderful at seventy-four to have composed such a masterpiece ?" You speak of Wagner. Put him out of your mind in connection with this. In the first place, Verdi detests Wagner, and would never have copied him, great as he was; and when you hear *Othello*, you will realise how limpid, how homogeneous, how truly Italian it is. But to continue.

As for a technical description of the music, why need I tell you that an irresistible torrent of chromatic scales and groups of three and four describe the tempest ; that Iago sings a brindisi in D minor, or Othello an air in A flat; that Desdemona's tears and laments flow in one key, or that Othello's rage and crime are expressed in another? When I say that from the beginning to the end Verdi has written four acts of grand and extraordinary music, you will know that a vocabulary more or less of set phrases can no more enhance the value of any opinion, than it could depict your appreciation of this masterpiece. No word · picture can adequately describe this ingenious work; no words can portray the enthusiasm it excited, nor the ovations it won for its composer.

The accepted thing seems to be to rave over the whole score, to find nothing bad. This may be national and friendly, but it is not being critical. Even Iago says, " I am nothing if not critical." The first act, as I have said, contains some glorious writing above mentioned, but the concluding duet is unequal in beauty and strength. Othello's music is very fine,

o

but Desdemona's opening phrases, "O mio superbo guerrier,"
are simply impossible. They are of superhuman difficulty,
and extremely awkward. Listening with the most attentive
ear, one cannot tell what Verdi has been trying to get at. The
number works up to the usual Verdinian climax, and the
second part contains a lovely dual phrase for soprano and
tenor, which every Italian was humming in the lobby during
the entr'acte, beginning:

> "E, tu m'amavi per le mie sventure,
> Ed io t'amavo per la tua pieta."

This, you will see, is most perfect Italian for Shakespeare's
words in the speech before the Senate:

> "She loved me for the dangers I had passed,
> And I loved her that she did pity them."

I think it would have been impossible to better translate
the immortal Bard's words, and it was immensely clever in
Boïto to have placed them in this love-duet. The finale is
graceful, but not original. It was almost ruined by the two
singers. It is writing of such scope and dignity that to
render it justice requires the utmost skill in the artists, and
the power and possession of steadiness and modulation; but
Madame Pantaleone's voice trembled, and was invariably loud.
When Tamagno sang, with one exception, I felt as if the Coli-
seum entire were being hurled in my face. This artist pro-
ceeds in blissful ignorance of the fact that there are some
people who do not care for so much voice at the expense of
even a little art.

The great passages in the second act are beyond anything
Verdi has ever composed. Notably the parlanti or recitative,
and the passionate, turbulent work for the band, preceding
the air "Addio sante memorie;" a superb solo sung by Othello
after Iago has convinced him that Desdemona is faithless.

THE NEW YORK
PUBLIC LIBRARY

ASTOR. LENOX
TILDEN FOUNDATIONS

TAMAGNO.

TAMAGNO AS OTHELLO.

THE NEW YORK
PUBLIC LIBRARY

ASTOR. LENOX
TILDEN FOUNDATIONS

This air should have been begun at least with some idea of expression, of regret, of tenderness, of sorrow. Would man or woman first touched in their supremest sense of honour scream their woe on the housetop, or shout it from the nearest convenient balcony? It seems to me, not. On the contrary, silence, secrecy, unbelief, vacillation, grief, are the sentiments to be first expressed in this air; Othello's very nature would have suggested that mode of expression.

Admitting that he would have published his woes, Othello, at first, was wary, subtle, incredulous. You will say that in an opera these things are difficult to express. I answer yes, especially when they must be expressed by a mere blockhead in the rough; but a man who is paid nearly two hundred pounds a night to sing ought to be able, even in a marketable sense, to outline the idea of the work he accepts money for, and is expected to perform. Nothing can make me believe that Tamagno has ever even intelligently studied his rôle. However, were Rossini here, he would protect him to his face, and say three things make an artist—voice, voice, voice; and if he spoke of his singing behind his back, would add of him, as he did of Prince Poniatowski's operas: "Il y a des beaux moments, mais des fichus quarts d'heures."

I shall not attempt to tell you in detail of the entire score. In the second act a credo for Iago is most noble music, but M. Boïto's poetry here is weak. If I understand it rightly, it is a very free adaptation of Iago's last speech with Cassio, act ii. of original. Iago speaks of devils, etcetera—you know the lines— and here M. Boïto gives him a tirade about what he believes and does not believe. As to music, Verdi is at the height of the Shakespearean situation. As the idea suggests, he is cynical, vain, weak, subtle, or perfidious. I never knew before that such qualities could be so expressed in opera. Here, Verdi is not betrayed but glorified by Iago, Victor Maurel, the incarnation of natural gifts, voice, intelligence, art, and experience. However, I will speak of him later.

Act third contains some magnificent pages, but in spite of talk to the contrary, the quartette will never equal the *Rigoletto* or any other great Verdi quartette. It was also so badly sung that it was difficult on a first hearing to make out what it was. I am not of the general opinion that the third act is a weak act. It may even be greater than the others, but its complex writing makes it less easy to understand.

The fourth is fraught with sublime sentiments, and carries everything before it : pathos, heart, resignation, and despair here reach their climax of expression. Verdi now rises to his greatest height. While we feel the humanity in every chord, we feel it only in the spiritual sense ; from the first bars to the last we are overweighted by the fatality of destiny; every measure breathes forth the doom of two irresponsible beings. Desdemona's recitative and willow song are the lamentation of the saddest of broken hearts, one broken without cause : broken through fatality, through mental darkness, and a blind groping after the impossible. In the following recitative and duet for the contre basse, unique in musical composition, are expressed Othello's long-pent-up feelings, his subtlety, his rage, revenge, and implacable decree. Desdemona on her couch, he comes on stealthily to the accompaniment of these significant sounds. It was impossible not to feel impressed, not to feel a tightening at the heart, and a sickening sensation creep from the heart to the throat. I can still see him prowling in Desdemona's chamber, can still hear the threatening murmuring orchestra, feel his footsteps near her couch, and hear the terrific crash of the brasses as I realised that the moment of death had arrived.

In all the range of operatic music I know of nothing so tender, so pathetic, so thoroughly heartrending as this act. Per-

THE NEW YORK
PUBLIC LIBRARY

ASTOR, LENOX
TILDEN FOUNDATIONS

VICTOR MAUREL AS IAGO IN VERDI'S "OTHELLO."
Scene—the tempest off Cyprus, Act ii. of Play, Act i. of Opera.

VICTOR MAUREL AS IAGO.
Act iii. *Othello*, Milan, La Scala, 1887.

THE NEW YORK
PUBLIC LIBRARY

ASTOR LENOX
TILDEN FOUNDATIONS

haps it is not so much the music as the sentiment : the music is not even wholly original, the sentiment is not even rare, but the expression of both is very rare. On hearing this composition you know that Verdi felt what he was writing : what he had of soul he put here, what he had in remembrance of a sad past, of ruined hopes, of early disillusions, he has put here. This was not writen by the Verdi who set down drinking-songs and mad cabalettas *ad infinitum,* but the Verdi who struggled with sickness and sorrow and fatality and despair ; the Verdi whom dire poverty attacked in his honour, the poor composer bound to write a comic opera, yet who felt his mood making his music ; the father who followed two little coffins to an early grave, the husband who closed the wife's eyes knowing that the seal set on those dear lids was one which eternity alone could ever tear away. Who may tell what phantoms of the past kept watch with his inspiration—dictated to the heart and guided the pen ; how the stone was rolled away from the door of years, and, at the reiterated stroke of inexorable doom, half a century of deadened emotions burst Time's callous barrier, and leapt forth in one irresistible wave of long-pent-up despair? And this is Verdi's last act of *Othello,* the most soulful, powerful, and touching of all his previous works.

The scenery, costumes, choruses, and orchestra were nearly perfect; the cast was certainly weak. Victor Maurel is the only real artist in the opera, and he is a Frenchman. In voice, acting, appearance, and dress he is the ideal of what an operatic artist should be, and the ideal of what any operatic Iago could be. He sang as even his best friends never dreamed he could sing, and his acting was the consummate work which we always have at his artistic hands. He entered at once into the fullest sympathies of the audience, and I could not help then and there contrasting the Iagos we have seen in other countries with the Iagos we always see in Italy. Iago even seems a *persona grata* to the public ; the qualities which raise a thrill of horror in the righteous Anglo-Saxon are received by this susceptible nation with placid contentment and relief. His vileness, ruses, and perfidy are accepted for their art, not their nature; his ingenious devices arouse heartfelt plaudits, and let me add that never will you hear a gallery god in Italy express any disapprobation with a successful knave. Had Iago not succeeded there is every reason to believe that *Othello* would be left out of the Italian Shakespearean repertory. On noting his more than prominence in this opera, rendered doubly so by Maurel's sublime creation, I could well understand Boïto's and Verdi's inclination to call their work *Iago*, and not *Othello*. Iago is essentially Italian, not in the sense of vice, but of artistic villainy : he reasons from the personal standpoint, and his reasons find a universal echo in the land which gave birth to such a student of human nature as Macchiavelli. Othello, you will see, is an inferior creature, and plays an inferior part.

Maurel will be well remembered as one of the most gifted artists we have ever seen at Covent Garden. His Iago ranks with Nilsson's Ophelia—to my mind the finest lyric creation on the operatic stage. His elegance, grace, subtlety, and exquisite style in Iago find their most perfect expression. I need not refer to his appearance, the beau-ideal of a handsome Venetian, whose years are but "four times seven," and whose graces in this artist's hands are the climax of elegance and histrionic art. But you will see him in London, and I am sure will allow that you have never witnessed or heard anything to equal his impersonation of this part. Tamagno, the tenor, looked and acted Othello, but he did not sing—he bleated. Desdemona has never been a favourite of mine in history, and the present exponent of the rôle suggested to me all my thousand unavenged wrongs laid at the door of Brabantio's daughter. Madame Pantaleone is an excellent person, but as Desdemona

THE NEW YORK
PUBLIC LIBRARY

ASTOR. LENOX
TILDEN FOUNDATIONS.

SIGNORA ROMILDA PANTALEONE,
Desdemona in *Othello*, La Scala, Feb. 5th, 1887.

she ought to have been suppressed the night before at her dress rehearsal. Her voice is naturally fine and dramatic, but she has no more knowledge of the pure art of singing than I have of the real science of astromony. She has a vile emission of tone in the medium open notes; the upper notes are clear, but rarely in tune. The lovely music assigned to Othello's wife must have splendid resisting powers not to have fallen flat in her hands or throat. In appearance Madame Pantaleone is likewise unfortunate : she is short, slightly cross-eyed, and of a physical plainness, which dwarfed the already insignificant Desdemona. She acted very well in the first and third acts, but not so well in the last. Of the other singers, I will add that Petrovitch as Emilia was deservedly hooted ; V. Fornari as Roderigo was not important to help' or hinder the work; and M. Paroli as Cassio was a really fair second tenor ; he, at least, knows how to sing, but Nature evidently never intended him to sing at La Scala.

The ovations to Verdi and Boïto reached the climax of enthusiasm. Verdi was presented with a silver album filled with the autographs and cards of every citizen in Milan. He was called out twenty times, and at the last recalls hats and handkerchiefs were waved, and the house rose in a body. The emotion was something indescribable, and many wept. Verdi's carriage was dragged by citizens to the hotel. He was toasted and serenaded ; and at five in the morning I had not closed my eyes in sleep for the crowds still singing and shrieking " Viva Verdi ! viva Verdi !" Who shall say that this cry wil not reëcho all over the world? At seventy-four this second conqueror may well exclaim : *Veni, vidi, vici, Verdi !*—Yours ever, &c.

CHAPTER XI.

Milan, Feb. 6th, 1887.

FIRST of all there is no second performance : to-night the tenor is ill, and opera postponed until—Heaven knows when ! What a pity !

In all I have written I have refrained speaking critically of Verdi. Not that it would not have been in my province, but until now I never could form an exact opinion of his talent. *Othello* seems to have made many things clear. In the old Verdi—but why the old Verdi? his last work has changed nothing. He is, on the contrary, not only as much the old Verdi as ever, but, if possible, more Verdi than ever. I still maintain none but he could ever have writen this opera. I utterly deny any Wagner influence. Verdi would have written as he has had Wagner never existed. That he has followed a secret influence of progress in musical composition I will not deny —but it is not a late influence. It is the same which he felt when he wrote *Oberto di San Bonifazio,* the same which dictated the noblest strains of *Nabucco,* the same which inspired the divinest measures of *I Lombardi, Trovatore, Rigoletto, Don Carlos, Aïda,* or *Traviata.* It is the old and young Verdi always struggling, always striving, always tormented by an ideal or visionary perfection to *which he has never attained ;* for *Othello* is not perfect. It has the same exquisitely depicted foreground ; the same background of enchanting but imperfect perspective ;

the same surface brilliancy of colouring ; but all the old under-
current of troubled thought and persistent endeavour, of trying to express in purest spiritual measures that which has ever
been vitiated by the shadow of materialism. This cloud, which
has always obscured Verdi's horizon of genius, this vague-
ness was Verdi's own self, his own character, his intelligence,
his mode of life, of being, living, and thinking ; and unless
Verdi could have been born again, he never could have extracted
a purer gold from his ore of talent. Verdi in one sense is a
caprice of Nature. As the ordinary mortal he is perfect ; as the
great genius he is incomplete. Had his life been otherwise, had
he not been the plaything of destiny and the victim of a too
early acquired popularity, he might have grafted the vine of his
musical disposition into a tree of majestic strength and power ;
but he did not, he could not : he lived his life, following the
mortal which was in him, neglecting to cultivate the immortal
whose germs were so widely but surely scattered in this too
earthly soil. Verdi's love-scenes are always the outpouring
of a mind which comprehends love as the ordinary nature
comprehends it. What there is of spiritual in his music is but too
often lent by our own feelings, or, perhaps, also the indefinite
sense of Verdi struggling against Verdi : his fire, his tenderness, his pathos, passion, or patriotism, are the most perfect
expression of our abnormal selves. He is a master of form,
and, like all ablest mechanics, while his execution never
betrays his craft, it still conserves the original stamp of the
artisan's mind. What we like, and have always liked, in
Verdi, is that he is intensely human. All the world is not
spiritual ; if it were only that, even Benedict would never have
said : " The world must be peopled." Verdi was a man of the
people, and if he ever went beyond that it was not his fault,
but the secret better vein which, hidden in his nature, in spite
of himself, sooner or later was bound to come to light. But

in music, as in other things, laws were made for the masses.
If you or I or any one think he is one rung above that middle
way, he is just out of the reach of the universal model ; he has no
right to complain if the mountain will not come to Mahomet.
The worst of it all is Verdi understood just what he was about:
his intelligence, combining the useful quality of mobility and
the shrewder sense of the peasant, realised but too well what
the general world wanted and required ; he could not resist the
temptation of satisfying a universal desire, and he yielded to
it as many have done—as we all have done, and all will do
while the world lasts. No, there is one exception: Boïto, the
next great Italian composer with the same talent, would never
have been a Verdi. But to return to the maestro. He wrote
for the masses, whom he understood. What Verdi has done in his
music is that from material measures he has eliminated vulgar
suggestions of materialism. The best part of his inspiration has
glossed over, turned down, and varnished what would otherwise
have been crude. Verdi is never brutal ; he touches the senses
by the softest chords. One may be stirred to the depths by his
noblest strains, but one is never irritated by a too abrupt ex-
plosion of passion ; in this he most nearly approaches his
great predecessors, Bellini, Rossini, and Donizetti. Verdi,
however, has a vigour they never had ; his melodies are supple,
flowing, and facile, his concerted numbers are magnificently
and dramatically outlined, while his grouping is strong,
ingenious, and bold ; but he lacks the supreme elegance which
characterised the masters above-named ; he has rarely, or never,
attained their spirituality, and at times a slovenliness of form
has even nullified the little of refinement which his really
inspired measures possessed. How different was Meyerbeer,
who adorned even trivial themes with so much grace that they
seemed much less vulgar than inspired ! The same may be
said of Gounod, perhaps the most supremely refined and

elegant composer the latter part of the nineteenth century has produced. Whatever his faults, they are rarely those of style or composition. I think you will agree with me that Verdi, however, of all these composers, had, perhaps, the most redundant, versatile, and happiest nature. His employment of it, with but four or five exceptions, is known to the world, and only at the last can we see mind dominating matter. One proof of Verdi's natural gifts was his distinct originality. He was the first Italian writer of to-day whose music could not be changed without occasioning a shock to the musicianly soul : we feel the same sensation when Mozart, Gluck, or Handel is tampered with. Even in Verdi's earliest days his music was exacting : it required being sung as it was written ; the slightest changing of a simple cadenza seemed heresy ; if an artist attempted such a thing, the audience speedily vetoed the pro-ceeding, and thus gave a proof of the rank in which they esteemed Verdi's genius and distinct originality. The same cannot be said of Bellini, Donizetti, or Rossini, whose fabric, on the contrary, seemed but the groundwork whereon to embroider new flowers of musical fancy. Verdi was the first to introduce the crashing brasses in voice accompaniment, the first to break away from the old slender voice supports. A singer once said to me : " He began by spoiling all the voices in Italy." But that was because the transition was too abrupt. Bellini to-day and Verdi to-morrow would have tried even the trained throat of a Grisi or a Malibran.

The secret, however, was that you could not sing Verdi and go to sleep over him. You will find that he rarely repeats a theme more than twice—witness the *Trovatore* and *Traviata* cabaletta, and then compare those interminable bars, for instance, " Sovra il sen " in the *Sonnambula*, or " Qui la voce " in the *Puritani*. The divinest phrase is repeated from six to eight consecutive times, and merely to think of it makes my modern hair stand on end : but I spare you further example. You, who know Verdi's music even better than I do, will understand exactly what I mean by these reflections. I cannot say comparisons, as Verdi cannot be compared, only contrasted. He is so totally out and away from other nineteenth-century composers that he must be judged—as, happily for him, he always has been—on his own merits and from his own standpoint. However, the public cannot yet judge of *Othello* for the simple reason that it has not yet been sung—one swallow does not make a summer, and one artist cannot complete an ensemble. As Verdi once wrote of *La Traviata* on its first performance and failure in Venice : " Was it the artists ? was it me ? *Il tempo giudichera —* time will judge." We will remember *Aïda, Rigoletto, Traviata,* and *Don Carlos,* but we will place *Othello* on the pedestal of a lasting fame.

To-day the city is still in an uproar over the great master's unanimous success. I have just come from a banquet, which, as it is destined to become historic, I cannot refrain writing you about—not about what we ate or drank, but about some of the people I saw, and the impression they made upon me.

The banquet was given by Verdi's publishers, the Ricordis, to celebrate the presence of distinguished Italians and foreign visitors to Milan on this occasion, and, although a feast in every sense of the word, was not the ordinary banquet-dinner or supper, but a breakfast, and such a one as has never before been given in the old Lombard city. I suppose that banquets and luncheons are usually pretty much alike, but certainly few of to-day have ever drawn together such a galaxy of literary and artistic talent as readily accepted the Messrs. Ricordis' princely hospitality. There were a hundred poets, writers, critics, painters, philosophers, and artists gathered together from Italy and all parts of the world to do homage to the last work of a great man, and to add the combined lustre of many

successful careers to the crowning brilliancy of one great
and preëminent genius. I shall not tell you of the foreigners
present, their names and works are already known to you, but
will speak more especially of the native talent on that occasion :
a perfect bouquet of Italian bloom. Long before dessert, speeches
were begun, and Verdi walking about in the rooms overhead
must have been shaken by the thunders of applause which fairly
pierced the ceiling. Among the toasts wit was not lacking, and
one impromptu pun in the dialect was as clever a thing of its
kind as I ever heard. The Mayor of Milan is named Negri, and
you know the name pronounced in Milanese means negro. After
several toasts and speeches Count Negri delivered one of the
most thrilling, beautiful, and pathetic of improvisations, in which
he referred to Verdi, of course, and *Othello*—the Moor of Venice
—naturally. When he had finished he was applauded to the
echoes, tears stood in many eyes, and maestro Boïto was so
deeply affected as to be absolutely incapable of speech. After
the peculiar silence that follows a brilliant oratorical effort,
one man's voice was heard : tears were in his eyes, but a laugh
on his lip, as he brought his hand down heavily on the flower
and crystal bedecked table and said, " E ver' dop', il Mora de
Venezia, g'he piu. ch' il Niger di Milan." I need not say that
tears were speedily changed to laughter, and from that time
forth flashes of wit made the round of the festal board. Among
the Italian galaxy of celebrities invited were De Amicis, whose
Constantinople ranks with Théophile Gautier's ; Michetti and
Boldini, two of the most brilliant painters of to-day ; Luigi
Gualdo, delicious poet and romancer ; Marchetti, the celebrated
operatic composer ; F. Paolo Tosti, whose songs are sung where
civilisation reigns ; F. Fillippi, the renowned Italian art-critic ;
Pascarella, poet, humourist, writer, and caricaturist : Fontana,
one of the finest dramatists in the Milanese dialects; Dario Papa,
a brilliant journalist ; the two most celebrated poets and drama-

tists of to-day, E. Panzacchi and G. Giacosa, the famous author
of *Una Partita di Scacchi.* Although there were a great many
others present, I shall only write you of those I had some conversation with, as it is easier for me to write of people after
I have looked in their faces or heard the sound of their voices.
And the women—don't laugh—but besides myself there was
only one present. She is the George Sand of Italy, and I—
well, I was not a woman on that occasion, only a writer—an
American—Heaven forgive me !—*bas-bleu.*

Before I tell you of the men, let me speak of Madame
Mathilde Serrao. She was born of Greek and Neapolitan
parents, and when yet a child began life as an operator in a tele-
graph-office ; but being a superlatively gifted woman, during this
time she managed to acquire an education and instruction little
short of marvellous, when you think of the slight opportunities
she had for study and reflection. However, she was born a writer
if ever a woman was, and began her splendid literary career by
articles which were printed here and there in various Italian
journals, and which not only drew public attention towards her,
but were immediately judged as works of great literary value.
After some years' consecutive labour, she left the telegraph-
office, and devoted herself to the career of art and letters.
In 1878, when barely out of her teens, she printed a romance
or rather a novelette, which was remarkable for literary
taste, intelligence, and the peculiar intuitive qualities which
gifted women alone seem to have possessed. Her book was
such a success that she was immediately assigned one of
the first places in Italian literature. She writes with ingenu-
ousness and great force, but her specialty is a fine, clear, far-
seeing mind, from whose eye she observes men and things,
and sets them down with as much fidelity as wit. She displays special force in descriptive scenes, and in scenes of
sentiment and profound passion.

While there is almost masculine vigour in her pen, no one would say that she writes like a man. On the contrary, the greatest compliment I can pay her is to say that she writes like a woman, and a very gifted woman at that. There is a robust audacity in her descriptions, a manner of setting forth the slightest object and of depicting the slightest trait, which seems almost to take one's breath away, it is so quick, so subtle, and at the same time so broad. Perhaps Mathilde Serrao is a great writer to-day, not because there are few writers in Italy, but because her style is peculiarly suited to our epoch : the last half of the nineteenth century being a particularly personal one, it throws the light of a strong personality on everybody and everything in or out of print. The clever or idiotic people that we meet in books we now recognise at dinner, or as they walk along the avenue or public promenade. They are the marionettes who figure on the literary stage of to-day, and the resemblance in the book, to the living in the streets, sometimes contributes the whole artistic baggage of the modern romancer. That which would have been an impertinence or want of tact one hundred years ago, to-day is a recognised art and a recognised talent. Madame Serrao had the whole of Naples by the ears by her first story, called *Piccole Anime* ("Small Souls"), as everybody imagined that he or she or somebody else was in this remarkable story. Madame Serrao's versatility is something likewise to be wondered at; stories of every sort simply flow from her brain. She has written, amongst other books, some tales for children, which have had remarkable success : amongst others, *Fantasie* and *Romanzo della Fanciulla* and *La Conquista di Roma.*

In 1875 she married Edward Scarfoglio, a well-known Roman publisher and writer, and together they founded a daily literary and political journal, published in the "Eternal City," called *Il Corriere di Roma.* It is almost unnecessary to say that the lion's share of the work falls on Madam herself : she not only takes part in the publication of the paper, but an infinity of other things connected with it. She contributes novels, stories, and criticisms of arts and sciences with as free, as liberal a hand as if she had nothing to do but go abroad and write up people and things.

Men have no curiosity, but of course you want to know just what Mathilde Serrao looks like. In personal appearance she is not altogether prepossessing : although her mother was a Greek, we find none of those harmonious lines and classic features which are supposed to be transmitted to the descendants of the native Hellas. On the contrary, Madame Serrao is plain, but sympathetically so. She is short and rather stout ; her dead-black hair is cropped close, and curls to her head, like the pictures of a Murillo's cherub ; her eyes are very large and black, her forehead is low, her brows are heavy, her skin dark, her mouth and teeth fine, and her expression, on the whole, extremely pleasant. But, to tell the truth, she looks more like a boy than a girl, and seems a young collegian masquerading in woman's garb. You will learn by this description that she is as original in appearance as she is in talent. I don't dislike that, however—she looks what she is: a personage. She converses very pleasantly, is very vivacious, witty, laughs as if she enjoyed it, and seems to have a faculty of immediately adapting herself to any sort or condition of person. She is at ease herself, and immediately puts others at their ease. I am sure you would like to know her. She is certainly one of the most celebrated and the most gifted of the sex to-day in Italy, and is very justly appreciated from one end of the peninsula to the other. And now for your more legitimate rivals.

The noble Signor Luigi Gualdo as a man is young, rich, handsome, and as a writer has one of the most facile pens in all Italy. He is not alone an admirable scholar, but he speaks innumerable languages with the fabled facility and purity of the Russian, of the Italian, his great compatriot, Cardinal Mezzofanti, or the Frenchman, Heilbuth, celebrated in our own day. Not only does Gualdo speak these different languages, but he writes in them as well. I always thought that people could only write well in the tongue in which they had lisped, and this I had made a rule ; but as there are exceptions to every rule, so an exception must be made in favour of Luigi Gualdo. His books written in French have been remarkably successful : they bear the stamp of a Frenchman's hand and talent. It is impossible to think that they have been written by a foreigner. *Une Ressemblance* and *Un Mariage Excentrique* have had great and undeniable success. Besides these works, he has published some charming novelettes in Italian, and two years ago published a book of verses in his own beautiful lan guage under the title of *Nostalgia*, or " Home-sickness " in the vernacular. Gualdo is the devoted friend of all the great writers of to-day. His social standing is bounded by the Quirinale in Italy and Buckingham Palace in London. You will meet him on the Roman Corso or the Parisian Boulevard, and among the renowned French *litterati*, his boon companions are the poet François Coppée, Halévy, Alexandre Dumas, and Paul Bourget, the æsthetic dreamer and romancer. Get these men together, and their conversation on literature, sciences, and arts reminds us of the legendary walks taken by Socrates and Plato under the trees of fabled Athens.

In the November number of *La Nouvelle Revue*, Gualdo published a charming short story called " A Venetian Adventure :" it is one of the most faithful pen-pictures of Venice that we have seen in modern times. Prosperity has not spoiled Gualdo ; yet, at the same time, we cannot help wondering what his career would have been had he not had a palace on

the Lake Como, and footholds in Milan, Rome, Florence, and
Paris.   As it is, he is a remarkable worker, and has added a
great deal to the Italian literature of to-day.   People have
said, and say, that this is a sterile epoch; that Italy, once
mistress of the world, is dead for ever in arts and letters; that
there are no Italian writers and no Italian poets; but I must
differ from them, as there are plenty, and amongst them Gualdo
is certainly one of the first.

In conversation he is brilliant, talks very well, and is
extraordinarily witty; above all, he has the keenest sense of
humour of any Italian I know, and a Yankee could not be
quicker at taking a joke.   His voice is beautiful and cultured,
and so full of good-nature and happiness that there is a very
mine of content in it; even if he speak casually to you
on the street, strangers passing turn at the sound of his voice,
and look at the man who possesses so charming and universal a passport.   It is a mystery to me how Gualdo finds time
for work, for whenever we meet he is just on the point of start-
ing off somewhere : his wardrobes are his trunks, and his couch
usually a sofa in some Continental sleeping-car : very certainly one-third of his life is passed either on the sea or in a
railway-carriage.   Yet, with all, he does a vast amount of
work — good, entertaining, and useful, which reflects great
credit, not only on his country, but on himself: he reminds
me of Macaulay's words: "Industry and a taste for intellectual pleasures are peculiarly respectable in those who can
afford to be idle, and who have every temptation to be dissi-
pated."

Marchetti comes next in my notes.   He is one of the most
distinguished Italian composers of the present day; was born
in a province of Bologna, near Camerano, 26th Feb. 1835.   He
was a pupil of the Naples Conservatory, and was studying in
the city at the famous time when *Trovatore* was brought out in

three of that city's theatres. Marchetti was also a scholar of
Carlo Contis, a very celebrated musician, at that time living and
teaching in Naples : his pupil showed in early life a distinct
aptitude for composition : the operas of *Ruy Blas* and *Romeo
and Juliet* are celebrated throughout Italy and South America,
and wherever Italian opera is performed in the various cities
of the world. *Ruy Blas* is certainly one of the most delightful
works to-day in the Italian repertory. There is a special love-
duet between Victor Hugo's Queen and celebrated minion,
which for passion, elegance, and style is worthy to be ranked
amongst the finest operatic compositions of the century.
Marchetti has never enjoyed the great reputation which his
distinct talent demands ; still, at the same time he occupies a
most honourable position in Italy, and is justly celebrated
amongst the Italian composers of to-day.

Marchetti is a very sympathetic man in himself, a charming companion, an admirable teacher, and a very pleasant,
obliging fellow.

Personally he is very striking in appearance, and any one
would turn to look at him a second time. He has a certain
individuality which bespeaks talent, that stamp of superior
natural gifts, to look at which causes one immediately to say,
"He is somebody." He is tall, with very black eyes, a full, rather
Roman cast of face, whilst hair and eyebrows and moustache
are a perfect salt-and-pepper. Marchetti was prematurely
gray, and has for years looked as he does to-day. I remember
last March I attended a concert at the splendid Barberini
Palace in Rome, and was attracted by one of the accompanists.
I said to a neighbour casually, " I haven't a programme, but
it strikes me that that man is a very remarkable musician, and
he accompanies divinely. Who can it be ?" She quickly replied,
" You surely cannot be ignorant of the fact that it is Luigi

Marchetti, one of the most delightful of Italian composers !
He is adored in Rome, adored in Naples, adored in Florence."

" And seemingly," I added, " adored everywhere else, if he
be the author of *Ruy Blas*."

Marchetti has composed some of the most charming and
elegant pieces in the repertory of chamber-music, amongst
others, " L'Anacreontica," " Di che ti lagni," " All' Amica
Lontana," " Il Bacio," " Il Tramonto," " La Preghiera,"
&c.   In 1881 he was elected president of the musical Ly-
ceum in Rome, a position which he has filled with admirable
care and admirable result.

There is a story afloat that he is writing a new opera,
shortly to be produced, libretto, the perennial *Midsummer
Night's Dream*. There is something very soft and amiable in
Marchetti's manner—I might say something very Italian. He
has a delightful speaking voice, a winning smile, and a certain homogeneity which is not without charm even to those
who are unacquainted with the sympathetic character of this
race. He seems to me a man singularly ingenuous and without
intrigue. Wherever I see him I hear the strains of *Ruy Blas*
or a very divine love-duet in *Romeo and Juliet*, and always say
to myself, " How is it possible that this man, who is really a
great composer, has not a greater position ?"   I am afraid he
never managed well for himself; he is one of those men who
do not work for fame, but purely and solely for the sake of
art.   I am sure he never did a thing to help himself along ;
and yet, in spite of this singular lack of ambition, he has made
a name which will be amongst the most honourable in the
record of Italian art.

Looking down the table, I saw an uplifted glass, sparkling
eyes, the lips moving, and I certainly imagined that the name
indicated by the sound, which I could not hear, was the name
of Verdi. The man with the glass was none other than Fg

Paolo Tosti, perhaps the most celebrated song-writer of the day, known throughout the world wherever there is a piano or a vocal Italian album, a pianino or Barbary organ. In personal appearance Tosti is most agreeable; he is small but compactly built, his head is shapely, and his face of an extremely agreeable cut. He has blue eyes, as blue as the Italian sky, or the Gulf of Naples when the sun is pouring over Capri. A blonde beard hides the lower part of his face, and partially conceals a very pleasant mouth and a very agreeable smile. Tosti merits his great success because he has not alone a very distinguished and original talent, but he is a man of vast musical information and practical musical experience ; he is one of the best-hearted fellows in the world, and possesses to an extraordinary degree the most valuable natural or acquired quality that any human being can possess. This gift is more than beauty, more than talent, or riches, or birth, or position : it is a simple word of four letters, called tact. I don't believe there is a man in this world who possesses this attribute in a more supreme degree than Tosti. He has not alone one of the first social positions in London, but one of the first musical positions in the great metropolis. I was thinking of it to-day when I saw him sitting opposite the Mayor of Milan, lifting a full glass, whose nectar bubbled up to the health of the great Verdi.

As I looked at him, his clear sparkling blue eyes, and his pleasant smile, I thought of his exalted position, and how much he merited it. I dropped my hour-glass of time, and the sands ran quickly back to fifteen years ago, when Tosti was a very humble violinist, second or third, I think, in the Valle Theatre in Rome, struggling and studying hard by day, and at night playing in the orchestra of the theatre ; humble, unnoticed, but always patient, watchful, and persevering. He used to sit in his humble corner, and stare up in the boxes of

the royal dukes and duchesses and princesses, not to speak of
her gracious Majesty the most beautiful Queen to-day on any
throne, Margherita of Savoy : he stared wondering and thinking about people then total strangers, never ever dreaming
that in so few years these far-away satellites would be not
alone his admirers, but his devoted and ardent friends. Tosti
is a Roman—that is to say, he desires to be called a Roman ;
but no matter what country claims him, he belongs to the
world of talent and success.

F. P. Tosti was born in the Abruzzi in 1848, and was educated
n the Eternal City. In early youth he managed to procure
excellent musical instruction. He worked with energy, and
dreamed of becoming a second Paganini ; but his talent was so
very humble, that for many long years he was obliged to content himself with playing second violin in one of the secondary of Roman opera-houses. I looked at Tosti, and heard his
voice, still speaking as he spoke to me yesterday—or was it the
day before ?—I have forgotten. In answer to one of my
queries, he said,

" Yes, it is true I began my career as a violinist. All my early
compositions were scoffed at ; and fifteen years ago—Dio mio ! I
can see myself there now—I was prowling about the streets
of Ancona. I hadn't ten soldi to my name, and for three days
I had lived on mandarines and stale bread. ' Healthy,' you
say ; yes, but very disagreeable. Three long days that I
wandered about that town, hungry, wretched, despairing ; I
didn't know where to turn or what to do. I only felt that I
had got away from Rome, and was bound to do something. I
saw that a prize was offered, a prize of 500 francs, by the
Florentine Art Society, for the best original song. In desperation I wrote one, sent it in ; there were other competitors—fifty,
perhaps—and, my dear friend, the very first song which was
rejected as utterly worthless was the one which later almost

made my fortune, 'Vorrei Morire.' Some way I got to Milan; I wrote two other ballads, both instantly rejected by the great publishers, Ricordi and Sonsogno, of Milan. Don't laugh when I tell you that those songs were my best efforts, those which set the seal on success, 'Ti Rapirei' and 'Penso.'

" I finally made up my mind to go to London; don't ask me how I got there, I never knew."

I said, " But to whom do you attribute that you owe your success ? to man, or woman, or—yourself ?"

He replied, " To one of your sex, and the best creature that ever lived. She befriended me in London; she is dead long since—God rest her soul! I can never forget her, and—and you know the rest."

This was the gist of what Tosti had told me, and looking at him as I did at the banquet, can you wonder that it came so readily into my mind ?

To-day his songs are sold by millions : he is the most successful living composer of chamber-music, and is not only idolised by the worshippers of popular melodies, but his talent is very original : he is an ingenious musician and excels in those touching, pathetic love-ballads, which alike touch prince and peasant. His compositions have not the elaborate pretensions which distinguish some of the song-writers of the present day; their simplicity does not always strike the chord simplicity should awaken; but more pretentious works shall be forgotten, and Tosti's will occupy a favoured and lasting place. Ricordi, who refused Tosti's first song, is now his principal publisher. This house pays him immense sums and royalties, beside 400 guineas for one song a month.

Tosti lives in London, 12 Mandeville Place, a charming house, filled with autograph portraits of the Royal Family, and a fortune in bibelots and bric-à-brac. He is chapel-master, musician-in-ordinary to her Royal Highness the aged Duchess of Cambridge, music-master to her Royal Highness Princess Beatrice, and is frequently invited to visit at Windsor, or Osborne, Balmoral, and other |royal residences; and her Majesty the Queen is pleased to consider Tosti not one of her most faithful, devoted, and agreeable servants, but one of her cherished and most distinguished friends.

CHAPTER XII.

FACING me at the banquet was a distinguished-looking man; he had black eyes and a pleasant smiling face; he seemed full of easy, interesting, and idle good-humour. I at once knew him to be somebody, and was not surprised later when he was presented to me as the famous writer Giacosa: still, you would never imagine him from his looks to be a poet; he appears hearty, and not worn by the poetic passions. An author and dramatic writer — yes, such he is, and one of the most celebrated in Italy. Besides his literary fame you must have heard of him recently in connection with the movement in Turin to present heretofore proscribed plays—the *Mandragola* of Macchiavelli, the *Aretino* of Boccaccio, &c., which have so long filled classic ook-shelves, but which proprieties since the Reformation have practically and publicly vetoed. First of all, Giacosa is against the Turin theatrical scheme—you remember that of bringing to light and publicly performing for students and litterati these works—and he has given lectures in Milan on the subject, one only a few days ago, discussing and denying either the utility or morality of such a thing; and although it would be difficult for me to enter into the question, like most women I have my ideas on the scheme, and find Giacosa brilliant but not convincing—I don't say wrong—I simply say not convincing. Macaulay, you will recollect, in his essay on the "Dramatists of the Restoration," said these words:

"The whole liberal education of our countrymen is conducted
on the principle that no book which is valuable either by reason of the excellence of its style, or by reason of the light
which it throws on the history, polity, and manners of nations,
should be *withheld from the student on account of its impurity.*"
The italics are mine, but does this not seem as well to apply
to Italy? Still, Macaulay may speak only of reading—not
publicly performing such works.

But to return to Giacosa. He is a Piedmontese, and was
born in Colleretto on the 27th October 1847, and is the
son of the very celebrated lawyer Guido Giacosa. The son's,
Giuseppe Giacosa, first works excited enormous interest, especially one, " A Can che Secca Cenere non gli fidar Farina,"*
and the work which made his name, " An Old Story : una partita di Scacchi." His next work was a play called *Triumph of
Love*, written in blank verse, which had a magnificent success
throughout Italy, and rendered the author's name as familiar
as a household word.

Giacosa then worked in collaboration with Marenco, and
really originated a new style of dramatic art—that is to say,
the idealic and legendary, so famous in the Middle Ages : added
to an extraordinary delicacy of thought and sentiment, Giacosa has the brilliancy and wit of a Sardou, and adds to his
model of the inimitable Goldoni's style, the perception and
progress celebrated in the best dramatists of to-day.

Amongst his other works are *Marito amante della Moglie,*†
Fratelli d'Arme,‡ &c. During the last eight years, Giacosa's
name has been celebrated for adaptation of various pieces from
foreign tongues into the Italian. I go back to the proposed
performance at Turin of the classical plays, for I cannot under-

* " To a Dog who eats Ashes it is useless to give Flour."
† " A Husband in Love with his Wife."
‡ " Brothers-at-Arms."

stand how a writer of his enlightened mind, of his superior
intelligence, could offer the reasons which he puts forth for
not presenting these plays. He has especially spoken against
the *Mandragola*, which, in spite of his opposition, position,
and undoubted authority, I am afraid will positively be given
in Turin the following season.

What with the *Othello* talk, the fall of the Ministry, and
the new horrors anent the Massowah massacre, Giacosa's lectures certainly have their share in creating a furore in Milan.
He sustains his position very well, and although it will be
impossible for intelligent minds to condemn and do away with
the classic Italian repertory, Giacosa has certainly advanced
some very wholesome ethics and clever ideas, which later may
not be without a fruitful harvest.

The next flower in my bouquet is Emilio Panzacchi, a writer
of the Romagnolo,* historical professor, professor of fine arts,
distinguished poet, critic, and essayist. Panzacchi was born in
Bologna in 1841, and published some admirable lyrics under
the pseudonym of " Lyrica." In personal appearance Panzacchi
has certainly been favoured by Madre Natura. His countenance bespeaks a man of superior intellectual fibre, and his face,
although round and full, has a sweet, almost pathetic, expression ; his black eyes are filled with an ever coming and going
happy light; but this changes when he smiles, his mouth falls,
and his countenance is clouded over by a strange melancholy
and sensitiveness. Panzacchi represents one of the great
Bologna newspapers, and is at present known as the translator
of Ernest Renan's and Alexandre Dumas's latest pieces. These
have been put into admirable verse and as admirable Italian,
things rare enough to-day in dramatic writers. Panzacchi is
a man not only of great intellect, but vast erudition. He

* The Romagnolo —ancient provinces of Central Italy, previous to
Italian unity under the dominion of the Pope

has all the Italian's fine musical intelligence, and spoke most delightfully on the great Musical Congress to be held in Bologna in 1888, which, according to him, will be one of the most remarkable exhibitions of the nineteenth century, and certainly one of the most remarkable ever held in Italy. The present *Othello* craze and affluence of strangers seem poor compared with that expected in Bologna. The foreign press are already invited, and should I happen to be present, you will please imagine me, not flirting, but talking literature to Japan, Persia, and the uttermost parts of the earth. The next thing I expect you will announce your intention of assisting at this ceremony. Panzacchi is one of the chief leaders in the movement, and certainly the responsibility of such an enterprise could not be in better hands.

And now for the noblest Roman of them all. Have you heard of Pascarella? If you have ever heard that name, you must have thought of how much it says. A man, a creature, anything called Pascarella must be some one or something. My Pascarella is the most original, the most ingenious, the most delightful of Italian poets. When M. Gualdo came up to me and said, "I want to present you"—looking at his friend, I interrupted, instantly crying, "I know whom, Pascarella;" then we all laughed and shook hands.

"He will write you a sonnet," Gualdo added. "Which, of course, I couldn't read," I replied; for Pascarella writes in the old Roman dialect, beautiful to listen to when spoken, beautiful to look at when scanned, but as unintelligible to a modern brain as the hieroglyphs on an ancient Egyptian obelisk. That for his writings; but as to Pascarella himself, his smile, his eyeglass jammed deep in one eye under one protruding brow, his low forehead, dark hair, and hairy skin, his soft eyes, diminutive nose, mouth, and almost featureless face, his quaint diminutive person; his small hands folded on his umbrella-handle, ready at any moment to dive into his pocket in search of his devoted and inseparable pipe, abandoned only to drink a health to maestro Verdi—yes, these are all that is most comprehensible, the language that appeals to all mortals, and these are—Pascarella.

Without speaking a word, we began an admirable conversation, and when the parts of speech intruded themselves upon our notice, we took up the thread of acquaintanceship as naturally as the thread of common chatter. Pascarella's manners are as original as his personality. Whatever he does is uncommon, or out of the common. When he speaks he begins at the end of a sentence or the middle, never at the beginning. Although he writes in dialect, he talks in a pure Italian, and not only never listens to the sound of his voice, but never seems quite to know what he is talking about. Strange to say, he never hesitates or stops, but glides on in delightful nonchalance ; there is no point put upon anything, but when he has finished, he also finishes — there is a point to everything. The sense of having heard something original dawns upon you ; from being original it becomes remarkable, and from remarkable develops into extraordinary ; then you glance up at this phenomenon, who has not changed his position, whose glass is still in his eye, whose smile is still on his lips, whose voice perhaps has ceased, but whose hands are still placidly folded on his umbrella's silver handle, waiting to dive into his pocket. You look at him, take him all in, and the word " Marvellous !" instantly escapes you.

That's it : Pascarella is marvellous. I still think it's his name, and say, " That man has not the right to call himself Pascarella without being marvellous." But besides his name and delicious art, he exaggerates his appearance by such ingenuity, even craftiness, that his defects add to his talent. He has remoulded his physique to conform with his mind ; what there is of comic in him is emblazoned in face, manner, costume, and gesture ; what there is of pathetic looks out of his sombre regard, pale, flattened countenance, in a way to bring tears to one's eyes. When you read his " Manechino," a serious lecture, and see himself in caricature illustrated by himself, you can well understand how he set the Roman and Lombard world laughing. When one reads his poem in the Roman vernacular on Villa Glori—history of a heroic struggle between the Pope's troops and the Italian volunteers—all the blood in your veins runs rife in patriotic fire, and the fountain of tears wept dry for our own honoured dead bursts forth anew, to water the graves of these heroic unknown.

This is Pascarella. He is not Bret Harte yet, but nearly approaches that great genius. Like the American writer, his blending of pathetic and comic is so forcible that he gives to the creations of his fancy the life we see in reality, the variations of mood and sense which sound up and down the gamut of human existence.

Pascarella was born in Rome, and can you wonder that amongst the Romans he—one of them—should be idolised? He burst upon his native horizon like a meteor ; he is as young in years as those young trees in the Pincio Gardens ; his fame is already national, and his sonnets sung wherever the Italian language is heard. I have not time—indeed, I cannot tell you of his alternate simplicity and pretension, his poverty and pride, his cunning and ruses and innocent naïvetés. This man, so gifted in verse and song, a student of human nature, sees through all the world, and never for a moment sees through himself or imagines that the world sees through him—he is such a character, a volume in 16mo would not adequately describe him. In Milan and Florence, as in Rome, he is a general favourite, his name is as fashionable as the latest perfume. Tosti simply adores him, and if you were in Milan, and in his company, I doubt not a week, a day, an hour even, would see you his devoted friend and admirer. I hear you say, "I leave for Italy by the next train."

The centrepiece to the bouquet, however, was missing—I mean to say, the only person present who was not present was the light of Italian letters, A. de Amicis. You remember I told you I had met him, and was preparing a pæan in his honour, when unforeseen events prevented his return to Milan, and although he was not at the banquet, his place was kept for him, like those familiar chairs placed for loved ones at family tables ; his absence caused his name to be but more frequently pronounced. Don't tell me that you don't know De Amicis ; do not tell me that you have not read his *Constantinople* : the former, perhaps, you cannot help, but the latter would be, in you, inexcusable. Read Théophile Gautier's *Constantinople*, read M. de Blowitz's *Course à Constantinople*, but don't fail to read De Amicis' *Constantinople*. He is the most popular amongst Italian contemporary authors. I say popular advisedly, as De Amicis' popularity being well won is well deserved. First of all, he writes brilliant, clear, and popular Italian, is a man who has travelled far and wide, and, thanks to his disposition and nature, a culture altogether beyond the ordinary ; for as a matter of fact the Italian travels very little, and his world lies between Etna and Mont Blanc.

De Amicis was born in 1846 in Oneglio, and began life a volunteer in the Italian army. He was an officer at Liguria, and suddenly burst upon the world an author, with a novel called *Baggette della Vita Militari*, which obtained an instantaneous and colossal success. He renounced the military career, began a course of travels, and wrote successively of voyages in Spain, Holland, Marocco, London, and Constantinople. With the exception of Gautier's work, I know of none so agreeable or so perfect as that of De Amicis. Beyond the magnificent and stirring descriptions of the City of Mosques, a chapter on the dogs—those wretched starving waifs, which fill street, lane, highway, and byway—is one of the most remarkable descriptions of modern Italian. De Amicis' works are translated into most of the modern languages; his style is fresh, flowing, and peculiarly earnest. He writes poetry and prose, and his pen is gilded with those idealisms, love of beauty, poetry, and sentiment, which the highest flights, the most daring Muse alone may know.

His descriptive style is scarcely less powerful. In pictures of mountains and valleys, of distant seas and far-famed lands, of temples and palatial halls, we see with his eye and feel with his sense of feeling and beauty. It is impossible to read one of his books without being impressed. We realise that while he is himself distinctly original in thought and expression, he at the same time never repeats himself, and his originality never contributes to falsifying of the picture : the peoples and scenes he describes are the people as he knows and has seen them, as you know and have seen them, as I know and have seen them. When you take up his volume, it is like shaking hands with an old friend ; when you read his pages, it is like renewing old acquaintanceship. You inquire after neighbours, casuals, even enemies : time has passed since the last meeting, perhaps a year—years. Some places are filled and—and some empty ; but do you think of that? The past, whatever it may have been, is yesterday, and you are reliving it all, with the pleasure of your last happiest twenty-four hours ; and the future—the future is, I hear you say "Let it be soon," my meeting with De Amicis.—Always the same, &c.

SIGNOR ARRIGO BOÏTO,
Author of *Mefistofele* and libretto for Verdi's *Othello*.

CHAPTER XV.

TO THE SAME.

Milan, Feb. 10, 1887.

My dear friend, according to an old promise, I am going to tell you all about maestro Boïto, and I dedicate this letter to him.

Arrigo Boïto is one of the finest living composers. He was born in Padua in 1842. His father was a noble of the Venetian province, and his mother a gentlewoman of Russian descent, birth, and breeding. At the age of five, little Arrigo began to play the piano very creditably. He was a thoughtful child, and became in time a most studious one. He was sensitive, modest, and so retiring that it was with difficulty his parents could ever induce him to play, even for members of the family. He began to develop so remarkable a talent that, at the age of twelve, he was sent to Milan, and entered the musical Conservatory as a pupil of the famous piano-teachers, Professors Mazzucato, Ronchetti, and Montiviti. For the final examination he wrote a composition with Franco Faccio, the present orchestra-leader at La Scala, called *Le Sorelle d'Italia;* and when this piece was played in 1861, it gained each aspirant a prize of 2000 lire, which enabled and obliged both to study a year out of Italy. Boïto, although a most accomplished musician, seemed chary of composing, and really began his career as a poet and librettist. In 1862 he wrote the words to Verdi's *L'Inno delle Nazioni,* for the Great Exhibition at London, and later on, the libretto for Bottesini's opera *Hero*

Q

and Leander, one of the most graceful and gracious books
modern verse has given us. In the mean time, Boïto was
secretly composing his great work *Mefistofele*. This claimed
his day, and stole sleep from his sleeping hours. His life was
the life that has so often been lived by genius: a wretched
existence of struggle with poverty, friendlessness, and despair ;
himself his own greatest enemy, for he often lived without
belief in himself. Nothing he did pleased him. He spent days
writing pages that in seconds he destroyed. He plotted, slaved,
always with the one idea, not of working for popular favour,
but of reaching a pure ideal through the medium of pure art.
After years of writing, Boïto brought out his *Mefistofele* at La
Scala. The work was not a success. He wrote and rewrote
it, and you know how it has since made a triumphant tour of
the civilised world. It is such a favourite opera in Russia that
the Emperor listens to some of its music at least once a day,
and is never happier than when humming "Lontano, Lontano,
Lontano," the refrain of the exquisite duo at the close of act
third.

You have heard about Boïto's writing the *Othello* libretto
how he longed to compose the opera himself, and not alone was
willing, but anxious, to efface his humble talent, and shine only
by a reflection of Verdi's glory. There is something touching
in the reverence and affection which Boïto bears towards the
great master. They are the traditions of a fine and generous
soul, a nature above all littleness, jealousy, or envy, the purest
sentiments of friendship, love, and veneration. I am sure,
when Boïto came out and gazed upon the sea of faces at La
Scala, no one so delighted in Verdi's success as he did. No one
was happier than he to think that every one present was
come to honour the crowning glory of Italian art. In the
circle of that last diadem, the younger master's homage was,
perhaps, the purest and most flawless gem. So they stood

together, these great men, and each had deserved well of his country. One wore the laurel, the other basked in its shade.

Having met Boïto at Teatro Manzoni and the banquet, we seem now to meet him everywhere. Like a strange word you see for the first time in a dictionary, then see it in every book you pick up for a week to come, the man for days invisible becomes ubiquitous : we meet him going to and coming from rehearsal, breakfasting at the Cova, or dining at the Rebbecchino ; paying a morning call on Signora D— or an evening call on Madame de V—, we meet him in the Galleria or on the Corso ; and every invitation for the last few days has been to see—Arrigo Boïto. Monday night a dinner at Contessa D—'s ; Tuesday night, dinner with Tosti ; ditto on Wednesday ; and—well, you shall judge if I have had a real opportunity at last of knowing this distinguished person.

Contessa D— has a delightful apartment in the celebrated Casa or Palazzo Crivelli. It is very cosy, and, of course, very simpatica. We assembled in the comfortable drawing-room at seven, where there is an admirable portrait with autograph of Napoleon I., given to her late husband, Count D—. Maestro Boïto, Madame Pantaleone, Franco Faccio, the Marquis F—ti, whose wife is one of the most perfect women, were among the other guests. By the time we went in to dinner, Boïto and I were very good friends. You remember I sat near him at the banquet yesterday, and, the ice somewhat broken, we began to talk—of course, the everlasting *Othello*. I noticed that if you pay Boïto a compliment he waves his arms and bows in a deprecatory manner. If you ask him a question he is very apt to respond at once, " Mon Dieu ! I haven't an idea;" when, of course, he has an idea. He has plenty of ideas ; he has, in fact, nothing but ideas ; he knows exactly what you are saying, and he waves his arms in—*vide* above. I believe he even knows exactly what you intended to say. Thought-readers, take warning.   Ask Boïto his opinion on any subject—he bows his head and listens silently, ever guarding a cold, modest demeanour; make any statement whatsoever, and he gives ear with such elaborate courtesy that you are sure he is meditating as elaborate a response ; instead, he hears you through to the end, bows with an acquiescent smile, which says plainly, "I take your word for it ;" or—more unflattering still—gives you to understand that either through indifference or unwillingness, he does not even deign to discuss the matter.   I think it was indifference last night : Boïto's whole manner said so plainly,

"Is anything on earth worth discussion ?"

I determined, however, to speak a few words about his poem *Othello* and some inadvertency brought me, this reply. I spoke relative to the suppression of the first act of Shakespeare's work.   Boïto said,

"I know what you mean.   It is generally supposed that Brabantio's words, ' Look to it, Moor : she hath deceived her father,' &c., is one of the primary reasons of Othello's jealousy.   I do not see it in that light.   The father said the words meaningly enough, but Othello repeats them idly : they come into his mind afterwards, when he rages jealously, as we remember a dream to which we cannot attach great importance, as it is but a dream.   And the finale of the third act you say is shocking.   So it is.   I admit it shocked me also more on the stage than I had realised in the libretto ; but, you remember, the scene took place.   Othello struck Desdemona before Ludovico."

"Yes, but not before the Senate.   And the concluding scene—'Here is the Lion of Venice,' and Iago's foot on the Moor's breast—"

A look on Boïto's face stopped me.   He smiled his cold patient smile, slightly lifted his arms and shoulders, and then dropped—the conversation.

You will admit that it was not encouraging, and I had wanted to discuss—O, so many things. Faccio then began on the opera, and the proposed performances at the Apollo in Rome. It seems *Othello* is to be brought out there with the same cast as here, only the artists' remuneration was a subject worthy of comment. Before the curtain goes up, three singers are to be paid nine thousand lire. Faccio laughed.

" I am for singers being well paid," he said, " but four thousand francs a night to Tamagno, three thousand to Maurel, and two thousand to the Signora," he indicated Madame Pantaleone facing him, " to put it plainly, is simple robbery. How can Italian opera continue? how can any theatre pay expenses? how can any impresario succeed who has such exorbitant demands to satisfy? and think, this outlay is before and besides other expenses. I repeat, it is outrageously pure robbery, and no singer in the world to-day is worth any such a nightly price, or justified in asking or taking it."

Faccio here settled his words with a glass of—no joke intended—barbera. We all signified approval. All? No, Boïto bowed; I must do M. Boïto the justice to say that he bowed, and looked as he always does when a question comes up. He again looked indifferent, even resigned, and said—nothing.

The prima donna spoke, and smiled a little smile.

" Nonsense !" she cried, " I am not exorbitant ; I see the others are paid great sums, why should I not be ?"

I wanted then and there to say,

" Well, if you place yourself on a par with Maurel, or even Tamagno, then the world must be going to end—by all means ;" and I thought of the Scotch saying, " Would the power," &c.

She exclaimed, " Why should I not be paid in proportion ? Mine is a chief rôle. I asked two thousand francs a night, and it was accorded at once."

Silence followed. No, not silence. Faccio still kept muttering, "Never mind; I have spoken the truth." After a discreet interim, just far enough off to be civil, and near enough to put a slight attachment between the woof of conversation and its accompanying thread, Vergil spoke:

"Maurel is a great artist: the greatest—the greatest baritone artist on the stage to-day. I have never heard—could any one surpass his performance on Saturday?"

Boïto's face lit up. You see, he can be enthusiastic!

"If you think well of Saturday night," he cried, "I don't know what you would have thought of him at the dress rehearsal. He was simply sublime. By far the most incomparable performance I have ever seen on the stage. Verdi fell on his neck and called him 'my superb Iago.' I hope he may sing as well again, but I don't believe in his lifetime he has ever-equalled, certainly he never could surpass, that effort."

Then the poet went on, and raved, simply raved, over Maurel. Faccio preserved an almost discreet silence. You will admit that it was a little humiliating at La Scala on such an occasion to have almost the sole honours in Italian opera borne off by a Frenchman, and that, too, at a moment when the two countries have their mutual upper and lower rows of teeth on edge.

Then a discussion arose about Maurel's voice. All agreed that it had never been in such form before, and Faccio hinted that Verdi had given this artist only occasional chords to sing against, which explained how his organ seemed so powerful.

"Which explains more than ever that Maurel is an artist," added Boïto concludingly. "His phrasing, art, and diction must be perfect, otherwise in that great theatre how quickly would any unsupported voice have gone to pieces, and for the very reason you have mentioned, completely wreck itself and its owner!"

Even Faccio admitted the justice of this reasoning.

. I see the poet does not trouble his head over politics. French, Italian, or Hottentot, Maurel is an incomparable singer, and he did not hesitate to say so.

Verdi was the theme, when we reached the drawing-room, and this time Boïto became, like everybody else, a touchstone of praise. I said to him,

. "How did you feel at such enthusiasm and repeated recalls? It must have been a strange sensation coming out before that . ea of faces, accompanied by such roars and billows of applause. Were you pleased? Were you nervous?"

"When I heard my name I was strangely touched," he replied. "I had not thought about it. I was up in a box with Signora Verdi when the maestro sent for us. We went to the stage, and when we were called he started, then turned in a half-dazed way for me. He took my hand. No, I shall never forget it." In spite of himself, Boïto's voice trembled, and his hand went half towards his eyes, which were filling with tears. "I can never describe to you how he took my hand : his touch —there was something so kind, so paternal, so protecting in it, and the clasp of his fingers so thrilled me that I felt the shock to my heart's core : it was an electric thrill, and yet so delicate I could scarcely realise that our hands had come in contact. Ah! Verdi said more to me in that single hand-clasp than he has said in all our previous intercourse : more than any one ever will say. I shall never forget it!"

Now will your believe it that we all felt like crying? There was something so pathetic in Boïto's voice that it was impossible not to be impressed, and I really believe, without knowing why, we would have all fell a-weeping : happily I remembered the closing scenes :

"And the being dragged home in the carriage," I said,— "how did that strike you? was it agreeable?"

Boïto laughed nervously.

" For fame, perhaps, not for comfort; on the contrary, it was very disagreeable. We left the theatre-door. There were crowds and crowds and crowds. Signora Verdi got in the carriage, I followed, and finally the mob let the master enter. We had only made a few paces when the yells began : ' Take away the horses, take away the horses, take away the horses ! We will drag the carriage back to the hotel !' Verdi demurred, but in vain, and I saw that we were in the hands of a rabble, a mob which had made up its mind to draw Verdi's carriage home to the hotel, cost what it might. The difference between Italian crowds and others is that there is no difference between their cries of joy or rage : their voices sound as threatening when they scream ' Long live Verdi ! as ' Down with the Ministry !' or ' Kill Verdi !' We finally persuaded the maestro to allow them to unharness the horses. This was done with wild yells something too utterly indescribable, and then began the going to the Hôtel de Milan. It was the first time in my life I had ever had such an experience, and I assure you, the question of honour put aside, it was likewise the most uncomfortable experience I had ever known. First we were lifted up, up, up; then suddenly, without an instant's warning, the vehicle was lowered, so that I thought we were going crash into the paving stones ; then suddenly uplifted again quite high into the air, then dropped quite as suddenly, shaking us almost as if some one had taken us by the shoulders. This went on all the way to the hotel, which was not far, but under those circumstances seemed miles away. At last we neared the Milan, and another wild yell broke out which simply curdled my blood. Signora Verdi was as white as a sheet, and Verdi was as pale as a ghost. Well, this kept on until, at last, thankfully I say, we reached our ultimate destination. We were deposited in front of the entrance, and I shall never forget Verdi's face as the carriage-door was wrenched open, and we—say, rather, *he*—turned to go.

As he got out, his foot yet on the step, he glanced back, with
an unsmiling face, an undescribable look, and giving me a sort
of desperate hand-grasp—such a one as a soldier gives his com-
rade before going into battle—he said,

"' Vi consegno mia moglie.'*

"I feared he would be torn to pieces, the crowd was simply
maddened, and snatching right and left at his garments ; but,
as you know, he 'got up stairs whole, and—and—and that is
all, except that I led the Signora into the hotel, and we
humbler mortals reached the house with difficulty, but without accident. Once there, glory was much more appreciable,
looking down from a high and safe balcony, than dragged over
the heads of men and looking at the crowds below."

Boïto stopped, and laughed a laugh I need not say we all
joined in. "Poor dear Verdi," he continued, "after such a
night of emotion, and at his age, too—seventy-four is not
twenty-four ! I wonder he was so brave with it all ; but that
hand-clasp—never shall I forget that, nor the bewildered heart-
broken ' Vi consegno mia moglie.' "

No one had ever before seen Boïto so much in earnest. All
present seemed as surprised as I was, for it is not often that this
taciturn man ever condescends to speak so freely of anybody
or anything. We then reminded him of the play *Francesca da
Rimini*, and Verdi's words recalled Malatesta's, where this latter
leaves his beloved to go to the war : the court is assembled,
there is a great crowd, and Malatesta, going towards Paolo,
cries in a desperate voice, "Vi consegno mia moglie." The
circumstance and Verdi's expression were similar, but you
may imagine the result was not the same.

Music was then called for, Boïto obediently went to
the piano, and Signora Pantaleone courteously consented to
sing the "Ave Maria" and prayer from Othello. It was really

* "I consign my wife into your keeping."

most kind in her, and whatever she may be as an artist she
certainly is an amiably disposed woman. I think it is the
one exception, certainly during my lifetime, of a singer getting
up the minute she was asked, and certainly of a prima donna
at La Scala singing the grand air of her success the night
before, without making beforehand the usual professional
apologies: "I am tired; I am hoarse; I really cannot get out
a note after dinner; I have no voice; eating so much ruins the
vocal chords; I did not sleep well last night ;" &c. &c. &c.

It seems incredible, but Boïto could not play a note of
Othello without the score before him. Then he accompanied
Madame Pantaleone as I have heard few composers accom-
pany.

When the air was finished, and the prima donna was
having the usual after-talk with a composer — this phrase
might be better, or that one worse, or something similar—
Contessa D— interrupted,

"It is curious, when Boïto sits down to the piano it seems
a different instrument; he doesn't make any fuss; his fingers
move over the keys so quietly that they scarcely seem to
touch them ; and yet every measure is soft, fascinating, and
enchanting."

The Contessa was right. The author of *Mefistofele* makes
no pretensions to be a pianist, and yet few professionals are
greater masters of expression ; one is not irritated by too
apparent technique, but one understands that he is as thoroughly versed in the *a b c* of his art as a Liszt or a Chopin.

As to the vocal part of the performance, the prima donna
sang much better than on the previous night. There certainly
was a great charm about her voice and manner ; she merited
more praise as Desdemona in private life than Desdemona
lying on her death-bed, visible to the great public of La Scala.

We were breathlessly listening for the fatal end, when an

interruption came from Faccio, the orchestra-leader, who was obliged to go to lead his band at the theatre.

" Social gatherings are very nice," he said, " but, alas ! the curtain must go up, and the orchestra and the people will not forgive it if the leader is not in his place."

Then came more music and conversation, and soon after Boïto, having an appointment with Verdi, also took his leave.

On rare occasions he had spoken about his work, but in the usual desultory fashion which said " I don't care to say anything about myself."

The door had no sooner closed after him than I begged Contessa D— to tell me all about him. I knew that Count Enrico and his mother were amongst Boïto's very oldest and most cherished friends, and I said,

" Where does Boïto live, and how does he work? I am not curious, but I am interested; I am dying to know all about him."

" Where does he live ?" repeated the Contessa ; then she laughed, such a pretty laugh, and answered in the Milanese dialect, " I don't believe he lives, he perches. We have known Boïto intimately for years, and know nothing about him. His house is a *casa misteriosa ;* he lives with a brother, or near a brother, a splendid architect; and at whatever time of the day or night you go to the composer's you find he is never there. ' Gin ' (Count Enrico) has missed him every time he has been to see him for—well, for years. Send a letter to him requiring an answer, he is never there : your letter is left ; you don't know its fate ; but he always turns up punctually at the appointed time, like a fairy, you know, in a pantomime. Last Monday was an exception ; for who in the world would imagine that two people would write notes saying ' to-morrow,' and neither one dating them ? He is the best friend in the world, the best fellow : invisible when he can do no good, but always on hand when

you want him. O ! you'd like to see his house, would you ?"
this was to me. " Don't flatter yourself you will. She won't,
will she, ' Gin '? So take your mind off that ; I know 'you
never will."

And I thought to myself, "You don't know me, madame.
I am not an American for nothing. I have made up my mind
to see Boïto's house, and the next time we meet I shall tell
you all about it."

We finally took our leave, naturally thanking our hostess
for the delightful evening : as I told you, I am not curious but
interested in him, and I shall tell you some more about him
when—

Later.

My letter was interrupted. I—I have seen his house! Now,
don't begin—don't say hard things about me ; don't fling at my
head that old, that eternal remark about women and curiosity.
I am a woman ; but this is not curiosity, it is interest.

To-night we dined with Tosti; Aldo Noseda, the witty paro-
dist of *Othello*, the inventor of the joke about the "viol of amore"
and other remarkable instruments for Verdi's new opera, one
of the brightest young journalists in Italy; Count D—, Vergil's bosom friend Massa, the fascinating Beau Brummell of
Milan high life, and Boïto. This latter was perfectly at his
ease, more so than I had ever seen him, and, as on the last
occasion of our meeting, was exceedingly amiable. You
will begin to think that I am worse than Boswell, of whom
Macaulay spoke in very free and not at all flattering terms; but
I sacrifice myself to a good cause. Boïto is a most gifted man,
and he is the present musical hope of Italy's future. When I lose
myself in detail on any public personage with *Othello*, I also
say, "It is the cause, my soul ; it is the cause." What would
we not give to-day if some friendly gossip over chianti or beer
had sat down and chatted of Dante's or Tasso's every-day life,

told the truth about Beatrice or Leonora, or, scorning delicacy, had frankly told of the Bard's escapade at Charlecot, or the reason why Anne Hathaway's name was the only one which did not appear in Shakespeare's will! Well, we drank neither chianti nor beer, but some very delicious extra dry, and before the froth had disappeared, someway we were all on the subject of *Mefistofele*. Were you aware of the fact !that two of the most charming numbers, at present the greatest success of the score, were not in the opera on its first representation, namely, the garden quartette, that charming inspiration in syncopes, and great prison air for Margherita in the prison scene, third act?

We fairly forced Boïto to speak of himself, and I asked him bluntly, "Is it true that you wrote these two numbers only to give way to popular taste,t that you bu don't like them yourself? that you say they are unworthy work, and you groan every time you hear them?"

"No," he said, "I don't groan unless they are badly sung. The quartette is not, perhaps, unworthy, but it is young, infan- tine. Were I to rewrite the opera once again "—you know he has already rewritten it three or four times—"which I have no intention of doing, I should cut out a great deal of the music allotted to Mephistopheles in the second act, which, at the second time of composing, I need not say, I thought about my best efforts."

Then followed more talk about this score, and he spoke of its performance at Drury Lane—how fine it was, and how adorable Nilsson appeared as Marguerite and Helen of Troy.

Boïto speaks very simply of his work when he does speak, but has the utmost lack of affectation of any man I have ever seen. He is so modest that it is difficult to believe that when he says "I," the first person singular means himself.

The question then came up about *Othello*, Wagnerism, the innovation of modern music, and the different style and changes from Verdi's first opera to Verdi's last opera; which latter, while intensely Verdi and none other, is the very quintessence of Verdi, and demonstrates in every page not alone the philosophy of musical composition, but the gigantic inroads into what is called music of the future; not Wagner, I protest. It is Verdi copying Verdi. At his best you recognise the handicraft. It is as personal as—well, were Raphael to copy Raphael.

Tosti then said to Boïto, " You may say what you like about this last work but I felt your influence throughout the whole score, and although I adore Verdi, a dozen times here and there in the music of *Othello* I recalled reminiscences, even identical measures, of *Mefistofele.* You can't deny it; can you explain it ?"

" O, *Dio mio !"* cried Boïto, " I can explain. I think you are mistaken about *Mefistofele.* The coincidence is simply that in an age of progress intelligent people all seem to hit upon the same idea and expression of idea at the same time."

" It is in the air," I said irrelevantly; "the same as when Columbus discovered America, the world was full of Columbuses."

" Yes," replied Boïto quickly, " you are right; those things are in the air ;" and before he could continue, Noseda interrupted laughingly,

"Yes, they are certainly in the air. Last night at Café Martini I heard a contadina scream out, ' Ah quel Boïto ! col suo progresso a guastà anch' il nostr' Verdi.' " *

Boïto had to join in the laugh in spite of himself, but I will do him the credit of saying that I don't believe the idea ever once entered his head that during their long and intimate collaboration Verdi had in the slightest way yielded to his influence in composition, or his advanced ideas on the philosophy of operatic writing.

* "Ab, that Boïto ! with his progress he has spoiled even our old Verdi."

Then followed a long dissertation on the subject. Of course Boïto shone preëminent. I shall not tell you all he said, as it would make this letter much too long; but he is very decided in believing and positive in asserting that, while he admires and recognises Wagner's talent—well, to quote his own words, " Verdi has no more to do with Wagner than I have with Dante."

By the way, I haven't told you of Boïto's personal appearance, nor the literary gods at whose shrine he worships. These latter are three poets, Dante, Victor Hugo, and Shakespeare.

Boïto has an air *très grand seigneur;* in spite of artistic life and, to some extent, Bohemian surroundings, this aroma clings to him, and it would be difficult to associate the idea of Bohemianism with such a man of the world. From his manner you might take him for a prince of the blood, a statesman, a diplomat, an ambassador, but never for an operatic composer. I have no wish to touch on arts, artists, or individuals, but Bohemia usually means eccentricity, rarely distinction. It is very odd, but I have found few professionals in any rank of life who in frequenting society, instead of preferring to look and dress like ordinary ladies and gentlemen, do not, on the contrary, by peculiarity in manner and dress, prefer to look like extraordinary individuals. They always seem to me not so much to wish to draw attention to their talent as to their appearance. This excessive vulgarity, this personal advertising and individual Barnumism, is the bane of artistic existence. Why should gifted people not appear in the world like other people ? Believe me, if you cannot make yourself remarked through your brains, you can never hope to through your apparel. Boïto is highly gifted also, but extremey well bred, and prefers being mistaken for a gentleman rather than a celebrity.

In personal appearance Arrigo Boïto is tall, very fair, with clear light blue eyes, light moustache, light hair, and a decided Slav or Russian hue of complexion. His countenance has a

Slav cast, and his features a decided northern cut. His cheek-bones are high, and cheeks very hollow; the habitual expres-sion of his face is one of coldness, at other times that of absolute impassibility. All his lifetime Boïto has frequented Bohemian men of letters, musicians, actors, artists, painters; he has lived sometimes with students, sometimes with poets; yet he speaks like a man who has been brought up at courts, who has never seen a world beyond that sphere where talent as a title comes after so many quarters of nobility. When one speaks to him of operas, or theatres, or artists, or com-posers, he has all the studied politeness we see in the Con-tinental well-bred amateur, but listens as if he were in the moon, and you from this globe talking the language of earth at him.

Unlike many celebrities, he is most at his ease when not talking of himself. He is learned, but not offensively erudite. His worship of poetry and his three poets reaches idolatry. Of course, he is at his best in the Italian or French authors; he reads Shakespeare very well in English, but told me he had learned *Othello* by heart in "François Hugo's * magnificent trans-lation and that of the Italian author Maffei." In conversing with Boïto, besides his genius you feel his nobleness of charac-ter, his simplicity, his kindness. More than that: in these venal days, when the most God-gifted regard their talent in the light of so much capital placed at so much per cent, and bound to bring in so much ready income, Boïto, who thinks only of art, who works for his art's sake, and not for money, seems to us a creature almost out of place in this modern world. Verdi received a great sum for *Othello :* he could never have written the opera he did without Boïto's libretto, yet perhaps the latter considered himself well paid with two hundred pounds. Boïto

* Son of Victor Hugo, translator of Shakespeare's complete works into French.

is an optimist; he believes in the goodness of human nature; he cherishes his illusions, and is as unsuspicious as credulous. He would take the last sou from his pocket or the last coat from his back to give to a needy friend. This without fuss, pretention, or reference to the fact. He is not understood by all the world, for although of a simple nature, he is not of maleable substance. He is a creature who cannot adapt himself to every one he meets, and who, ninety-nine times out of a hundred, will make a poor impression for one occasion when he will please.

I thought of all these things as the conversation went on, which, by the way, when Boïto took part in it, was always to a purpose. Finally it was proposed to go to the play, and we all started off to the Teatro dal Verme, a very fine opera house, where opera and spectacle are given, and where at the present moment they were performing Marchetti's *Ruy Blas*, the opera being supplemented by the charming ballet of *Sieba*.

The Dal Verme is a very sympathetic house, very large, with a splendid acoustic—one of the favourite, in fact is the second opera-house of Milan. I have heard some great artists there, notably La Galetti, decidedly the finest operatic singer I have ever heard in my lifetime; certainly none ever equalled her for beauty of voice or phrasing. She has imprinted so indelible a memory on the Dal Verme stage, that no matter what prima donna sings or what is going on, you can still see her dark face back of the footlights, hear her glorious voice and passionate accents, and follow every movement of the divinely inspired Favorita.

We spoke of her as we made our way into the boxes, and Boïto was loudest in words of praise. He had heard her, but not, as it happened, here. I firmly believe that this was the first time the composer has set foot in this theatre for years : everything seemed new to him, and he enjoyed the performance like

R

a child. He especially enjoyed the ballet, which, although but a one-horse affair for Milan, was still far superior to any first-rate Continental performance. We paid visits and received visits in our boxes, and had a long chat with the lovely Contessa D— V—, who occupied her own charming loge in the first proscenium. The theatre was packed, and O, so many pretty women, amongst others the beautiful Marchesa d'A—a, of whom I have so often spoken. And now for the great attraction—not the opera, not the ballet, but—you shall judge. All eyes were attracted to a grand tier box, and I saw her Grace the Duchess of B—, who, in addition to the usual family jewels, wore a most curious ornament—a necklace nothing more nor less than a yard of hangman's rope! This *corde de pendu* was studded with superb diamonds and emeralds, which fell on her grace's velvet dress like Roman candles on a 4th of July greensward. The cord itself lay in all the touching innocence and simplicity of virgin hemp, and on looking at it, fair and unwrinkled, one would scarcely imagine it had had the honour of launching a soul into eternity. None other, I believe, than the famous Hartmann, Nihilist, Socialist, Communist, assassin— Heaven knows what! Can you imagine wearing such a thing? I would as soon have had all the cobras in their native jungles hanging about my neck; but they do say nothing brings luck like a piece of the *corde d'un pendu.* I need not add we all wanted a look at this ingenious amulet. I think, however, were I the possessor of such jewels as belong to her Grace I would bedeck myself with the mineral products of the earth, and consider myself lucky in being able to face destiny without the hempen talisman. I asked Boïto if he had looked at it, and as he shuddered, of course I knew he had. Give me a man for curiosity: they are all alike.

After this hangman's business you may readily imagine that although in an operatic theatre in Milan, listening to *Ruy Blas,* and looking at some very pretty women on the stage and off, our conversation became characteristic ; we left *Ruy Blas* and Spain to hurl ourselves headlong into the regions of Nihilism, Socialism, hangmen, and horrors. The evening finished—I never knew how—but night and I had a dire struggle. I woke up fifty times, either being blinded by 4th of July rockets gone wrong or strangled by the combined yards of hang- man's rope used for traitors since George Washington signed that Declaration of Independence. However, once awake, I had it out with Aurora. The hours passed, and as soon as feasible I prepared for—

And the composer's house : perhaps you think I have for- gotten all about it ? At midday we saw the maestro taking breakfast at the Café Cova with M. B—, the gifted musical critic of *La Revue des Deux Mondes.* To my surprise Boïto at once cried, " I hear you want to see my house, and I remem- ber you once said you had no curiosity."

" Both are true," I added. " I wish to see where you work and study ; that is interest, not curiosity. I am interested and not curious."

Then he smiled, a very unbelieving smile, and—and bowed the bow before described.

" Name your hour," he said.

" To-day, at four ;" I replied, and at four precisely we pre- sented ourselves in the Via Principe Amadeo. The composer lives with his brother, Camillo Boïto, one of the most able and celebrated architects in Italy.

I must confess that when I saw the house, the ordinary square white Italian building, the Contessa D—'s words, " Boïto lives in a *casa misteriosa*," flashed into my mind, and I could not help saying, " How like many things the world describes and knows all about ! it is the very antithesis of what rumour has pictured." Surely there was nothing mysterious.

about this place; and now that I knew him, or fancied I knew him, Boïto himself was no longer a mystery. The house is a new one for Milan, with the usual lofty rooms and large square chambers. As we entered, the composer was seated talking with Professor Erlich of Berlin, one of the delightful critics, obliged morally to hear *Othello* again, despairing inwardly and outwardly because he was obliged to leave town without having heard it a second time. Naturally he can't wait; Tamagno is ill; will there be a second time? I glanced hastily about the apartment, and Boïto's eyes followed mine. I must have showed some surprise, for he said, with a fine ironic smile,

" You see my home is a very simple one, after all." Could the Contessa have told him ?

" But where do you work ?" I interrupted.

He waved his arms with the old familiar gesture; it said, " Here—there—everywhere."

" Here !" I repeated, aghast ; "impossible for any one to write music in—a—room like this ; it looks too prosaic, too cold, too precise, too—too uninspiring, too—too respectable."

Boïto smiled. " And what do you think of this one ?" he said, leading the way into an inner chamber. It was much more *simpatica* than the other. It was narrow, long, and crowded with antique furniture, a mass of objects, and reminded me of some sculptured cave in the Middle Ages, where spoils had been stored after a battle. The room, in fact, was just the width of a large window looking on the street; against the wall was a piano—an Erard, if I am not mistaken ; a swinging bracket held a number of classical books, and the window-ledge, was covered with books, musical instruments, odds and ends. A couch at the further end of the room was covered with an embroidered tapestry which looked like some far-away object lying on a cloud. On a rack above the piano were a dozen or more globes or brass bells. The maestro took up one of them, and as

I asked what it was, a curious reverberation was heard in the room : it seems they were sound - conductors, or something of that kind; but I could not make them out, and need not attempt to describe them. I said to the maestro,

"And this where you compose?" He smiled in the affirma- tive, gave one look around, and we then returned to the first apartment.

This room, as I have said, seemed very cold and ceremo- nious, yet a bright fire was burning in the Italian stuffa, or porcelain stove—the only one, by the way, that I have seen which gave out any warmth or suggested that there was a fire within it.

A long sofa was set out, and a portfolio opened upright on it was filled with photographs of celebrated works. I then noticed some book-cases furnished with imposing-looking volumes, pro- tected with glass doors, which appeared hermetically sealed ; everything was in such order, however, so scrupulously, method- ically clean, that I could scarcely believe it to be the apart- ment of a poet and musician. Believe me, it is quite as original as its owner. I am still suspecting unfair play, and that, fore- warned, it must have been got up like that for the occasion ; still, that would have been unnecessary: it is one of those stereotyped rooms which naturally wear the stamp of eternal order, cleanliness, and routine.

Boïto was in a delightful humour, and talked very pleasantly on many topics. He also referred to his *Mefistofele* again, and said that it was soon to be brought out at the Grand Opéra of Nantes: he told me he even counted on going to France to assist at the representation. Speaking of opera, I was indiscreet enough to ask to hear some of *Nerone*, the new work so anxiously awaited throughout Italy. Conducting me to his study, he then sat down and played some of it, but I have only a very dim idea of what it was. He also hummed a barcarolle, a most delightful piece of composition, excusing himself at the time, saying, " I cannot sing a bit. I haven't even the ordinary composer's voice. Ask Tosti to sing it : his singing is perfection ; he can do it more justice than I." I don't know how Tosti sings it, but Boïto's performance certainly was most perfect.

I asked him if he would ever come again to England. " Who knows," he said, " that I may not come to — "

I added, " Bring out *Nerone* after its triumph at La Scala ; let us hope that it will be very soon." Then I said good-bye —was it good-bye, or only a rivederci ?—Yours ever.

P.S.—Of course the most important thing comes in the P.S. You ask me about singing-teachers, &c. Milan is still the best school in the world for vocal study, and the town as usual filled with male and female aspirants for lyric fame. However, there are now a few hundreds less, with music-scores under their arms, tearing through the Galleria night and day, than there were ten years ago. At that time the city was one grand operatic caravanserai, and the thousand voices, each yelling in a different language, " I want to be an operatic singer," caused a confusion of tongues, " than which," to quote Poe, " the Tower of Babel would have been a quiet and comprehensive affair." Now, however, the operatic rage is somewhat subsided, and the few caterpillars once crawling on operatic legs are preparing to don the butterfly's gossamer and float to less sunnier, to—less ethereal skies. If you have any women friends who want to study music, and insist on Italy, send them here. The great Galletti is as incomparable a teacher as she was an incomparable singer, and I can recommend her most highly.—Yours ever, &c.

THE NEW YORK
PUBLIC LIBRARY

ASTOR, LENOX
TILDEN FOUNDATIONS

REPUTED HOUSE OF DESDEMONA,
Grand Canal, Venice.

CHAPTER XVI.

Milan, Feb. 11, 1887.

EVERYTHING is over, and we leave Milan to-night : this after-noon I had a last chat with Verdi. I need not say he was most amiable, and that I found him the same old Verdi I had known in Paris, only a little quieter, perhaps a little more staid—shall I say it ?—a little more gentle than before. There was a something sad in his manner : I could see that he was deeply chragrined about something, and that something is the big poster at La Scala, saying " Riposo." Verdi is tired, worn, and nervous ; can you wonder at it ? At his time of life, to pass through such a series of emotions would be enough in them-selves to render a younger and stronger man ill. Also the weather has changed—cold rains, hailstorms, and biting winds send people spinning and shivering through the Piazza ; faces are downcast, and the city seems in mourning. Even the triumph of last Saturday is far away, one of those vague delicious dreams, which, on awakening, leave a sense of having walked through perfumed meadows, but in a strange land. There is always some bitter to Verdi's sweet. Milan has always been destined to be the scene of his greatest triumphs, but also of his greatest humiliations. The King has given him another smart decoration, but if the sovereign could heal Tamagno, I think the composer would be more indebted than even to be allowed to call his Majesty cousin.

Sounds of many voices came to us from the adjoining

chamber. Crowds were in there — a delegation come to bring Verdi—the earth, as we would say in America—simply many honours, more triumphs, but most—municipal bores. I think Verdi is proud enough, but rather tired of it all. This is Thursday, and there is no second performance to-night. It seems a farce, quite like *Le Locataire de M. Blondeau,* a piece I once saw at the Palais Royal theatre : still—the tenor is ill. That unfortunate artist is obliged to lay up, and the other singers must remain *in statu quo* until he gets better. I asked Verdi if it was hoarseness, temper, or tenor. He raised his eyes and said :

"Tenor? Perhaps ! But you know he is really suffering."

"It is a thousand pities."

"Yes, it is at least *one.*"

Verdi spoke absently.

I can see the maestro is longing for the quiet of Sant" Agata. Even those amiable joyful voices in the next room are enough to grate on tender nerves. Honours! Honours mean fame and glory, but a great many disagreeable things besides. The maestro would leave Milan to-day if he could, but etiquette and the La Scala commissioners require that every composer shall personally assist three times if living— *à la* Edmond About—I don't know how many times if dead— at the first performances of his work. Verdi in this must do as others have done, and as he himself always has done. He made a precedent in the matter of rehearsals which has brought down envy and annoyances—not on his head, it was well protected, but on the heads of the Ricordis, the theatre managers, &c., and things are bad enough without the composer fleeing the camp. Now, a word once and for all about theatrical shortsightedness. Can you imagine a great opera-house like La Scala calmly paying twenty or thirty thousand pounds to produce a new opera, and refusing to pay forty or fifty more

THE MOOR'S HOUSE AT VENICE,
Canale Grande.

THE NEW YORK
PUBLIC LIBRARY

ASTOR. LENOX
TILDEN FOUNDATIONS

to engage substitutes in case a principal singer falls ill? Could one believe such a state of things? Not only that, but the *Othello* artists have been singing *Aïda* all the season, and by stopping it for the new work took off the only paying opera; hence the theatre is closed in mid-Carnival. Times have sadly changed when the greatest traditional opera-house of the world is reduced to such management and such straits. Naturally the loss to La Scala is enormous. I don't say who deserves this, but I do say such impresarios certainly merit no sympathy.

Of course you realise that it is also a real misfortune for the critics, especially they who felt called upon to judge a second performance of *Othello*. I don't need to hear a second; my mind is made up. I repeat, the opera is Verdi all over; it is as Italian as the Lake of Como, and as beautifully put together as the cathedral. Verdi's *Othello* is, indeed, a Gothic structure and the crowning effort of his life.

But the maestro.

We talked and talked, and I said : " They tell me your next work will also be Shakespearean. Don't say no. I am going, but it is not good-bye. On the contrary, I shall return to Milan to assist at your *next* great triumph."

I could have gone on for hours—most women can, and do, but I had to go. However, I reiterated my last words.

Verdi smiled—he smiled all over his face and eyes, as the children say. He came with me out into the passage, and only as my foot was on the staircase did he speak.

" Au revoir," he said, still smiling; then added, mysteriously coming closer to me, "another opera? Mademoiselle, connaissez-vous mon acte de naissance?"

FINIS.

APPENDIX.

IN this short work on so many subjects, although writing with some irrelevancy, I have tried to be exact in the matter of historical data, epochs, and events. Still, on re-reading my book, I find in the chapter treating on Signor Giacosa and other eminent Italians, an inaccuracy, or rather an omission, with regard to the proposed public performances in Italy of hitherto proscribed Italian plays, which must be rectified viz. *Macchiavelli, La Mandragola,* the works of Cardinal Bibbiena, Signor Aretino, &c. I find that I have said either too much or too little respecting these works; and my words as they now stand may prove misleading to the amateur or the student of classic dramatic literature. I have spoken of forthcoming public performances in Italy of the above-named pieces, and have omitted to mention certain public representations of *La Mandragola* at Florence—the Teatro Nuovo, on the evening of January 21st, 1887—and similar recitals at Naples and Turin during the winter of 1886-1887. I may also add that the above representations were for the benefit of male enthusiasts only ;* whereas in the time of Leo X. ladies of the Court and society in general brilliantly filled box and amphitheatre. But in spite of universal howling against the wickedness and immorality of the time of Leo XIII., the female sex was rigorously excluded from the Naples, Turin, and Florentine performances ; the audiences on these occasions presenting from platea to gallery a dismal array of black coats and masculine faces.

And this in the year of our Lord 1887—the enlightened and, if such a thing ever existed, the only true woman's rights century !

"O tempora, O mores !"

B. R.

---

* The *Mandragola* was first represented in Florence before the year 1520, by the celebrated Cazzuola company ; and in Rome in the year 1520, before His Holiness Leo X.

CPSIA information can be obtained
at www.ICGtesting.com
Printed in the USA
BVHW031722110419
545239BV00004B/173/P